4320

MAKING PEACE WITH SPAIN

The Diary of Whitelaw Reid,
September–December, 1898

THE PEACE COMMISSION IN JOINT SESSION

William P. Frye (standing); left to right—John Bassett Moore, George Gray, Cushman Kellogg Davis, William Rufus Day, Whitelaw Reid, Rafael Cerero, Wenceslao Ramírez de Villa-Uruttia, José de Guarnica, Buenaventura de Abarzuza y Ferrer, Eugenio Montero Ríos, Interpreter Ferguson, Emilio de Ojeda.

UNIVERSITY OF TEXAS PRESS, AUSTIN

4320

Making Peace with Spain

THE DIARY OF WHITELAW REID

September–December, 1898

Edited by H. Wayne Morgan

Library of Congress Catalog Card No. 65–13517
Copyright © 1965 by H. Wayne Morgan
All rights reserved
Manufactured in the United States of America
Printed by The University of Texas Printing Division, Austin
Bound by Universal Bookbindery, Inc., San Antonio

EDITORIAL NOTE

The Diary which Whitelaw Reid kept during the Paris Peace Conference that ended the Spanish-American War in 1898 is an excellent source for the study of late nineteenth-century American diplomacy. It offers fascinating glimpses of men and events in both Europe and America. It is also a rare full inside account of the secret proceedings of an important diplomatic conference.

Reid dictated the Diary to a secretary, who transcribed it to a clean typed copy, upon which Reid himself later made minor corrections and additions. He undoubtedly kept the Diary chiefly as an *aide memoire* for any future work he might write on the conference or on his public career in general. At his death, the Diary was deposited with his papers in the Manuscripts Division of the Library of Congress.

Preparing the document for publication has presented the usual troubles associated with editing. To avoid crowding the pages with excessive notations, I have changed, added, or deleted punctuation and altered sentence structure without notice where such revisions did not affect the meaning of the text. Added and paraphrased words are indicated within brackets. Certain omitted passages are indicated by three dots. These omitted sections are comments on Reid's social life, expressions of his opinions on matters extraneous to the conference, redundancies, or other passages that seemed irrelevant to the main story of the text. I have deleted nothing materially affecting the process of diplomacy. At all times I have tried to intrude with the minimum of editorial comment, and to allow Reid to tell his own story in his own style.

The formal reports, testimony, and protocols of the conference were published in U.S. Senate, 55th Congress, 3rd. Session, Document No. 62, *A Treaty of Peace between the United States and Spain* (Washington, G.P.O., 1899). These papers may be helpful in following the daily proceedings. (The document is cited in the footnotes as *Treaty of Peace*.) The Commission's full formal records are in the National Archives, Washington, D.C., filed under Special Missions in Record Group 45 (cited in the footnotes as *Records*). *Papers Relating to the Foreign Re-*

lations of the United States, 1898 (Washington, G.P.O., 1901) contains a considerable, though not exhaustive, number of the dispatches that passed between Washington and Paris during the conference (cited in the footnotes as *For. Rels., 1898*).

The Commission's secretary, John Bassett Moore, kept voluminous correspondence, drafts, notes, and minutes, which are deposited with his papers in the Library of Congress. They may be used by special permission. The papers of William McKinley, John Hay, and Whitelaw Reid in the same depository contain much correspondence on the peace settlement in general.

H. Wayne Morgan

University of Texas

CONTENTS

ILLUSTRATIONS

The Peace Commission in Joint Session . . . . *Title Page*

Following page 132

President William McKinley
Signing of the Armistice Protocol for Spain,
    August 12, 1898
Members of the American Peace Commission
William Rufus Day, President of the
    American Peace Commission
Whitelaw Reid in Later Years
William P. Frye, Member, American Peace Commission
Cushman Kellogg Davis, Member, American Peace
    Commission
George Gray, Member, American Peace Commission
John Bassett Moore, Secretary, American Peace
    Commission
The Young Whitelaw Reid
Whitelaw Reid, a Contemporary Caricature
Eugenio Montero Ríos, President, Spanish Peace
    Commission
Buenaventura de Abarzuza y Ferrer, Member, Spanish
    Peace Commission
Rafael Cerero y Sáenz, Member, Spanish Peace Commission
José de Guarnica, Member, Spanish Peace Commission
Wenceslao Ramírez Villa-Urrutia, Member Spanish
    Peace Commission
Emilio de Ojeda, Secretary, Spanish Peace Commission

MAPS

MAKING PEACE WITH SPAIN

The Diary of Whitelaw Reid,
September–December, 1898

INTRODUCING MR. REID

There was just enough chill in the September evening air to make the formal clothes required by the occasion feel comfortable. And who could fail to be warmed and pleased by the setting? The White House glowed in soft light, and the air inside seemed charmed by the rustle of silk dresses and the bright splashes of colorful furniture in a historic setting. The President's hospitality was already legendary, and not even war and the prospect of making a difficult peace deterred him from his usual thoughtful inquiries and charming manner. Nor was Whitelaw Reid, one of the circle of select guests, a man to overlook any of these details, or the comforting and impressive picture they presented. Below the surface of the talk, behind the faces of the men and women present, beyond the glow of lights and the feeling of power and place, he saw the beginnings of a historic occasion. The time was September, 1898; the place was Washington; the problem was settling the war between the United States and Spain.

Mr. Reid was an honored and influential friend of the President's, and McKinley spared nothing in making both his gratitude and his expectations for success clear to Reid and the other distinguished men present. They knew that much of America's future lay in their hands.

Mr. Reid was accustomed to the Administration's ear, and his was a familiar, if often peripheral, figure in the circle that advised the President. Since 1895 Reid had supported McKinley, first in his nomination and then in his election to the Presidency. Himself a lifelong Republican and the Party's nominee for the Vice-Presidency in 1892, Reid had long spoken with much power through the pages of his New York *Tribune*. Honors and emoluments had come to him, especially in the years since he first supported the man whose genial countenance and deft hand were familiar in public and in the private councils that made national policy.

Whitelaw Reid's origins and early life did not promise such an exalted prospect. Who would have thought that anyone born in frontier Xenia, Ohio, as he was on October 27, 1837, would attain national or international prestige? Notoriety, perhaps, in view of the rustic surroundings, but hardly statesmanship. Yet there was much in Whitelaw Reid's family background and geographic situation to help him rise to riches and power. His family, of Scottish-English-Irish stock, had fought the American wilderness in the eighteenth century. He had in himself and in his surroundings the urges for self-help and independence that made many Americans great in his century. He matured in an area rich with economic and political possibilities. The web of roads and waterways that crossed the Ohio Valley in the early nineteenth century, linking it to both east and west, made it a crossroads not only of goods but of thought and ambition. The coming of railroads meant greater speed, a new economy, larger chances of power in the community. The labor of generations had made the area habitable, tamed its Indians and land, built its mines and transportation, raised up a rustic but solid society. It had opportunities, especially for its young, in politics, law, business, and all the outlets of energy that went with what the men of that time called "progress."

Reid's family insisted on a proper education for their son. He did not object, for he had a taste for books, literature, and the arts that later set him apart from others in his profession. Ohio boasted many colleges that by the day's standards were outstanding. The Scotch-Irish immigrants, and others, brought with them the thirst for knowledge. Many New Englanders had also extended their tradition of learning and education to the area. For four years Reid worked hard at Miami University amid books and congenial friends, graduating with honors in 1856.

There was about him, as was often the case in young men of his day and upbringing, a touch of the prude, which was offset, however, by his graciousness and a serious approach to studies and duties. His motto was not uncommon, even trite: "Labor omnia vincit." He was a driving worker throughout his life, exemplifying before long the American myth of rags-to-riches that his generation so loved. He studied hard most days and many nights at Miami, absorbing literature, rhetoric, history, and some science. His infrequent vacations to New York prompted expressions of disapproval. "It is awful to think of the wickedness of this great city," he wrote home. "It has produced an effect upon me which I think time can never efface."[1] He was wrong, of course; he later lived in New York, and loved it.

Safely graduated, he looked about for a profession. His education had fitted him for the things associated with the mind. He had begun writing for the school yearbook and paper while in college, and he already liked the smell of printer's ink. In 1857 he managed to control the small but

[1] Royal Cortissoz, *The Life of Whitelaw Reid*, 2 vols. (New York, Charles Scribner's Sons, 1921), I, 22.

locally important *Xenia News*, from which he exercised his talent for observation and discussion of the men and events around him.

Party battles fascinated the Ohio and the America of the 1850's. Interest in politics seems almost innate in most Americans, and the great crisis of the slavery question was at hand. Reid entered the newspaper field when his talents could draw an audience and find an outlet. Since 1854 he had been a strong Republican, hating both slavery and talk of disunion. Reid could not have escaped embroilment, even had he so desired, because Ohio was a border state, not far from the physical presence of the Peculiar Institution in Kentucky, and populated with a motley blending of Democrats, Free-Soilers, Abolitionists, and secessionists.

An early Lincoln man in a state that generally favored Salmon P. Chase, Reid managed to make few enemies for himself and many friends for his candidate. Even as a beginner in a rustic newspaper he showed more than a reporter's interest in news. Though the roar and clatter of the presses fascinated him, he sprinkled his columns with book reviews and editorials on the arts, literature, and culture. He quickly developed a talent for meeting and reporting on visiting luminaries, who graced the lyceum circuits of the day. He was still often severe, but he could also be charming, and his physical appearance was proof of his grace. Careful in dress, fluent in speech, warm in approach when he wished, he made his way among people easily. "I remember him as a tall, graceful youth with an enviable black moustache and imperial, wearing his hair long in the Southern fashion, and carrying himself with the native grace which availed him in a wordly progress scarcely interrupted to the end," an old acquaintance recalled.[2]

True to his intuitive convictions, Reid worked first for Lincoln's nomination and then his election. He hoped, as did most of his countrymen, that the outcome would not precipitate the long-predicted crisis. When war came, however, he went to the front as a reporter, feeling it his duty to publicize the Union's struggle. As a war correspondent, the mature Reid utilized all his talents. He was often at the scene of battle, and just as often near historic men and events. He sent word pictures of his encounters to a newspaper chain for eager and impressionable readers. But there was more than good reporting in these dispatches. There was the conscious effort to kindle the spirit of resistance to rebellion, to probe behind the men and events to see their larger motivations. He was

[2] *Ibid.*, I, 63.

among the best reporters of the war on either side. For vividness, reality, and good sense, his accounts had few peers. They had, as he himself said later in another connection, "the smell of fire upon them." He later drew on these experiences for two books—one on Ohio's role in the war, and another on the South at the war's end—which also revealed him as more than a mere reporter. Though not a trained historian, he had more than average insight into the events of his time.[3]

War took him also to Washington, where he often angrily reported the stupidity and confusion he saw on the battlefields and behind the lines. But he also watched the political process at work. He was for a time clerk of the House Military Affairs Committee. From that post he gained access to some leading men with whom he was later connected, and insight into their actions. Edwin Stanton, "Bluff Ben" Wade, Salmon Chase, Henry Winter Davis, Thaddeus Stevens, John Hay, John Sherman, Horace Greeley—these and many others were his guests and associates.

Peace at the War's end left Reid with a sizable reputation in the newspaper world and some influence in politics. His tour through the defeated South, where he often gathered information in disguise so that Southerners would not suspect him as a Yankee reporter, filled him with the hope that reconstruction might be swift and easy. "They admit they are whipped," he said of the people he saw, "but the honest ones make no pretense of loving the power that whipped them."[4] He was so confident that reconstruction would be swift that he invested in cotton acreage, hoping to turn a quick profit, as the postwar demand for the South's staple crop rose. But he was disappointed. His "plantation" produced more swamp water than cotton, and he abandoned the venture.

His talents, in any event, lay elsewhere. The Gilded Age that emerged from the war was an era of "personal journalism," when powerful editors and publishers imprinted their personalities on their papers. E. L. Godkin, Horace Greeley, James Gordon Bennett, Reid himself, and the most famous, or infamous, of the late-comers, William Randolph Hearst, dominated American journalism.

Reid was considered briefly for the editorship of *The Nation*, the new liberal weekly. But the post went instead to E. L. Godkin, with whom Reid often disputed the issues of the day. The War had brought Reid and Horace Greeley together in Washington, and the *Tribune*'s editor was

<hr>

[3] See Reid's *After the War: A Southern Tour* (Cincinnati, Moore, Wilstach and Baldwin, 1866); and his *Ohio in the War*, 2 vols. (Cincinnati, Moore, Wilstach and Baldwin, 1868).

[4] Cortissoz, *Whitelaw Reid*, I, 122.

impressed by the young man's personality and reportorial ability. In 1868 Reid joined the newspaper's staff in a somewhat vague capacity, and in 1869 became managing editor.

Reid disliked what later decades called "yellow journalism," though he knew the value of colorful reporting. Essentially responsible in his outlook on world affairs, he wished to maintain and expand the *Tribune*'s record for integrity and full news coverage. His early role on the newspaper was that of the coordinator. Here he revealed the talents for compromise and conciliation that later made him an effective diplomat. He was unassuming though authoritative in manner, often cool, always silently demanding of the best in his associates. He was usually impersonal, though he could be the soul of courtesy and assistance. As Greeley retired and then died, Reid's talents sharpened with new authority. In time he became the actual head of the paper, pursuing a policy of personal control. But he never lost his knack for group management and conciliation. And no aspect of publishing the paper, from setting type to gathering advertising to distribution, was too small for his attention.

Reid always sought more than news coverage, and valued brains in his associates. "In making a newspaper, the heaviest item of expense used to be the white paper," he once said. "Now it is in the news gathering. By and by, let us hope, it will be the brains."[5] He widened the paper's scope of interest. He did not remove the *Tribune* from politics, which was always its staple fare, but channeled it slowly and successfully into the mainstream of American cultural life. Broadened coverage and new departments, together with better reporting and smoother production, brought literary figures like Bret Harte, John Hay, Mark Twain, Henry James, and Rebecca Harding Davis as contributors. The expansion revealed the new director's own cosmopolitan tastes.

Reid was deeply interested in politics, and as Reconstruction and "Grantism" unfolded in the 1870's, he occupied an anomalous position. He wanted to be a good Republican, where his inclinations naturally lay. But he could not stomach the harsh Reconstruction program of the Radical Republicans. And he could not support Grant after it became obvious that the General was utterly incompetent to occupy the White House and was in fact too often a popular front for his nefarious friends and party managers.

In 1872 Horace Greeley joined the Liberal Republicans, along with such eminent reformers as Carl Schurz and Charles Francis Adams, to

[5] *Dictionary of American Biography*, 15, p. 484.

bolt the Republican Party, or at least to try to cleanse it. Though he opposed Greeley's acceptance of the presidential nomination, Reid supported his chief when the latter won the Democratic and Liberal Republican endorsements and ran against Grant. To the end of his days Reid disputed the charge that "Old Horace" had greedily sought public acclaim. ". . . I should hardly have said he had a passion for office," Reid noted, revealing his shrewdness in assessing men. "What I did think was that he had a passion for recognition."[6] The campaign brought added labors, but Reid was accustomed to long hours. Jay Cooke left a sharp memory of seeing "Whitelaw Reid's tall, muscular figure, clad in a long surtout far below the knee, wearing a scotch cap, his long hair brushed back, and his eyes closed with weariness, going home on the Third Avenue cars at one, two, or three o'clock in the morning."[7]

Greeley's defeat and death did not dampen Reid's or the *Tribune*'s political work. Momentarily abandoning the Republican Party, he supported Samuel J. Tilden in New York politics. His influence was greater now, for he controlled the paper. Despite his opposition to Grant, Reid was never really a political independent. The chill aloofness and detached intellectuality of the mugwump reformer was not to his liking. He feared the decline of responsible government as illustrated in Grant's two terms, and combatted it vigorously. He supported Tilden on the state level. He abandoned him when he ran for President in 1876, however, because Rutherford B. Hayes pledged himself to a realistic national program and to ending Reconstruction. It was one thing to have Democrats in command of New York, and quite another to risk their controlling the national government. Reid opposed two basic national Democratic demands, a lower tariff and "soft" money. He wanted easier Reconstruction, reforms in the civil service, and a cleaner and more efficient national government. But he wanted a revitalized Republican Party to accomplish this.

Though not a personal friend of Hayes, his position gave him influence, and he worked hard to secure the Ohioan's election. When the disputed election of 1876 was over, his further searches helped reveal the "cipher dispatches" by which the *Tribune* proved that Democratic hands had not been entirely clean in the jobbing that characterized the contest. Tilden's supporters, like those of Hayes, had used questionable methods in searching for electoral votes. It all brought not only satisfaction but wider recognition and more authority in national politics for both the

[6] Cortissoz, *Whitelaw Reid*, I, 200.
[7] *Ibid.*, p. 250.

Tribune and its publisher, who was now becoming an influential Republican and a national figure.

Thus far work had been the keynote of Reid's life, and he was single as he verged on middle age. The situation was remedied by his marriage in 1881 to Elizabeth Ogden Mills, daughter of the California millionaire Darius Ogden Mills, whose wealth had first poured from the great bonanza of the gold rush. The elder Mills, wiser than the miners who took the glittering metal from the earth, built his enterprises to endure. After the Civil War he became a powerful factor in the Golden State's banking, transportation and hotel enterprises. He was more than the millionaire so typical of the era. He was also a philanthropist, whose benefactions supported the Lick Observatory, the Metropolitan Museum in his adopted New York, and the New York Botanical Gardens.

Well established, prosperous, noted socially in a wide circle, important politically, Reid now settled into the grooves properly accorded to the successful men of his time. He enjoyed his newspaper work. He liked to dabble on the periphery of politics. Gnawing desires for office soon worked on him. He entertained, travelled, and maintained his cultural connections. Every era has its special symbol of wealth, and in the age that many called Gilded, the millionaire's lavish home bespoke the extent of his fortune, or perhaps his bad taste. For Reid, the sturdy walls of "Ophir Farm," a castle near White Plains, New York, reflected his success. The visitor who approached it rode through fine lawns and formal gardens. The great house was secure in its crenelations, towers, and heavy windows. And it was not unpleasant. It was no worse than similar houses, and both its interior and its guests revealed the owner's varied interests.

In middle life Reid began to suffer from asthma and he searched for health in the globe's drier quarters. After travelling in Egypt and North Africa he settled at last in the still frontier environment of Phoenix, Arizona, where he spent much of each winter, retaining a firm control of the *Tribune*. His illness was not permanent, and disappeared gradually with the years.

Public service, which he could easily afford, now beckoned for the first time. Since diplomacy seemed both a logical reward and a natural field for him, in 1889 he accepted from President Harrison the ministry to France. It was the proper spot for Reid, whose cosmopolitan tastes fitted perfectly with the French capital of the *fin de siècle*. He did his share of tedious and often frustrating diplomatic labor, negotiating two treaties, on pork imports and extradition. But he also devoted time to the artists, writers, and intellectuals who filled Paris in that decade. He also travelled in Egypt and throughout Europe and the Near East, adding to the "Big America" feeling and cosmopolitanism that made him an early expansionist.

In 1892 an even more signal honor came; he was chosen as Harrison's running mate on the Republican presidential ticket. Though he was defeated, Reid later congratulated the victor, Grover Cleveland, on much that he did during his hectic second term. Reid and the *Tribune* supported the stubborn President's maintenance of the gold standard, his action against labor in the Pullman strike, and some of his policy exerting American influence in Venezuela in 1895. Cleveland's innate conservatism was not so different from Reid's, though the President lacked the publisher's polish and charm.

The arid years of depression that followed 1893, deepening into gloom and despair that seemed at times to border on revolution, revitalized the Republicans, and produced a new candidate, William McKinley. Reid had known McKinley when the Ohioan was a congressman, and favored his growing presidential aspirations. As governor of Ohio between 1892 and 1896 McKinley was in a prime position for elevation to the White House. Though momentarily suspicious of McKinley's past favorable stand on bimetallism, Reid liked his high-tariff record, and he could hardly fail to like the man himself. Genial, charming, courtly as only the men of his generation could be, thoughtful, calm and well reasoned in his view of the political situation, and experienced in politics, McKinley had much to recommend him. He spent his whole life in conciliation, and now that the Party faced dissension, he was its ideal standard bearer. His stand on protection, his long tenure in Republican councils, his Ohio origins, and his lack of enmity toward his opponents on the silver question made him a natural presidential candidate.

McKinley opposed and defeated the Republican machine masters like Thomas C. Platt of New York and Matthew Quay of Pennsylvania, and this opposition to bossism naturally appealed to Reid.[8] As McKinley's organization under Mark Hanna began consolidating his boom, Reid gravitated toward his camp. Since he approved of McKinley and shrewdly saw that it would be fruitless to oppose the people's apparent will in favoring the Ohioan, Reid and the *Tribune* supported McKinley as it became obvious that he was the leading contender.[9]

[8] McKinley to Reid, March 21, 1896, *ibid.*, II, 204.
[9] Reid to Stephen B. Elkins, February 28, 1896, Reid Papers, Library of Congress.

Practical politics aside, Reid also thought that McKinley was the man of the hour. As was his habit, he deluged the candidate with advice. McKinley clearly saw Reid's value and power, and kept him informed of his campaign's progress.[10] He did Reid the honor of consulting him on the important currency plank of the party platform. For a time Reid worried lest McKinley's success make him the target of all his opponents. He counselled the use of caution and deftness, talents that McKinley already had in abundance. "A boom for '96 which starts in '93 is in danger of withering before harvest time," he warned.[11] But the expert hand of Mark Hanna guided the organization that brought success at both the Republican convention and at the polls in November, 1896.

Reid belonged to a generation of statesmen who felt that, publicly at least, offices should seek men. He thought he should sit in McKinley's Cabinet, having contributed funds, influence, and his personality to the victory. But McKinley was not anxious to have the publisher at his elbow. While he recognized Reid's power in the GOP and his talents as a publisher and diplomat, he thought him too inclined to talk, a besetting sin to the cautious Ohioan.

Isolated in Phoenix while McKinley formed his Cabinet during the winter of 1896–1897, Reid deluged the President-Elect with advice and warnings that reinforced McKinley's hesitation to admit him to his Administration's inner councils. Reid wanted to be ambassador to England, but the President made a wiser choice in John Hay, who was almost ideally suited to cement the growing Anglo-American diplomatic accord. Reid also wanted to be Secretary of the Navy, but the President gave that post to Massachusetts' John D. Long. Reid's hand was never heavy, but his intent was obvious. McKinley could not afford to be unkind or ungrateful. And he could not yet afford to anger New York's Republican boss, Thomas C. Platt, by appointing Reid to office. Reid's efforts failed for the moment, though not for want of trying among his friends. "I have ceased thinking about Reid," Hay wrote McKinley; "he thinks enough about himself for two."[12]

But Reid was not left idle. In 1897 he headed the special United States mission to celebrate Queen Victoria's Diamond Jubilee. Warmly received by the Queen and official London, impressed on every hand by

[10] McKinley to Reid, December 30, 1895, February 19, 1896, *ibid.*

[11] Cortissoz, *Whitelaw Reid*, II, 199; Reid to McKinley, April 2, 1896, Reid Papers.

[12] Reid to Hay, February 8, 1897, Reid Papers; Reid to McKinley, January 2, 1897, McKinley Papers, Library of Congress; Hay to Reid, January 17, 1897, Reid Papers; Hay to McKinley, February 16, 1897, McKinley Papers.

evidence of growing solidarity between the two countries, and welcomed into the enjoyment of British culture, Reid found the special embassy rewarding and pleasant.

More serious and momentous events, however, crowded such pleasantries from American minds as 1897 closed. Reid had long predicted trouble, perhaps war, with Spain over Cuba. As early as the 1880's Reid was an expansionist, wishing to see the American flag wave over an empire. Shortly after the election of 1896 he told McKinley bluntly: "Some day we will have Cuba, as well as the Sandwich Islands [Hawaii]. To that extent I believe in Manifest Destiny."[13]

He was right. The war came, contrary to the President's wishes and in spite of his labors, and its results were far more complex and significant than its causes. It was, John Hay once said, a splendid little war. Theodore Roosevelt recalled that while it wasn't much of a war it was the only one we had. Its consequences were not small, for at its end America faced a dilemma. Should she accept the foreign territory she had conquered during the war? Should she acquire the Philippine Islands, presumably won at the Battle of Manila Bay on May 1, 1898? Reid did not hesitate, recognizing fully that America was at a crossroads. She could take the new path of world power and responsibility, enlarging her role in world politics and commerce, or she could continue in relative diplomatic isolation and at commercial disadvantages in the world's markets. In June, 1898, an interview published abroad quoted Reid as saying that the country must keep what it had won. He was an expansionist, or as others said, an "imperialist."[14]

The arguments with which Reid sustained his view well represented the expansionists' ideal. He thought that the United States must have foreign possessions such as the Philippines before she could gain admission into the circle of great powers like England, France and Germany, which made world policies. Believing in America's mission to extend abroad the best parts of her institutions, Reid and millions of his countrymen felt that the country could not shirk either the opportunities or the necessities of her new position.

Future military status and national defense were also involved. The United States needed a larger navy to police her coasts, to protect her nationals in foreign commerce, and to make her presence and policies felt in world diplomacy. This required coaling stations, cable landings,

[13] Cortissoz, *Whitelaw Reid*, II, 214.
[14] *Ibid.*, p. 224.

and harbors. This appeal to national pride subtly reinforced the call to duty, symbolized in the concept of "taking up the white man's burden."

To some who wavered for a time, like William R. Day, the final appeal of duty was very strong. The President and his advisers, relying on the best information available, believed the Filipinos incapable of self-government. Could the United States morally leave them to civil war and bloodshed? The administration policy makers thought not. In another sense the Islands were a laboratory, to which American ideals of self-rule and democracy could be transplanted. The idea of mission was never stronger than in this instance.

The United States could hardly abandon the Islands, as Senator Gray suggested to his colleagues on the Peace Commission. They would pass back to Spain, which seemed too weak to hold them. They might then go by default to an unfriendly competitor in the Orient, like Japan or Germany. That would be unwise policy, as the President so firmly told his commissioners. American acceptance of only part of the Islands would invite endless misunderstandings with whoever acquired the remainder. An American protectorate over the Islands would have been unworkable and without precedent, involving responsibility without control.

And as Reid, McKinley, and other expansionists pointed out, the United States presumably had a great deal to gain from commerce with the Philippines. Their acquisition might ultimately revolutionize the oriental balance of power, for the United States could use them as a steppingstone into the supposedly lucrative Chinese markets. The flame of trade beckoned brightly in the East. America already had interests on the mainland, in the form of religious missions, diplomatic embassies, and traders. These could now be extended if the United States accepted its new role in the Orient. That much of this glittering prospect did not materialize should not detract from the force with which the expansionists honestly argued otherwise at the time.

The opposition to overseas expansion was instant and bitter. The arguments in favor of acquiring empire and entry into world affairs seemed rational to many men. But the arguments against this action swayed a diverse and articulate group of "anti-imperialists." Legally, they argued that the Constitution forbade acquiring territory not intended to be admitted into the Union as states. Morally, they argued that the United States had no right to pursue a war of conquest. The nation had commendably fought to free Cuba. To seize the Philippines by force would make the conflict no more justifiable than one of England's or Germany's imperial wars. No one should force the Filipinos, or anyone else, to accept American rule, they argued. That was not America's rightful mission. To do this would undermine the Constitution and America's historic principles of liberty and self-government.

If confidence in America's abilities and future role as a world power sustained men like Reid, fear of power's complications motivated men like Senator George Gray. It might lead to militarism at home, and dangerous, unpredictable conflicts with other nations abroad. The anti-expansionists thought that oriental trade was deceptive. In any event, commerce could be won peacefully and without the moral, fiscal, and political costs or risks of world power. On both sides of this complex and historic question, belief and animosity entwined together, and ran deep into the American conscience.

This was the background against which President McKinley formed his own policy and chose the men to write it into a peace treaty. His own attitude was often murky, and his talents at dissimulation and creating opinion were never better used. He first appeared not to desire overseas expansion; the Philippines seemed to come as an accident of war. But Dewey's squadron went to Manila by presidential order, and McKinley knew the risks he and his country ran in attacking the Islands.

For a time in the summer of 1898 he seemed to favor retaining only Luzon, the major island, as a naval base. But that was clearly impossible, and he steadily allowed himself to appear to be "persuaded" to take all the Islands. Events carried him to the logical conclusion of the policy he had long since accepted. In July, 1898, he signed the congressional resolution annexing Hawaii with references to "manifest destiny." It seemed no great leap of logic or policy to acquire the Philippines in the final peace treaty. Aware of the demands of strategy and commerce, wishing to take America into world affairs as a force for idealism and democracy, the President steered a course through public opinion until he was sure the people supported expansion. The call of duty was strong. He wished to uplift the Filipinos with American rule. The call of reality was equally strong. International politics, commerce, military strategy, the whole future of the Pacific basin, demanded that the United States accept its new role. Diplomatic isolation was over.

The President revealed his early commitment to expansion in the Peace Commission he chose. Realizing that the treaty would face fierce opposition in the Senate, which must approve it, he chose three senators to help negotiate it. Two were expansionists: Minnesota's powerful Cushman K. Davis, Republican chairman of the Foreign Relations Committee, and Maine's expansionist Republican, William P. Frye. But it would be unwise to pack the Commission, so McKinley persuaded Delaware's antiexpansionist Democrat, Senator George Gray, to speak for the opposition. William R. Day, an old and honored friend of McKinley's, then retiring as Secretary of State, would speak for the Administration as president of the Peace Commission. To balance the politicians and to gain influence with a major newspaper, McKinley asked Reid to go to Paris. It was an admirable and strong Commission, carefully chosen to minimize the dangers that faced the treaty and expansionism.

Paris, the city of treaties, welcomed the American commissioners with traditional hospitality. Though the French had emotionally favored the Spanish during the war, the Foreign Ministry spared no effort to insure neutrality during the negotiations. Spacious rooms at the Quai d'Orsay were set aside for the discussions, with high windows opening onto a pleasant terrace and river view, graced with marble trimming and busts of famous Frenchmen. Inside, ornate ceilings, heavy draperies, rich rugs, and liveried servants bespoke the majesty of France. In the center of the room, under a massive chandelier, stood the conference table, covered in green felt.

The men of the Spanish delegation, who met with the Americans first on October 1, were stiff with formality and mournful dignity, but were courteous and proper. They seemed, like their country, elderly. Their names in themselves were imposing, with titles that flowed behind them like ribbons in the wind. Generals, nobles, senators—however fictitious their pretensions to power might seem to such brash newcomers as the Americans, few were unmoved by the simple fact that the country these men spoke for had once ruled most of the New World. Proud Spain had already lost one empire and now she was to be humbled again.

The work involved in preparing the American case for the peace conference was both complex and arduous. Each morning the American commissioners met in Reid's hotel room to discuss the coming session's proposals, and to settle among themselves upon a policy, or at least an approach. They worked hard and long hours, Reid often complaining that their only exercise was the one-eighth–mile walk from the hotel to the conference room. Occasional drives, the inevitable dinners and luncheons, sightseeing in the cold of a Paris winter were their chief diversions. But the formal conferences, the witnesses giving testimony, the calls from other diplomats, and the official presentations and receptions left little free time.

Reid profited from his earlier diplomatic experience in Paris, and from his travels. Though the governments he had earlier dealt with officially as the American minister had long since fallen, the men he had known were still available, and added to the cordiality of the atmosphere. His reputation gave him more contacts among foreign diplomats than his fellow commissioners. In this, as in so many other roles during his life, he acted the part of middleman or go-between. Though he strongly stated his own expansionist views on the retention of all the Philippines, he also calmed the nerves and tempers of his colleagues. John Hay, now Secretary of State in Washington, felt that Reid more than anyone else was responsible for the final treaty. While that may have been the exaggeration of a friend, there is no doubt of the importance of Reid's contribution to the final document.[15]

The chief questions were the status of newly freed Cuba, and the acquisition of the Philippines. The Spaniards, no doubt like most Europeans, could not believe that the United States would not annex Cuba. They persisted in trying to transfer the enormous Cuban debt and the island to the United States. The Americans stubbornly resisted both ideas, and in the end won, though only after forcing the conference to the point of rupture. Reid's dinner conversation with the Spanish ambassador to France, Sr. León y Castillo, did much to convince the Spanish commissioners that their efforts were hopeless. The November congressional elections in the United States brought Republican majorities, and ended Spanish hopes that the American people would reject expansion. At last only the Philippines remained, and the Spanish accepted the inevitable and surrendered their claims. In return for a money payment the United States acquired an Oriental empire. The momentous conference, which had achieved a treaty with significance in all its ramifications for the future place of the United States in the world arena, was over.

The treaty was finished, but the problems it contained were not. Returning to the United States, the three senator-commissioners entered the great debate of early 1899 on the acceptance of the treaty. The bitterness of the anti-imperialists, now enlisting in their ranks several powerful Republicans like Senator George F. Hoar, Speaker Thomas B.

15 Hay to Reid, November 3, 1898, Reid Papers.

Reed, and Andrew Carnegie, knew few bounds. The problem was further complicated on February 4, 1899, by the outbreak of hostilities between the Filipinos and the Americans near Manila, beginning the long guerilla war that lasted until 1902. The treaty was accepted in the Senate on February 7, 1899, by only one vote more than the necessary two-thirds. But in the months and years that followed the bitterness remained. Reid himself lost some old and honored friends. "It is a matter of congratulations, however, that you seem to have about finished your work of civilizing the Filipinos," Carnegie wrote him as the casualty lists came from Manila. "It is thought that about eight thousand of them have been completely civilized and sent to heaven. I hope you like it."[16]

Reid did not like the costly and vicious guerilla war, but he defended overseas expansion as a historic necessity. In speeches, pamphlets, and books like *Our New Duties* (1899), and *Problems of Expansion* (1900), he upheld America's new role in world affairs. Though he admitted that American foreign policy had many faults, he did not abandon the expansive policy he had so long and so well espoused. He congratulated Theodore Roosevelt for seizing the Panama Canal Zone in 1903.[17]

The first year of the new century symbolized many changes. President McKinley died at the hands of an anarchist assassin in 1901. Across the ocean Queen Victoria had died, ending an era that bore her name. Old issues and attitudes were passing, and the pace of change—some men called it progress—quickened.

In Reid's own circle Theodore Roosevelt brought energy and a fresh outlook to the Presidency he assumed on McKinley's death. If he was less subtle than his predecessor, he was more vigorous, and both Presidents pursued policies that Reid supported and helped formulate. Reid and Roosevelt were often together, for the publisher was still a powerful force in the Republican Party. Roosevelt knew him as a friend and as a political power, and was bound to call him to prominence in his Administration.

Though he was now over sixty, an age at which many men retire from active life, Reid still faced his fullest years. In 1902 Roosevelt made him special ambassador to the coronation of King Edward VII. The task gave Reid the chance to wine and dine with the great and famous. Parties, receptions, and state occasions made the mission happy and rewarding for him. He was pleased to note and report to Roosevelt the

[16] Cortissoz, *Whitelaw Reid*, II, 261.
[17] *Ibid.*, p. 292.

growing accord between the two nations, which to his mind augured well for a stable future.

He had other duties. He still controlled the *Tribune*, though it was gradually passing to his son, who began work at the bottom to learn the trade, and who would assume command in 1913. Whitelaw Reid was a regent of Stanford University in California. He also worked closely with the School of Journalism at Columbia University, and with the state university of New York.

He had one final diplomatic labor. In 1905 Roosevelt appointed him ambassador to England, the post Reid had always most desired. He had hardly reached his embassy when he assisted Roosevelt in matters relating to the Russo-Japanese War. His long reports to the President revealed his old flair with the pen and his keen eye for colorful detail and interpretation. Though usually rather outwardly sober, he could be humorous. He was once asked by W. E. Gladstone: "What does your Republic do to reward distinguished public services from private citizens?" Reid thought a moment and answered: "There are only three things we can do. If they live at the North, we can invite them to lecture; if they live at the South we can call them Colonel or General; wherever they live, if they can get votes enough, we can send them to Congress and let them take the consequences."[18] All who met the Ambassador could agree that he filled his post with much dignity and taste.

He was a diplomat of the old school, given to deliberation and methodical weighing of alternatives available. Fortunately for him there was no great crisis between England and the United States during his ambassadorship. But he did much to increase the growing diplomatic cooperation between the two powers. He was a wise choice for the closing Edwardian era.

In 1907, Oxford honored him with a degree. He helped Mark Twain visit the University to accept his degree, drawing a typical thank-you note from the creator of Huck Finn and Tom Sawyer. "The dates are exactly right; they couldn't possibly be better. I wanted two engagements, and only two; . . . They and Oxford leave me seven days for private dissipation and last good-byeing with old friends, whom I shan't ever meet again without their haloes. And there are one or two whom I shan't ever meet *with* them. I am sorry for that, for they are among the best of the flock."[19]

In his last years in the English post Reid saw many familiar faces

[18] *Ibid.*, p. 334.
[19] *Ibid.*, pp. 380–381.

disappear. Edward VII died, and the brief age to which he lent his name closed, little suspecting that the gaslights that were its hallmark would soon give way to more fearful fires on the Continent and around the world. Reid saw the building world tensions, and his old suspicion of German designs sharpened. But he was not to see the final conflagration end the old order he had worked so hard to preserve. On December 15, 1912, he died quietly in London. His passing produced extraordinary responses from his hosts, including a solemn service at St. Paul's and a personal message from King George V to President Taft.[20]

And so his long, eventful, and fruitful life passed, leaving behind it a legacy of accomplishment in several fields. A leading newspaperman, more than an occasional diplomat, a power in his party's politics, a supporter of some of the best in his era's culture, he would be missed. Of all his legacy, perhaps the record he left of his part in the Peace of Paris is most significant and most interesting. It reveals not only the workings of his mind and of the peace conference, but also suggests the complex currents that carried his country into the realities of world power in the twentieth century.

[20] *Ibid.*, p. 450.

THE DIARY

CHAPTER I

Organizing the Conference: Problems and Persons

Washington, [Wednesday,]
September 14, 1898

Calling at the White House this morning, [I] encountered Mr. Bart-lett, the lawyer of the [New York] *Sun*. Subsequently, Senator [Cushman K.] Davis came in, and he and I were invited into the cabinet room to-gether, where we found Professor D. C. Gilman of John Hopkin's [*sic*] College. The President [William McKinley] mentioned that he was just urging upon Professor Gilman his duty to serve on the board to investi-gate the War Department, and I warmly reinforced his position, repre-senting that a call of this sort by the President of his country, for an im-portant and delicate service, which he had not sought, was one which he could not refuse unless for the most convincing personal reasons.[1]

There was a little talk with the President about the work of the Com-mission, but he was rather disposed to put off everything until Senator [William P.] Frye and the other members should be present. He seemed still to hope for Senator [George] Gray, although Gray was engaged in a law suit which, owing to the very recent date of his appointment, he had been unable to push off.[2]

The President asked me to come back and drive with him at 5 o'clock,

---

[1] McKinley was at this time engaged in establishing a presidential commission to investigate charges that corruption and incompetence had dictated wartime policies in the War Department under Secretary of War Russell Alger. Gilman did not join the commission, which was finally formed under the chairmanship of General Grenville M. Dodge of Iowa. The commission report, which exoner-ated Alger of the charges of corruption, did much to draw attention to the need for military reform.

[2] It is interesting to note that at a date as late as 1898 it was not considered questionable for a United States senator to engage in private law practice while holding public office.

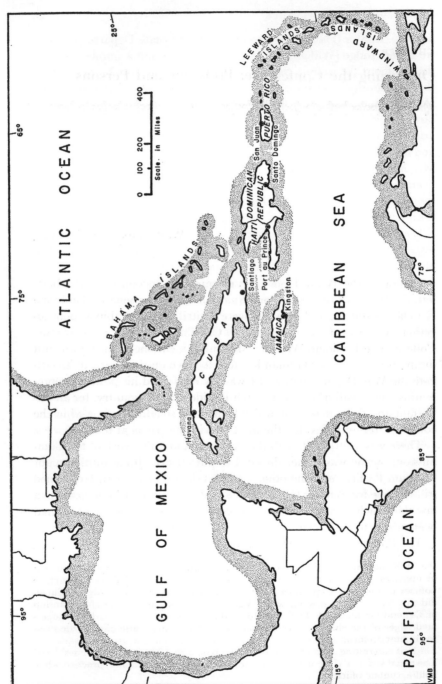

The Caribbean Area

and the Senator [Davis] and I went over to the State Department. Here we found Judge [William R.] Day, who entered into a number of little details about the sailing, the order by the President for the payment of the Commission, personnel of the staff, etc. I noted that each of the Commissioners excepting myself seemed to be allowed a private secretary; so I made provision for having one too. The Secretary [Day] called attention to the payment allowed for the service, and gave Senator Davis and myself checks for the first installment. Mr. [John Bassett] Moore and Mr. MacArthur, the Secretary and Assistant Secretary [of the Peace Commission] were also presented, and there was some little talk about the documents, which they were preparing to have with us, especially documents relating to the Philippines, and [referring] to the Cuban debt.

Lunched with [M. G.] Seckendorff at the Metropolitan Club, and subsequently repaired to the White House, where I found the President had already gone out driving with one of the cabinet, but had left word for me to wait. He returned a few minutes later, and we took a drive through the grounds of the Agricultural Department. He seemed timid about the Philippines and oppressed with the idea that our volunteers were all tired of the service and eager to get home. "The whole shooting match wants to quit," was the way he expressed it. I tried to impress him with the notion that this was only a temporary feeling, due to the sudden stagnation in military operations, and the depression of prevailing sickness in semi-tropical climates in mid-summer. But he still insisted that if the temper of the soldiers could be taken as any criterion of that of the people, the country was in no mood for further military operations or for any extension of territory, which might imply the necessity for them [military operations] in the future. I combated this idea moderately, but not with much apparent success. I concluded it wise not to introduce any personal subjects, on which I had already told him that I wanted a private interview after the meeting of the Commissioners the next day.[3]

Seckendorff dined with me at the Metropolitan Club. Subsequently,

[3] McKinley's remarks reported here ought not be taken too literally. It is true that he seemed to many to be unsure on what to do about the Philippines, and that he appeared to bow to public opinion in finally retaining the Islands, but there is considerable evidence that long before the peace conference opened he was determined to acquire the territory, and that he was at this time engaged in creating public opinion to support his decision. Drawing opinions from other men was a favorite weapon of his, and he was not likely to reveal to Reid at this time any final convictions or secrets. See H. Wayne Morgan, *William McKinley and His America* (Syracuse, Syracuse University Press, 1963), pp. 398–399, 402–412. The same author's *America's Road to Empire* (New York, John Wiley and Sons, 1965), contains a fuller discussion of the problem.

on going down for coffee, I encountered Judge [Charles] Denby, whom
I had not seen since he was sailing from San Francisco for his post at
Peking thirteen years before. He at once began with expressions of his
lively sense of obligations to me because of my letters to him from Paris
advising him of President [Benjamin] Harrison's intention to retain him
in office. The subsequent talk turned largely on the possibilities for
American trade in China and on the extreme importance of the Philippines to us to that end. He thought we certainly ought to hold Luzon,
and inclined to think that we should hold the whole group. In fact, as he
began to talk freely, he expressed himself more and more positively in
this direction. John Russell Young came in and joined in the conversation, without expressing any positive opinion on this point.

[Friday,] September 16th, 1898.

At the hour fixed for the meeting of the Commissioners at the White
House this morning, Senator Davis, Judge Day, and myself were present,
but it was said that Senator Gray could not get away from court. We
waited nearly three quarters of an hour for Senator Frye, who finally
appeared, brisk and cheerful, with a laughing statement about not having wanted this task, but having referred it to his wife, in the confident
conviction that she would settle it his way. On the contrary, he said,
"She informed me at once that I was going to go. I had told her that of
course she couldn't go on account of her always being seasick, but she
told me that of course she would go, and that she wouldn't think for a
minute of having me fail to go." Finally the President indicated his desire to begin business and motioned us to seats about the table. Senator
Davis had established himself at the President's left, and Senator Frye
was near him; Judge Day was at the foot of the table, and the President
beckoned to me to take the place next to him at the right. He began by a
reference to the protocol, and to the wide divergence of opinions that
seemed to exist in the country as to the unsettled questions concerning
the Philippines. He said he had prepared some instructions covering the
main points of our duty, but had left the final decision as to the Philippines to be filled out after the present consultation. He then asked Senator Davis to express his views.

Senator Davis said his general impression was that we certainly should
retain coaling stations in the Ladrones and also in the Carolines, if that
were practicable. As to the Philippines he believed it to be a great oppor-

tunity for the United States with reference to trade in the East, as well as with reference to its naval power. He thought Manila of the utmost importance, but believed that the proper defense of Manila would require the territory back of it. He also thought that the islands adjoining would be found rich and desirable, and thought it would be a mistake to abandon them. As to the islands in the extreme southwestern portion of the archipelago occupied by Mohammedans, namely, Mindanao and the Sulu group, he was not clear. He thought he should be willing to let Holland take them, as she had possessions in that neighborhood, was a friendly power, and not likely to be an unfriendly neighbor.

Senator Frye, who was next called on, referred particularly to the moral features of the case. [He] said that he thought that while there was some difference in New England as to the policy [of overseas expansion], and while some important newspapers like *The Boston Herald* and *Springfield Republican*, representing a considerable public sentiment, were opposed to any increase of territory, he thought the larger and better part of New England believed it impossible for the United States, with any show of consistency or morality, to return to the dominion of Spain territories which had once been wrested from her. He had an impression that the conscience of the religious community was going to make itself felt effectively in this direction, although he admitted that he wished to get a little further light. On the whole, however, this talk was decidedly in favor of holding on to the whole of the Philippines as well as to all the Spanish West Indies. He also considered the Carolines and the Ladrones important.

Continuing on around the table, the President next called on Judge Day, who spoke in a strongly conservative sense against the desirability of any further territorial acquisition by the United States. He believed that with Cuba, [and] Puerto Rico in the Spanish West Indies, which he thought it clear that we would be compelled to retain, or be responsible for, we had already undertaken a very large task. He would like to get out of the Philippines with the least possible responsibility in that quarter. They were remote, had no direct relation to us, [and] would not have been thought of as a desirable acquisition but for the war; he did not see why the war had made them any more desirable. They comprised a great multitude of islands, anywhere from six hundred to several thousand, embraced a great variety of races, pure and mixed, including many still in a state of savagery, and also a great variety of religions. A large section at the south was under the control of Mohammedans, who had never been conquered by Spain, and who were believed to be depraved, intractable, and piratical. He thought the United States had enough on its hands now, that it had really not taken possession of this portion of the Philippines, at least, or indeed any portion excepting the harbor and bay of Manila, and that it was under no obligation to assume responsibility for any more. To the humanitarian argument that having freed them from the yoke of Spain we ought not to return them to it, he replied first that we had not freed them excepting in Manila, and second that there must be a limit to our humanitarian enterprises. Because we had done good in one place, we were not therefore compelled to rush over the whole civilized world, six thousand miles away from home, to undertake tasks of that sort among people about whom we knew nothing, and with whom we had no relation. Judge Day's statement was given with a good deal of precision of manner, following notes which he had evidently jotted down in advance, and was undoubtedly effective.

The President next called on me. I began by reference to his talk the previous evening about the temper of the volunteer army, first asking his leave to refer to it. I spoke of this as undoubtedly serious, but insisted that it would be a great mistake to base a permanent policy affecting the largest questions of national interest on territorial expansion upon a purely temporary condition arising from malaria among the new troops, and the prevalence of nostalgia. Leaving out of sight, therefore, what had seemed to me the argument having the greatest weight in the minds of those opposed to taking any more [territory] than we could help, I rapidly repeated first some of the arguments in my *Century* article[4] as to the clear obligation upon us not to leave Cuba without, at least, a better government than the one we had destroyed. [We could not] return to Spanish rule, which we had declared too bad to be endured in the West Indies, any country which the fortunes of war had enabled us to free from the same rule in the East Indies. I dwelt upon the obvious necessity for coaling stations, spoke of the desirability of getting a point in the Carolines as well as in the Ladrones, and referred to a communication from Edmund L. Baylies, Vice-President of the Scrymser Pacific Cable Company, as to the necessity of one island in the Carolines as a landing point for a cable stretching from San Francisco to Manila, with landing points only on United States territory.

I then spoke of the various schemes which had been presented with

---

[4] See Whitelaw Reid, "The Territory with Which We Are Threatened," *The Century Magazine*, 56 (September, 1898), 788–794. The article is somewhat indefinite on the solution to the Philippine problem, but Reid advanced in it the basic arguments on expansion for which he was already well known.

reference to the Philippines, mentioning the proposals: (1) that we should take only Manila; (2) that we should take only Luzon; (3) that we should divide Luzon at the peninsula in the southern part; (4) that we should turn Manila into a free city, like the cities of the Hanseatic League, guaranteeing its independence; [5] that we should take all of the Philippines excepting the Mohammedan part; and [6] that we should take the whole of [the Islands]. I spoke of the great importance of the Philippines with reference to trade in China, of the difficulty morally of taking one part and abandoning the rest to Spain, and of the political difficulties flowing from the same policy, which, it seemed to me, would be merely organizing in a worse shape exactly the trouble we had been suffering from in the West Indies for the past three quarters of a century. The islands it was proposed to abandon to Spain were much nearer to Luzon than Cuba or Puerto Rico were to Key West, the necessities of constant intercourse were much greater, and it was obvious that the friction would be constant and the provocations to war far greater. I believed it too difficult to hold Manila alone without the island to which it belonged, or to hold any other harbor on Luzon. The hinterland seemed to be a necessity .

I believed also that the commerce of the Philippines themselves with the United States would be very considerable. Our possession of them would give us an enormous advantage in the vastly greater commerce that might be cultivated with China. I believed their possession valuable to the whole country, but especially important to the Pacific coast. We were at present at a disadvantage in commerce on the Atlantic Ocean, and could hardly expect in our time, or in that of the next generation, to catch up with Great Britain. We already had, however, an enormous advantage on the Pacific Ocean. The acquisition of the Sandwich Islands [Hawaii] greatly strengthened us in this field. If to this we now added the Philippines, it would be possible for American energy to build up such a commercial marine on the Pacific coast as should ultimately convert the Pacific Ocean into an American lake, making it far more our own than the Atlantic Ocean is now Great Britain's. Such a possession therefore would tend to stimulate our shipbuilding industry and commerce, and could not but add immensely to the national prosperity.

I strongly deprecated the idea of making two bites of the cherry. I was not so much concerned about whether it would be immediately popular or not, though on this point I had little doubt of the popular tendency. What concerned me more was whether it should be left to the people of a succeeding generation to dwell on the magnificent opportunities that

Providence had thrown in our way, and to record that the men in charge of public affairs at that time were unable to comprehend or grasp their opportunities, and had thus thrown away the magnificent future that should have belonged to the nation.

I stated the proposition that the commerce which existed of necessity, and should naturally therefore give the greatest profit, was that between the inhabitants of different zones, exchanging articles which, in each case, the other needed and could not produce. Commerce between inhabitants of the same zone was less natural and less necessary. The articles which one people could produce, another people might under similar circumstances produce, and the trade might thus be imperiled or destroyed. Our true national interest, therefore, was to seek a development for our commerce particularly with countries who needed what we had to sell and could not produce, and who could offer us in exchange what we needed and could not produce. The Philippines seemed to me to meet these conditions; so did China. The control of the Pacific Ocean pointed almost exclusively to a commerce under these conditions and seemed to me therefore to offer the largest and best commercial future for the country.

The suggestion that we should take any part of the Philippines as a war indemnity, though plausible, seemed to me unnecessary. We had taken the capital of the country, the center of its Administration, the point from which it was controlled. In doing so, we had taken prisoner practically the whole Spanish army of occupation and destroyed the whole fleet. The war left us masters, therefore, not only of Manila, but of the archipelago. It was ours, therefore, by right of conquest.

I deprecated undue alarm about the difficulty of administering these distant possessions. What Great Britain had done successfully, a kindred people need not be less skillful in [doing]. No doubt it would involve material reforms in our civil service, which would be an advantage anyway. The Constitution interposed no obstacles and there would be little difficulty in so modifying our present territorial system as to adapt it to any of these islands whenever it might be thought best to relieve them from military rule. But they should be governed permanently as colonies, never with the remotest idea of permitting their admission as states in the Union.

The President then remarked that he believed the acquisition of territory was naturally attractive to the American mind, . . . but thought it would probably be more attractive just now than later on, when the difficulties, expense and loss of life which it entailed, became more manifest.

He thought we could not possibly give up Manila, and doubted the wisdom of attempting to hold it without the entire island to which it belonged. Beyond this he did not seem inclined to go. He thereupon read the instructions, which were explicit on other points, and indicated that he would fill out the gap with reference to the Philippines in the sense of the opinions he had just expressed.[5] He closed the meeting after some remarks about the satisfaction he had in enlisting our services. [He desired] that we should use our best judgment on the Philippine question, and accumulate all possible information. [He suggested] that, after hearing from [General Wesley] Merritt and [Admiral George] Dewey (to the opinion of the latter of whom he seemed to attach great importance), we might find it necessary for the safety of Luzon to provide also for acquiring some of the smaller islands near it.

After the others had taken their leave I sat down with the President for the talk on personal matters for which I had asked the day before. I began by saying that I hoped he did not imagine that I did not appreciate to the full the very high honor he had done me since his administration began in [appointing me] to two very high and distinguished positions. I did not depreciate in the least their importance, although the fact remained that neither of them was of my seeking. For that matter, I had never been an office seeker. My record on that matter was clear and precise. Three successive administrations had offered me three of the highest diplomatic positions in the gift of the government. The offers of [President R. B.] Hayes and [President J. A.] Garfield had been successively declined. That of [President Benjamin] Harrison was accepted, and the post [of minister to France] was held three years (until the work the [State] Department especially desired was concluded) and was then resigned, constituting one of the very rare instances in our entire diplomatic history in which so high a position had been given up merely from a preference for private life. The subsequent nomination for the Vice-Presidency [in 1892], as he knew, came to me absolutely unsolicited. After it came I had done more pecuniarily than any other candidate the Republican party had ever named, if not double as much as any. Against my own wishes and protests [I had also] been forced into the campaign work to an unusual extent, and at the cost of three years [of] dangerous ill health.

When the President, however, had done me the honor unsolicited, and while he was still only a candidate for the nomination, to say that he

[5] For the full text of the President's instructions, see Appendix II.

desired to have me, in case of his election, as one of his most intimate friends, constantly at his elbow for consultation throughout his administration, and had accompanied this by the remark that he could not say more, since he was making no promises or offers of places, I had naturally construed this as practically making me one of his official family. [I] had taken some steps with him, in consequence, on which otherwise I should not have felt at liberty to venture. I had recognized the difficulties he encountered when he came to make up his cabinet, and appreciated, if I did not fully share, his anxiety about beginning a quarrel with Mr. [Thomas C.] Platt.[6]

The situation now, however, was this: A vacancy had occurred in London by the transfer to the State Department of the man [John Hay] whom I thought the best fitted in the country for that position. The President had done me the honor to intimate to various people, in a more or less public way, that in his judgment I was the person next best fitted for the vacant post at London. This fact had gone before the country, and indeed the nomination had been announced as practically settled. Thereupon, Mr. Platt filed a twelve-page protest, and the proposed nomination was laid aside. To be left therefore in the position of having been chosen by the President of my country for this important place, and having that President then told that he must not appoint me because one man in the State of New York had issued a decree proscribing me, was, I confessed, a situation which seemed to me disadvantageous, if not humiliating, not only to myself, but to the President of the United States. I did not think either could afford to let it rest there, and as for me I must frankly confess that it left a taste of bitterness in the distinction of the present place [on the Peace Commission].

These ideas were elaborated a little in various ways, but the above was the essence of it. The President repeatedly interrupted me with expressions of assent. Towards the close he said: "You do not need to dwell upon this, there are some things which I cannot say, but you surely know the depth of my affectionate friendship, and how fully you

6 Thomas C. Platt, at this time a Republican senator from New York, was a bitter enemy of Reid's, whom he considered a reformer and mugwump. Platt had run the Republican machine in New York for years. He had criticized much of McKinley's program, and took the lead late in 1895 and early in 1896 in an effort to combine Eastern party bosses to prevent McKinley's nomination. The President himself had placated Platt, though he kept a careful watch over him, and controlled him indirectly through patronage. Reid's concern here was ill-founded, as were his apparent hopes for the ambassadorship to England. McKinley was not seriously considering him for the post, but was using his name to make Platt agree to his final choice, Joseph H. Choate.

can depend upon it. I see the situation perfectly. You did not need to say one word; you do not now need to say one word."

A few sentences followed on other topics, and I took my leave to return in the evening for the dinner.

This was small and comparatively informal. The members of the cabinet were all present, together with Gen. [H. C.] Corbin, Secretary Moore, and Mr. [Alvee A.] Adee. Mrs. Day and Mrs. [Lyman] Gage dined with Mrs. McKinley upstairs. Our dinner was in the private dining room back of the elevators. I sat at the left of the President with Attorney General [John] Griggs next me. My talk with the President during the dinner was on general subjects. But with the Attorney General it fell upon the Pacific Railroad, and he gave in some detail his views concerning the obligations of the Central and Southern Pacific Railroads, and the way he could enforce them. He seemed to think he could bring Mr. [Henry] Huntington down.

After some chat in the corridor after dinner, I left the rest smoking and went up to pay my respects to Mrs. McKinley and say good-by. I found the ladies at work over a game of euchre, with a young nephew of Mrs. McKinley holding the fourth hand. He at once gave place to me, and the game went on. I had the misfortune to beat Mrs. McKinley in one game, but recovered myself soon, and presently said good-by to the ladies and rejoined the party downstairs.[7] Before 11 o'clock we all took our leave of the President, and I had time to get into a travelling suit and catch the midnight train for New York. [I spent] the next day at Ophir Farm, and sailed on the day following.

[7] Ida Saxton McKinley suffered from chronic nervousness and ill health, complicated by a form of epilepsy which often made her irascible. She was a semi-invalid most of her life, but the President was devoted to her. Her favorite pasttime was playing cards. As Reid notes rather drily here, she did not like to lose, and was spoiled by her husband, who contrived for her to win when she played with him.

CHAPTER II

Organizing for Diplomacy

[Paris] Wednesday, September 28th, 1898.

All the Commissioners met again in my private room at 10 o'clock. Judge Day raised the question of organization of the Joint Commission, or whether there should be any. The example of the Joint High Commission at Washington was cited, in which, by general agreement there was no organization, and only the simplest and briefest protocol of the daily proceedings. A remark in the English Parliament in defense of this proceeding was quoted to the effect that if there had been an organization and formal record of the proceedings and debates the [resulting] treaty might have been imperiled and the proceedings would have been indefinitely prolonged. Judge Gray explained the manner in which Lord Herschell had finally been selected as president of the present American and Canadian Commission.[1] The members generally agreed at the end that no organization was necessary or desirable in the present case— it being held that it was best to recognize no individualities, and nothing that could suggest the possibility of a debating society or votes. The two nations appeared by such representation as they chose, and were the only individualities to be considered. The Commissioners of each nation, after a full hearing of the other side and a full consultation among themselves, [could] express the decision of their nation.

There was a good deal of talk as to the language in which the proceedings should be conducted. None of the American Commissioners spoke Spanish, while two or three of the Spanish Commissioners were said to speak English, and only a minority of the Commissioners on each side were known to speak French. Under these circumstances it seemed

[1] In 1898 Canada, the United States, and Great Britain accepted a *modus vivendi*, whereby a joint high commission sought to negotiate the outstanding differences between Canada and the United States.

to the Commissioners best that the American proceedings should be conducted in English, having their Spanish interpreter present to repeat whatever might be necessary in Spanish, and leaving the Spanish Commissioners to adopt their own course.

I repeated the explanations received indirectly, but confidentially, a day or two before from the [French] Foreign Office as to the plans of M. [Théophile] Delcassé for receiving the [American] Commissioners today, and enabling them to meet the Spanish Commissioners at breakfast tomorrow. I also had Mr. Blanchard [a secretary] prepare for Secretary Day, and a number of others, acceptances of the invitation from the Foreign Minister, which had been received late last night, following the form of one I had myself sent in French. Senator Frye and Judge Gray, however, preferred to send their replies in English. . . . I also communicated to the Commissioners the substance of a private dispatch received for me by Mr. Inman Barnard [a newspaperman] from Port Said, announcing the arrival of Gen. Merritt and his staff at that point; giving their names, reporting them all well, and explaining that they departed immediately by the P.&O. steamer and should arrive in Paris Sunday evening.

Renewed reference was made by Judge Day to the importance in his opinion of the letter from Admiral Dewey, which Gen. Merritt was expected to bring.

The members had mostly brought in their sets of the series of confidential documents printed for their use by the State Department. There was some talk about the belief of our Embassy in Paris, that Spanish spies were endeavoring to secure copies of these documents, and above all to secure a copy of the instructions which were still locked up in my safe. The discussion caused one or two of the Commissioners to retire hastily to their rooms to gather up the documents which they had left scattered about, and put them in safe places.

Secretary Day then mentioned a report he has had that M. [Jules] Cambon was likely to be in Paris with some statements about the real meaning of the [armistice] protocol, and the agreements and explanations which had preceded it, that might have the effect of giving the Spaniards some opportunity to complain. He said he thought it desirable, therefore, at the outset that every Commissioner should know precisely what had occurred. As soon as the protocol was signed he had dictated a memorandum of the preceding conversation, of which he believed no copy was in existence save the one which he held in his hand. He proceeded to read this. It detailed the various efforts M. Cambon had made to have the terms softened; his repeated complaints that he thought they were harsh; and his final representation that, in the language of the protocol, the words "possession of the Philippines" originally used would sound to the Spanish very harsh. On this President McKinley had suggested the substitution of the word "disposition" for "possession," and to this M. Cambon had assented, whereupon the protocol was signed. The Commissioners were generally of the belief that M. Cambon's interference in this matter had resulted in an advantage to the United States, the word "disposition" in the opinion of Senator Davis, Judge Gray, and others being more comprehensive and suitable than the word originally used. . . .[2]

There was a brief meeting in my room in the afternoon about half past two o'clock, at which there was little talk excepting of generalities. The Ambassador [Horace Porter] arrived a few minutes before three o'clock, and took Secretary Day and one of the other Commissioners with his [Porter's] secretary, Mr. [Henry] Vignaud, in his carriage to the Foreign Office to be presented to M. Delcassé, the Foreign Minister. The remaining Commissioners, with Mr. Moore, accompanied me in my landau. We were received in the usual style at the Foreign Office, and shown immediately into a smaller reception room (the one to which I was accustomed being at the moment under repairs), where we were received by M. Crosier, the successor [to] Count d'Ormesson as Chef du Protocol. As I entered towards the last, the Ambassador presented me as Mr. Reid, but Crosier in a moment grasped my hand in both of his with the characteristic French effusion, exclaiming in French: "Oh, the former Minister, whom I already have the honor to know very well. We need no introduction."

Some miscellaneous conversation followed, and the members glanced about the room, looked out of the window at the garden, and finally seemed to grow a little weary. Senator Gray and one or two others asked me if it was not getting a little slow, and if we had not better go, the Ambassador not having made them understand clearly that M. Crosier, who had received them, was not the Minister of Foreign Affairs himself.

---

[2] Jules Martin Cambon, French ambassador to the United States, acted as agent for the Spanish government in August, 1898, in securing the armistice that concluded the war. Though, like most of his countrymen, he was personally more pro-Spanish than not, he conducted himself with admirable skill. What the Spanish thought McKinley agreed to, and what McKinley agreed to in the armistice negotiations were two different things. For exchanges of correspondence and dispatches relating to Cambon's role in the whole affair, see *For. Rels. 1898*, pp. 942–957.

I explained to them who he was, and that we were apparently delayed by some ambassador who had got the start of us with the Foreign Minister. It must have been ten or fifteen minutes before the double doors were thrown open, and the members were ushered into the room of the Minister, who greeted each at the door, and then had seats arranged in a semi-circle about one end of his table. Mr. Day took his seat nearest the Minister; as the group arranged themselves I sat next, and the Ambassador sat at the other end of the semi-circle opposite the Minister of Foreign Affairs.

M. Delcassé opened the conversation with a polite expression to Mr. Day of his pleasure at meeting the American Commissioners, and of the pleasure France had experienced in being in any way useful in reaching the present situation. Mr. Vignaud took a seat a little behind and between him and Mr. Day and translated to Mr. Day. Mr. Day expressed his gratification at the action of the French authorities, and at the good results which had apparently followed, as also with the personal conduct of M. Cambon. The Minister expressed his great pleasure that M. Cambon had been found agreeable and useful. He explained how carefully France had refused to be drawn in any way into any movement hostile to the United States during the progress of the war. [He] said that he had been in frequent communication with our ambassador in order to make clear the position of France. The Ambassador interrupted to say that communications of this sort had frequently taken place between them, and that there had been no hint at any time of any concert with other powers against us. The [Foreign] Minister referred to the invitation he had sent to the Commissioners for breakfast tomorrow. [He] said he had likewise invited the Spanish Commissioners [and] hoped that it would be agreeable thus to initiate their meeting. Having accomplished this work of bringing the representatives of the two nations amicably face to face at his breakfast table, he and his government would henceforth in this matter efface themselves. After a few more complimentary expressions on both sides the Commissioners took their leave, returning immediately to the hotel. All seemed pleased with the reception and noted with satisfaction the distinct intimation that France had no further share in the negotiations thus to be begun between Spain and the United States. . . .[3]

[3] Throughout the Spanish-American conflict, from 1895 to 1898, most of continental European opinion favored Spain. This resulted naturally from Spain's European position, her monarchical ties, and the fact that Spanish bonds had been purchased rather widely in Europe. The French, it should be noted, despite

Thursday, September 29th.

The Commissioners met in my room a little after 10 o'clock. A dispatch was read from the President acknowledging ours of the day before advising me that the order countermanding the assignment of Gen. [John C.] Bates, the London military attaché, to us would be issued and mentioning the arrival of Gen. [Francis V.] Greene, whose information seemed to the President interesting and important. He proposed that if we desired it Gen. Greene should be sent over. After a few moments talk it was agreed that since Gen. Merritt was to arrive on Sunday evening, it was better to await his arrival before deciding that we needed also to have Gen. Greene sent from the United States to furnish information on the subjects Gen. Merritt was supposed to cover. A dispatch in this sense was prepared and sent to the President. . . .

Gen. [William] Draper, Ambassador from Italy, made a brief call of ceremony. The Commissioners then proceeded in my carriage and another. . . . first to Pirou the photographer, where twenty minutes were given to hurried sittings; and afterwards to the Ministry of Foreign Affairs.

We arrived about three minutes past the half hour, and the servants at the door advised me that the American Ambassador had arrived a few minutes before, and that the Spaniards had that moment gone up. Taking Judge Day with me I immediately led the way up, the servant at the foot giving the usual battle axe salute as we mounted the staircase. We were received at the door by M. Delcassé and immediately presented to M. [Eugene] Brisson, the French Premier.

The next instant I saw the Spanish Ambassador, Mr. Castillo [Fernando de León y Castillo] making his way towards me. He shook hands with great cordiality, and immediately expressed his pleasure at renewing the old friendship. [He] inquired after Mrs. Reid, [and] said that Madame Castillo was still out of town, but would return in three or four days. After an exchange of a very few sentences of mutual compliment, [he] plunged at once into business by reminding me that he had been especially pleased at hearing the news of my appointment, because he was sure I would appreciate their situation. They were poor and defeated, and it became a great and powerful nation like ours, in the moment of its first great victory over a foreign power, to show itself as

American suspicions to the contrary, were at great pains to be formally neutral as hosts to the Peace Conference.

magnanimous as it had been successful. I avoided a direct reply at the moment. After the luncheon was over, he resumed the subject in the smoking room, repeating to me again, very earnestly in French the phrases: do not forget that we are poor; do not forget that we are vanquished; do not forget that after all it was Spain that discovered America; do not forget that this is the first great war you have had with a nation on the continent of Europe, or with any foreign nation; that you have had an astonishing victory, and that you cannot complete it without showing magnanimity.

Aside from this, to which I merely gave a general assent, the conversation consisted entirely in reminiscences of our former services in Paris, recollections of colleagues, amusing reference to the rapidity with which I had begun to speak French on my first visit, after having professed entire ignorance of the language, etc. His old first secretary (or *conseiller,* now minister to Belgium and one of the Spanish Commissioners) [Villa-Urrutia] also came forward to renew the acquaintance of eight years ago. [He] told me that he, like Mr. Vignaud, had had sufficiently long experience in Paris, almost to claim to be permanent secretary to the Embassy.

We had gone in to the table without special formality, excepting that the Minister of Foreign Affairs led the way with the American Ambassador, and M. Brisson, the Premier, followed with the Spanish Ambassador. On the left of M. Brisson sat Mr. Day, while on the left of the Minister of Foreign Affairs sat the President of the Spanish Senate, and Chief of their Commission [Eugenio Montero Ríos]. Between Mr. Day and myself sat another Spaniard, Guarnica y Díaz, and on my left sat M. Gall, Chef du Cabinet for the President of the Republic, M. [Félix] Faure. I found my Spaniard with only a few words of English, and he soon fell back on a harsh French in which we exchanged conventional and common-place remarks. From M. Gall, on the other hand, I was able to recall many particulars concerning French public men whom I had known, the changes in their positions, etc. In the brief conversation before going in, Mr. Castillo had told me that four of their Commissioners spoke English. But my experience with the gentleman at my right convinced me that the amount of English he would use in our discussions would not probably convey much instruction or conviction.

The other members of the American Commission made the best of a somewhat difficult situation, but none of them talked much, and our Ambassador [Porter] himself seemed a little quiet. The luncheon, however, was in every way well appointed, and our Commissioners in the smoking room expressed themselves as considering it a most dignified and elegant function charmingly carried out in all its details.

. . . It should have been mentioned above that in the meeting in my rooms in the morning the subject of the order of procedure was discussed and the time when we must decide upon & be prepared to present our ultimatum on the Philippines. Senator Frye and others thought it desirable to retain open minds on this subject until Admiral Dewey and Gen. Merritt had been heard from, and also perhaps until Commander [R. B.] Bradford could be seen. Secretary Day urged the necessity of reaching as speedy a conclusion as possible. I finally suggested that, at any rate, there were many questions connected with Cuba and Puerto Rico on which Spain was acting much too slowly for the spirit of the protocol. It might be wise to insist upon an adjustment and speedy disposition of these questions before we approached the Philippines. It would probably be wise to have them raise any questions they had concerning Cuba and Puerto Rico under the protocol, force decisions on these points, and above all get the evacuation of Cuba thoroughly under way before we took up the more difficult question. Before starting out for the visit to the Foreign Office, the Commissioners seemed substantially agreed upon this point.

Friday, September 30th, 1898.

The Commissioners met in my room at 10 o'clock. Senator Davis was not feeling very well, and left before the meeting was over.

. . . There was more talk on the question of what should be first brought up when we approached business, after the exchange of credentials and full powers, which, it was assumed, would occupy the session tomorrow. I repeated my suggestion that pending the further information we were awaiting from the Philippines, it was most desirable to begin on the points which the situation might seem to raise concerning Cuba and Puerto Rico. Judge Day pointed out that we were bound at the outset to assume that all these were settled finally by the protocol. I agreed to this, but remarked that by a quiet statement to this effect at the outset, we should either commit the Spaniards to it, or should draw their fire, which last was precisely what we wanted.

In connection with this subject, I called attention again to a letter from Madrid in the *Temps*, of which I had spoken the day before, and a copy of which had also been sent in by the Naval Attaché of the Paris

Embassy. None of the members having given it any attention, I took the letter and read a free translation of the latter half of it. All agreed that it was probably the most plausible and probably the most accurate and complete forecast that had yet been seen of the expected attitude of the Spanish Commissioners, and Secretary Day gave orders to have it translated and typewritten for the benefit of the Commissioners.

Almost at this moment a letter from some place in Switzerland was handed me, which proved, on being opened, to contain simply the card of Mr. McCormick (late Second Secretary in London) together with a copy of a recent letter in the *London Standard*. I had before heard that the *Temps* and the *Standard* had the same correspondent in Madrid, and that he had close relations with [Prime Minister Práxedes Mateo] Sagasta, and was apt to express the views which Sagasta wished promulgated. On examination the English letter proved to be almost a reproduction of the French one, and it was accordingly given the Commissioners to save the trouble of having the typewritten translation of the other.

The Commissioners were unanimous and emphatic at the close of this reading and discussion in the opinion that it was desirable first to draw out the Spaniards on the questions of Cuba and Puerto Rico.

Judge Day expressed a desire to have Mr. Stickney, the [New York] *Herald* correspondent who was with Dewey at the battle in Manila Bay, examined. I happened to have in my hand a memorandum from Mr. Barnard explaining that Mr. Stickney left Paris yesterday for London to make arrangements with a London newspaper for correspondence from China and Japan. Great regret was expressed at his absence, and it was thought desirable to see whether he could be induced to return. I explained to the Commissioners that I knew Mr. Stickney had the impression that Admiral Dewey's views were tending solely towards the occupation of Subig. I also explained the idea Mr. Stickney had expressed while in Paris that Russia was attempting to form an alliance with Japan, and that the inducements held out were great and not unconnected with the Philippines.

Lieut. [William S.] Sims, the Naval Attaché of the Embassy, appeared with a few more reports from his secret-service correspondent in Madrid. [He] asked whether we would retain this service at our expense, the Navy Department having instructed him to close up all the work of that sort he had been doing during the war. His name and some details of his qualifications were imparted confidentially. It was finally concluded to let him continue for a week or so in order that he might see whether he could do anything to shed further light on the plans of the Spanish Government, and confirm or qualify the statements in the Madrid correspondence of the *Temps* and [London] *Standard* about the instructions to their Peace Commissioners. . . .

It should have been mentioned above that Judge Day laid before the Commission two letters concerning the Philippines. One from one of our consuls and the other from a British firm at Manila, with branches at Iloilo and elsewhere. The consul gave some account of Spanish impressions and wishes, and then added his own strong belief that the reported plan for dividing the Philippines between Spain and the United States would lead to endless trouble, and be found impracticable. The British firm protested strongly against any idea of a division, showing that it would greatly reduce the importance of Manila, would scatter the trade and make it more expensive, and [would] tend to disorder in the islands and general confusion. Senator Frye vigorously expressed his concurrence in the views of both letters.

Between calls during the afternoon I found time to read carefully the confidential pamphlets prepared for us by the State Department, containing the correspondence with Dewey, Merritt, and [Oscar] Williams. [I] was struck by the fact that both Dewey and Merritt had clearly expressed views much more favorable to the character of the inhabitants of Luzon than those heretofore attributed to them, or generally held in America.

Saturday, October 1st, 1898.

The Commission met as usual in my rooms at 10 o'clock. A communication from Commander [John C.] Colwell, Naval Attaché to the London Embassy, was read, explaining that he had dispensed with the secret agency he had maintained in Spain, not having heard promptly from us any desire for its retention. The Commissioners were quite satisfied, several of them expressing a strong dislike of this whole spy business, and added that Lieut. Sims' man would at any rate probably give us more of that sort of stuff than we wanted.

Professor Moore read a very important confidential memorandum from the [Spanish][4] Legation at Washington which strongly sets forth

---

[4] The word "Spanish" is stated in the original text, but is an obvious error. What country is intended is unknown, but the context suggests Japan or possibly Germany.

their entire acquiescence in our procedure in the East, the satisfaction they would feel if we retained the whole of the Philippines, and their belief that Spain is quite unable to control them or preserve order. If the United States did not care to undertake alone the responsibility of such preservation of order, they would then be willing to unite with us and with another strong power (obviously pointing to Great Britain) in a joint protectorate. The question came up again as to the order in which the various topics should be taken up in our negotiation.

The members had by this time all reverted to my recent suggestion that we should deal first with Cuba and Puerto Rico, leaving the Philippines to the last. Judge Day had asked Professor Moore to prepare a little memorandum in this sense, which indicated that the natural order of business for the Commission would be the order in which the various subjects coming before it were stated in the protocol. The questions Spain was likely to raise in regard to Cuba were then mentioned, including rights of Spaniards remaining in the country, public debt, etc. Senator Davis remarked that as Spain had already agreed in the protocol to yield all sovereignty over the island of Cuba, her Commissioners had no occasion to negotiate on those subjects at all with us; that Spaniards, for instance, remaining in Cuba came under the constitutional guarantees themselves. Professor Moore suggested that it would not be wise to take this position, since the United States had not as yet undertaken to annex Cuba, and since the only control it proposed at present to exercise over it was that of a military occupation.

This led to a reading of the instructions concerning Cuba and the consideration of an article in the proposed treaty, which practically adopted the language of the protocol. The question arising as to what was really meant by "immovable property," Senator Davis said he had a vague recollection that the civil law gave a definition of real estate differing from [that of] the Common Law. Dr. [José Ignacio] Rodríguez was sent for to explain this point. The Doctor gave the definition in the Spanish Law substantially as it is in the English, holding that immovable property or real estate included all that was attached to the soil. He also explained that all the municipal buildings in Cuba were government property, as well as the buildings directly occupied by the Spanish authorities. . . .

Some further discussion was then had as to what should be our policy about meetings. It was generally agreed that it would be better, if possible, to arrange with the Spanish Commissioners to have only one meeting a day beginning at 2 o'clock in the afternoon. This would enable us to have our own private meeting every morning and to avoid the Foreign Office breakfast, which was generally considered desirable. Senator Frye was the only Commissioner inclining to meet at the Foreign Office every morning, interrupting the proceedings for a short breakfast there and continuing till the afternoon.

The question arose as to how we should go to the first formal meeting, and I proposed that it would be better to go in a body and in carriages, at least to the first meeting. I offered my own landau and Mrs. Reid's victoria for the purpose, which were promptly accepted.

In the course of private conversation this morning Judge Day indicated to me a much stronger tendency than at any time heretofore to come over to the views I have expressed concerning the Philippines. He regrets it very much, but begins to think it may be a necessity of the situation. Senator Davis hinted to me also that Senator Gray was beginning to take the same view.

The Commissioners reassembled in my room at 2 o'clock in the afternoon, and some desultory conversation on the probability of the Spaniards springing some of the questions foreshadowed in the Madrid letter to the *Temps* ensued. I predicted that they were going to raise the question of our capture of Manila after the protocol had been signed, and having deprived them of the means [of] preserving order in the rest of the archipelago, and Judge Gray in the evening reminded me of the prediction.

At twenty minutes past two, Senator Frye not having yet appeared, it was thought best that the rest of us should go on. I took Day, Senator Davis, and Judge Gray in my landau, leaving Mrs. Reid's victoria to bring Senator Frye and Secretary Moore. As we reached the Foreign Office a battery of photographers seemed to fire upon us in succession. We were shown immediately to the further portico on the front, not the one usually employed in entering the Foreign Office. Here we entered a vestibule where a French attendant received and gave checks for coats, etc., quite after the fashion of an evening reception. In the next room was found a buffet with wines, cold dishes and cigars and cigarettes. From this several doors opened into the Salle des Conférences, where a long table was arranged with portfolios and writing materials opposite each chair. Ample provision was made for at least two or three times the number of members in the Joint Commission.

Two or three minutes later the Spaniards began to arrive. As they were coming, the Frenchman who seemed to be in charge of the rooms . . . came to me, as the only one with whom he could communicate, asking what he should do about the crowd of newspaper men at the door. I explained to him that it was the sense of our Commission that no communication was to be made to them or received from them during the sessions, all the members dwelling with emphasis upon this view. The Spaniards and Americans met with great courtesy, which presently thawed into almost an appearance of cordiality. Villa-Urrutia joined me in the talk to the Frenchman about not permitting representatives of the press to invade the premises or send in questions, and emphasized the fact that the guardians of the hall must be careful to have no communication with them. He dwelt upon the fact that it would be a matter of honor for the Spanish representatives to give no information to the press, and that the proceedings must be absolutely secret. A few moments after the hour, we all entered the large room. Secretary Day was taking a place on the side facing the windows, when some of our Commissioners beckoned to him to take the other side, evidently preferring to make the Spaniards face the light. All fell into their places on the opposite sides of the table, the President of each Commission sitting nearest the end, and the others apparently in the order of their appointment, excepting that Senator Gray fell into a place beside Senator Frye.

The proceedings were opened by our exhibiting our full powers and showing them copies, to which they responded in like manner. Their President, Montero Ríos, then immediately raised the question as to the nature of the record that should be kept of each day's proceedings. His proposition was elaborated at tedious length, and apparently looked to a full record of everything that was proposed and pretty nearly everything that was said. His remarks were translated by our interpreter, Mr. Ferguson, who stood at the head of the table after the manner of a witness before a court, while Mr. Moore sat at the head of the table making memoranda. Montero Ríos talked sometimes for three or four minutes before stopping to permit the translation, and Mr. Ferguson's rendering was therefore necessarily a condensed summary rather than a literal translation, though the Spaniards did not seem to realize this for the moment.

Secretary Day replied, expressing the agreement of our Commission in favor of as brief and simple a protocol as possible. Montero Ríos talked again in the same sense as before and once or twice his remarks were briefly supported by Abarzuza. Finally I grew weary of what seemed to promise an endless discussion on a trivial point, having no apparent object excepting to create delay and needless formalities and technicalities, and jotted down [some] memoranda on the margin of

which I wrote my signature, and passed it to Judge Gray, who on reading it immediately added his signature and passed it on to Senator Frye.
It thus finally reached Secretary Day, each Commissioner signing it in
turn, and the Secretary without reading it repeated substantially its
proposition, leaving out the word "written." I suggested that we present
it formally to them. Day hesitated a moment and finally arose and he
and I consulted behind the chairs of the others. Mr. Moore, it seems,
had suggested that the word "written" might tempt the Spaniards into
loading down the record with endless documents, which they would
claim had to be inserted because they were written. [He] thought it
better to follow the spirit of my suggestion without actually adopting a
form of resolution. I assented and this soon led to the agreement in
which the Spaniards seemed to concur heartily, that the two secretaries
should prepare a brief protocol each day on which they should agree
before the subsequent meeting, this to be then submitted to the subsequent meeting for approval or correction. We all anticipated, however,
that Mr. Moore would find the Spanish secretary still desirous of
making a longer record than we wanted.

Judge Gray proposed that a Committee of one from each side might
properly draw up a brief form of order of procedure to be submitted to
the next meeting. The Spaniards assented and named Villa-Urrutia as
their member, whereupon Secretary Day named Judge Gray as our
member.

This seemed practically to finish the work of the preliminary session,
and the Americans supposed we were about to adjourn. It had already
been agreed that the next meeting might occur at 2 o'clock on Monday.
Suddenly Montero Ríos remarked that before adjournment he desired
to present a paper on which he desired to ask that action should be taken
at our next meeting before any other subject was taken up. Secretary
Day at once remarked that it would be desirable to have the document
read immediately, and it was handed to our interpreter for that purpose.
Mr. Ferguson glanced at it for a moment and then proceeded to read it
in a tolerably clear and direct fashion in English. The American Commissioners were able to gather that it was a renewed assertion of the
Spanish claim that Manila had been wrongfully taken after the signature of the protocol; that we were consequently bound to restore the
status quo; that the insurrection and bloodshed recently reported in the
Visayas were directly due to this situation, to the acts of our allies, the
Tagalog insurgents, and to the fact that we had been distributing arms
to them, while keeping the Spanish soldiers shut up at Manila deprived

of their arms. We gathered also that their "demand" for the restoration of the *status quo* was made in a somewhat peremptory fashion, and was intended to be interposed as an obstacle to any other negotiations until this question should be settled. Secretary Day simply remarked that the paper would be taken under consideration and that we should be able to say something about it on Monday. We thereupon adjourned by general agreement without a vote, stopping in the buffet for cigars and for five minutes general conversation. During this the question of communications to the press was again raised by Secretary Day. There was a unanimous agreement, made especially strong and earnest on the part of the Spanish Commissioners, that the proceedings were to be kept absolutely and sacredly secret.

The Americans who had arrived a minute or two first, were also the first to take their leave. We returned in the same way to the hotel, where the Commissioners immediately assembled again in my rooms.

Here we discussed at some length the nature and motive of the document which had been sprung upon us. The translator and typewriters were busy in the offices below producing separate copies of the English translation for each Commissioner.

There was some discussion during this period of our exact rights at Manila under international law. The other Commissioners seemed to think there could be no question that we were entitled to hold both by the protocol and by conquest. I threw out the suggestion that there were authorities, even among the most noted American writers, which might suggest the Spanish contention that whatever had been taken by our forces after the signing of the protocol, but before they received news of it, might be the subject of a reclamation upon our part by the Spaniards. Judge Day replied that this would undoubtedly be true if a peace had been signed. But he did not think it would hold good as to a mere armistice, and asked that the secretary look up and arrange the authorities. The other Commissioners rather quietly assented to this view, though I observed that neither Senator Davis nor Judge Gray seemed very clear about it.

When the translation was brought to us, it was read over carefully aloud, each member following the reading on the copy in his hand, and Senator Frye and others expressing from time to time some surprise at the peremptory nature of the demands.

The suggestion of Secretary Day was at once agreed to that we ought to communicate its substance quite fully to the President together with our opinion that the matter had already been dealt with in the correspondence between the State Department and the French Ambassador in Washington representing Spain, and that we were without authority to revise the conclusions therein reached, or take up the subject. He thought we should add that the Commissioners were unanimously disposed to reply to the Spaniards on Monday in this sense, and should ask his instructions.

The correspondence between the State Department and M. Cambon, which had taken place after our documents had been printed, and on the eve of our sailing, was then read. I noted particularly that the question raised as to our right to hold Manila under international law by virtue of a capture occurring after the signature of the protocol was very lightly touched upon in Mr. Day's letter. After our meeting was over, I took an opportunity, in his room, to call his attention to this fact, and repeat my recollection that some eminent American authorities did not sustain his contention.

Secretary Day immediately began with Mr. Moore the preparation of the dispatch outlined above, and about six o'clock it was finally approved by the Commissioners, and sent to the office to be put in cipher.[5] . . .

Sunday, October 2nd, 1898.

. . . Shortly after luncheon Mr. [James Gordon] Bennett called, the first time I had seen him in five years. He is perceptibly older, and the expression of the face has grown heavier. . . . The talk was cordial and on general subjects, but by and by he introduced the question of news of the Commission, explained that while he knew he could not get direct news, and did not think it proper that it should be furnished him, [he] thought, at times, I might give his man Mitchell pointers of importance. . . . He spoke severely of [James] Creelman of the [New York] *Journal* as a dangerous person not to be trusted. On the question of the Philip-

[5] The peace commissioners wisely declined to enter the tangle outlined by the Spanish here. A declaration at this time from the United States favoring the *status quo* in the Philippines and restraining Filipino rebels would have amounted to a refusal to accept sovereignty over the islands, as both sides clearly saw. "We propose to reply that these demands having been presented to the Government of the United States, were answered by notes of the Department of State to the French Embassy of September 5 and 16, and that any further demands as to military operations in the Philippine Islands must be addressed to the Government at Washington, and consequently that we can not join in the proposed declarations" (Day to McKinley, October 1, 1898; *For. Rels. 1898*, pp. 916–917).

pines he was quite convinced that the present popular judgment was in favor of their retention. He believed that owing to the composition of the Commission, I really held the balance of power.

Later in the evening I talked with Judge Day about the American authorities on the right to hold captures made after the signature of an armistice, but found him dwelling upon the great distinction between captures after an armistice and captures after a declaration of peace. . . .

CHAPTER III

Making Calls and Taking Testimony

Monday, October 3rd, 1898.

Judge Day came into my room half an hour before the time fixed for the meeting. I took the opportunity to recur to the suggestion that on the questions of international law involved in the assumption that we hold Manila by right of conquest, as well as by virtue of the protocol, and therefore were justified in holding the Spanish army as prisoners, depriving them of their arms, and leaving Spain to that extent without means to repel attacks by insurgents upon Spanish people in other parts of the Philippines, we might be confronted by some of our own legal authorities. . . . I attached importance to the subject because of my fear that their effort was in some way to draw us into a position in which we could not be justified in the eyes of Europe by [inter]national law. They would thus pave the way for what I believed they were scheming for, an opportunity to ask for arbitration, and secure the sympathies of Europe in demanding it. . . .

We were all agreed that in any case the notion of surrendering Manila was not to be thought of. [We] also agreed in the desire to avoid, if possible, having the Spaniards seem in the eyes of Europe to have any advantage over us on a point [where] authorities could be cited on both sides. The commonsense view [held] that captures made before the suspension of hostilities could be communicated by the swiftest means must stand. The best remedy for existing difficulties was to hasten a final settlement of the Philippine question.

[Secretary of State John] Hay's reply to our dispatch of Saturday night to the President was presented and read. It simply said "Your dispatch of yesterday approved by the President." Thereupon we took up the tentative draft of a reply to the Spanish Commissioners based upon the lines suggested in the dispatch to the President, with a few modifications. It was agreed to have it first prepared by Mr. Moore, and copies were ordered to be prepared for the Spaniards in English and Spanish.

Next we took up tentative drafts for a proposition as to the order of business, merely suggesting that the Peace Commission follow in this respect the lines of the protocol; and then [we] offer[ed] articles as to the surrender of sovereignty in Cuba and the cession to the United States of Puerto Rico, other Spanish islands in the Western Hemisphere, and the island of Guam in the Ladrones. As originally prepared the proposition also included a reference to the Philippine Islands as the subject next to be taken up, and a reservation of the right to introduce other topics. On my suggestion both these paragraphs were stricken out, leaving the proposition to be presented today to extend only to the questions obviously fixed by the protocol. On the suggestion of Senator Davis, the words "public domain" were inserted in the draft, referring to the cession of the public property. In the description of the islands ceded, "Puerto Rico and other islands," I raised the question whether or not there would be any advantage in having it read "and all other islands." Senator Davis and Senator Frye both desired this change made, but Secretary Day argued that it would be wiser to follow the exact language of the protocol. [He] held that "other" in this sentence was just as strong as "all other," and was re-enforced by Mr. Moore's suggestion that in the parallel French column in the protocol, the phrase was "les autres." Senator Davis said he would then like to have the word "the" put in before "other." But it was finally agreed to follow the exact language of the protocol. Any benefit derivable from the use of the word "the" [would be] secured by the reference to the French text. The understanding of the Spanish Government that they were surrendering the last vestige of their possessions in the Western Hemisphere, [could be] shown by reference to one of their letters concerning the protocol at the time.

I exhibited to the Commissioners one of the Cuban bonds, in order that the nature of its guarantee might be fully understood. Mr. [Darius Ogden] Mills had procured it confidentially for me. . . . I explained that I was also trying to get a copy of one of the Philippine bonds without anybody's knowing . . . it. Secretary Day asked to have the Cuban bond long enough to have its exact language copied by the Secretary, and it was left with Mr. Moore.

There was some inquiry about Gen. Merritt, whose appearance before the Commissioners had been rather expected. I read them a private memorandum setting forth that the newspaper representatives of the [New York] *Journal* in Paris were claiming that Mr. Conway, who had been sent by Mr. Creelman to Marseilles to interview Gen. Merritt, had secured from him an interview of 900 or 1000 words, which had been cabled by him last night to the *Journal* in New York. In this it was reported that Gen. Merritt had indicated that Admiral Dewey was strongly in favor of the retention of Luzon, quite contrary to the statement of Admiral Dewey's views which Mr. Stickney had previously given.

Judge Gray was not able to be at the meeting this morning, being confined to bed with a recurrence of his toothache and neuralgia. Shortly after the other members had gone Gen. Merritt's cards were brought in. He had merely left them in the office, however, and gone back to his hotel.

At ten minutes to two the Commissioners assembled again in my room, Judge Gray being now present, though with a badly swollen face, and four of us went in my landau to the Foreign Affairs Office, where we found our secretary and Mr. Villa-Urrutia struggling over the wording of the protocol. We still found that the Spaniards were endeavoring to force into the record of Saturday's proceedings a statement that we had agreed that the daily protocol should contain not only proposals made whether adopted, rejected, or laid aside, but also the arguments in favor of such as might have been rejected. We had a brief session at one of the small tables at the end of the room over the form which our secretary presented, made some modifications in it, and then explained to the Spanish Commissioners that we were ready for business.

They first read their Spanish protocol, and our secretary then read the one we had agreed upon. Mr. Day pointed out the difference and Montero Ríos at once began arguing as to the necessity of having the record exhibit not merely the proposals, but, in important cases, the arguments. Mr. Day replied with precision and skill. But both made the mistake of talking a considerable time without giving the interpreter a chance to translate what was said, [and] a large part of the force of each argument was lost upon the other side. Finally, Mr. Abarzuza made a rather plaintive little appeal in English for the right to file arguments in important cases. All the members of both Commissions participated briefly in the discussion. It finally ended in an agreement to a proposition by Secretary Day that the point in dispute might in the light of today's discussion be probably arranged by consultation between the two secretaries, who should report what they agreed upon at the next meeting.

This struggle over the protocol of Saturday's meeting had lasted nearly an hour and a half. The obvious purpose of the Spaniards was to secure an official record for the protests they are undoubtedly preparing to present on every question of international law and at every point at which they can interpose delay to the inevitable results. Since they have to consent to the dismemberment of their country, they wish to make the process as slow as possible, and to be able to show to their countrymen that they protested and struggled at every turn, using every resource to avert their unhappy fate.

The moment they finally agreed that the secretaries should try to arrange the question in dispute, I whispered to Secretary Day that now was our opportunity to present our proposition concerning the order of business, and our proposed treaty articles for the surrender of Cuba and the cession of Puerto Rico and Guam. The instant after the Spanish President inquired whether there was anything more that could be done at this session, Secretary Day immediately took the opportunity to have our secretary read our proposal. They asked to have it first read over in English and then to have our translator turn it into Spanish.

The scene during the reading was picturesque, and in the highest degree dramatic. Montero Ríos looked as if he was losing his last friend on earth, and the others obviously experienced considerable emotion also at being thus brought face to face with the results of the war [in] the Western Hemisphere. The feeling of profound sadness was still more apparent, on the part especially of Montero Ríos and Abarzuza, when the Spanish translation was read, but they bore themselves with dignity and courtesy.

At the close of the reading Montero Ríos suggested that these provisions were of such importance that, while they undoubtedly related to things established by the protocol, it was desirous to examine them in minute detail before incorporating them in the final treaty. He would ask therefore an adjournment until next Friday afternoon for that purpose. The American Commissioners consulted rapidly, and then suggested that perhaps they might be able to reach a conclusion by Thursday, explaining that some of the Commissioners had official duties elsewhere, which made their early return to the United States important. The Spaniards intimated that they would yield on this point if it were urged, but remarked that Tuesday was practically lost to them, since both Commissions were expected on that day to be formally presented at the Élysée. The American Commissioners thought it might be better to yield on this point, and therefore agreed promptly and considerately to an adjournment until Friday at two o'clock. There was again an interchange of mutual courtesies in the ante-room lasting only for a moment or two, and the Americans again left first, most of us taking pains to

shake hands and take our leave rather ceremoniously of each of the
Spanish Commissioners. They were still apparently depressed, but as
always extremely courteous. The American Commissioners, on the other
hand, were a little surprised and more than satisfied at the quiet way in
which our refusal to join in their demand for the *status quo* or consider
the question had been received. [We were also surprised by] the readiness with which, after declaring that this question of the Philippines
must be settled before any other business was taken up, [the Spanish ac-
cepted] for consideration the new business which we presented.

. . . As soon as I could escape from some callers in the afternoon, I
walked around to the L'Athenée [hotel] to look for Gen. Merritt, who
had left his cards earlier in the day. He was seated in the office, and was
obviously gratified at the meeting. After a moment's talk, I urged him
to come around informally to dinner at once to meet Secretary Day. He
had very little time to dress, but presented himself in our parlor almost
on the stroke of the hour, looking magnificently healthy and rosy with
his recent exposure to the Philippine climate and his thirty-five days'
voyage since. Secretary Day led the way in pouring a volley of questions,
to which we all contributed our share. He [Merritt] was enthusiastic
about the Philippines, and declared the climate the finest in the world,
barring the fact that there was a good deal of rain. [He] was delighted
with the [Filipinos], declaring them a kindly, courteous, grateful, tract-
able people, eager for United States' protection or for annexation. [He]
was against the friars and wanted them driven out of the country.[1]
[He] was not the least little bit in favor of giving up anything we had
conquered. [He] spoke in warm praise of his army and in general made
a frank, soldierly, enthusiastic talk. . . .

Tuesday, October 4th, 1898.

General Merritt appeared before the Commissioners this morning,
when they met, as usual at 10 o'clock in my rooms. After a little preliminary talk, and some reference to a long interview with him which

[1] The Filipino insurgents who have revolted against Spanish rule in 1896 cited
as one of their reasons for revolt the excessive privileges granted to the Catholic
Church, the vast holdings of the friars, and church interference in politics. As the
Diary shows, the Church was at great pains to have its legitimate interests recognized, and shrewdly chose an American, Archbishop Chappelle, as its spokesman.
The vexing question of payment for confiscated church lands, or "friars' lands,"
was not finally settled until the administrations of Roosevelt and Taft.

had appeared in the [New York] *Herald* this morning, which he said was fairly correct, but in which he had tried to avoid mentioning anything beyond facts which were accessible to everybody, Secretary Day asked him a question which led to his production of the written reports which he had brought from Generals, Staff Officers, Admiral Dewey, and others. The Secretary [Day] read these in full, the General introducing each one by a little statement about the opportunities he had had for information, and the importance which he (the General) attached to the facts and opinions therein.

The papers by Gen. Greene, Major Bourne, Admiral Dewey, and the Belgian Consul attracted the most attention, those of three of them from what they contained, and that of Admiral Dewey from what it did not contain. The latter paper seemed especially disappointing to Secretary Day and Judge Gray. All of us in fact had expected from the Admiral some expression of his opinion with reference to the desirability of retaining the whole archipelago and of what he would prefer, whether a coaling station, a single island, or the whole group. Instead, his letter appeared to be merely an amplification of the dispatch which he had previously sent in reply to the first government inquiry as to which island would be preferable in case the government should desire to retain any. On this point he was entirely clear as to the superior importance of Luzon. Before the Commission separated for lunch, it was agreed that a dispatch should be sent intimating the narrow scope of the Admiral's letter and inquiring again whether it would not be desirable to get from him through the Navy Department a distinct statement of his opinion on the larger question. Senator Frye seemed as eager for this as Secretary Day . . . He thought the opinion of the Admiral (if we could get it) would carry greater weight with the country, on account of his reputation, than that of any other living person. He was inclined therefore, even against the Admiral's apparent unwillingness, to try to extract an opinion from him.[2]

Gen. Merritt spoke with scant respect of Consul General [Oscar] Williams' written opinion and of his attitude, but thought highly of Gen. Greene, Major Bourne, and the Belgian Consul.

---

[2] Dewey's opinion was highly valued because of his public stature, his firsthand evaluation of the Philippines, and his supposed technical competence. In view of subsequent developments, General Merritt's explanation given here takes on credence. Dewey won a hero's welcome on returning to the United States in 1899, and was spoken of for a time as a presidential candidate in 1900. Whether he favored retaining all the Philippines in 1898 is still not clear, but the balance of his statements and dispatches shows that he supported the move.

In the course of the conversation the General showed very clearly his belief that the inhabitants of Luzon were a much better class than had been indicated, [and] that the government of them would be comparatively easy. They would utterly refuse to return to the dominion of Spain, and our withdrawal to that end would probably result in horrible massacres. The island was valuable, the climate not as bad as had been painted, and at the season he was there [was] entirely agreeable, excepting for the constant rains. [He said] that the City [Manila] was attractive, rich, and prosperous. Sufficient native troops could easily be recruited [and] the revenues from the island, even with the operation of the oppressive Spanish taxes, would be ample for all the expenses of administration. He considered us in honor, as well as in interest, bound to hold it. There were also indications that he would incline to hold the whole group. . . .

At half past four o'clock, Ambassador [Porter] arrived with his secretary to escort the Commissioners to the Élysée. I had retained our landau for the same purpose. We went accordingly in the two carriages, Secretary Moore and Mr. MacArthur following in a third. Judge Gray and Senator Davis accompanied me, together with Gen. Merritt. At the Élyseé, we were met by the Chef du Protocol, M. Crosier, and in a moment or two were shown through the various ante-rooms, receiving salutes from members of the staff, as we passed, to the room of the President.

It was the same room in which I had first been received by Mr. [Sadi] Carnot, and in which I had last seen Félix Faure. He [Faure] stood now in his usual place behind the table, but advanced at once to receive each in turn, the Ambassador presenting first Mr. Day, next myself. Seats were shown, and as the company happened to group itself, Secretary Day sat exactly opposite the President, with Senator Davis and General Merritt on his left, myself, Judge Gray, and Mr. Frye on his right, the Ambassador at the right hand of, and a little behind, the President, Mr. Vignaud next him, and Mr. Moore and Mr. MacArthur behind the Ambassador. All were in the usual afternoon street dress, with frock coats, silk hats, gloves, etc. The President was dressed the same way, but all the military attachés in the rooms through which we passed were in full uniform. Gen. Merritt was also in citizen's clothes.

Almost immediately after the presentations had been finished, and the President had asked us to be seated, Secretary Day arose and, speaking in English, stated that he had been instructed by the President of the United States on the occasion of this presentation to deliver to President

[Faure] a copy of a telegram, . . . which he proceeded to read. To this he added an expression of the gratification the Commissioners felt at their reception in Paris, and at the action of the French Government with relation to the business at hand.

The President stood like the rest of us while this little address was made, but immediately on receiving the dispatches took his seat, motioning to the rest to do the same. He then replied briefly and gracefully, expressing his gratification at our visit, [and] his hope that we would feel that we were welcome to the capital of France. [He assured us] that while we at home were in the habit of treasuring the memory of Lafayette, we were now among a people who treasured equally the memory of Washington. [He] said he was very grateful to the President [McKinley] for his charming dispatch, and should not fail to reply to it within the afternoon.

Then he proceeded to address a few remarks to several of the members, first inquiring of Secretary Day as to whether it was his first visit, etc. Finding that Secretary Day replied in English, he immediately fell into English himself, speaking it with some hesitation, but not incorrectly or badly. He next addressed me in French, kindly saying that I was already well known to them, and that they were very glad to welcome me back again. . . . I replied that the President [Faure] did me as always much honor. He made some inquiries also of Gen. Merritt and one or two others in the same way. His formal speech in reply to Secretary Day had been translated by Mr. Vignaud; but the other remarks when he spoke in French were not translated. The Ambassador said next to nothing. A pause coming in the President's inquiries about the members, Secretary Day rose to take leave, and after a few mutual expressions of good will each in turn shook hands with the President and bowed himself out of the room. . . .

The Spaniards had been received in precisely the same style about half an hour before us.

Senator Gray was particularly pleased with the bearing of the President, and remarked that no royal personage could have done it with greater dignity or greater grace. . . .

In the smoking room after dinner [this evening], Gen. Merritt fell into some confidential talk. I asked him why Admiral Dewey had not furnished his opinion on a subject concerning which the President [McKinley] had been particularly anxious: *viz.,* what was really in his judgment the best policy for the United States to pursue with regard to the Philippines? Whether to hold only a coaling station, to hold only

the island of Luzon, or [to] take the whole archipelago, and particularly,
whether the whole archipelago was susceptible of safe division either
from a naval or economical point of view?

The General at first expressed a little unwillingness to say anything
about Admiral Dewey, whom he spoke of as his friend, and with whom
he said his relations had been entirely cordial. This last, however, he
seemed to qualify a moment later by the remark that the Admiral had
been a little stiff sometimes as to what the navy would or would not do
in the matter of cooperating in attack. [Dewey] had been careful to keep
his ships and himself out of the range of fire, and was evidently resolved
not to injure ships or risk the loss of any life in bombarding Manila in
order to aid the army in capturing it. He said that at no time during the
bombardment did the Admiral or any of the important ships of his
squadron get closer than two miles to the shore. He said [that] some of
the vessels commanded by younger and more impetuous officers worked
their way farther in.

On my returning to the question why the Admiral did not give the
opinions which he must have known the administration asked, the
General said that he liked the Admiral too well to attribute motives.
[He said] that it was tolerably obvious that he had his eye on the future,
and did not wish to express any opinion which would make him un-
available as a candidate for the presidency. He then mentioned that
Senator [Redfield] Proctor had been writing letters on the subject to
Admiral Dewey, and even (rather jocosely, he thought) to the President, declaring that Dewey might be forced into being a candidate. He
said that undoubtedly the idea had made some lodgment in the Admiral's mind, and had not been entirely dismissed. The General left
clearly in my mind the impression that Dewey did not intend to express
himself on the broad question of policy as to the Philippines without
being fairly forced into it.[3]

[3] Most American consular officials in the Orient had long pressed their home
government to expand into the lucrative Asiatic trade. When Aguinaldo revolted
in 1896, American consular officials in Manila, Hong Kong, and Japan led him
to believe on their own authority that the United States favored his revolution.
Oscar Williams, consul at Manila after January, 1898, was especially pro-Filipino
and had been reprimanded by the State Department for his effusive, colorful, and
naive evaluations of the situation, and for his public statements. Merritt argued
in his testimony before the Peace Commission that the insurgents were rather low-
class soldiers and posed no serious threat to American occupation. He ridiculed
Williams' idea that they represented the best element of the Islands, or loved
liberty, or could set up a republic. Merritt's testimony fortified the belief of Reid
and other expansionists that the Islands would have to be acquired to insure order

Wednesday, October 5th, 1898.

There was a rush of calls this morning while I was trying to dictate. . . . All the other Commissioners had assembled in my room before Judge Day arrived. He came accompanied by Mr. Moore, and it was evident that he had been in the office preparing a long list of written questions with which he intended to begin the formal examination of Gen. Merritt. As soon as a few of these questions indicated the line he was taking, and the thoroughness with which he had prepared himself, Senator Davis and Senator Frye seemed to take the hint, and began preparing lists of questions also. Presently Judge Gray asked me for a pad and began making notes too as the questions of the examination seemed to suggest them. The private secretary of Senator Davis, who is also the Secretary of the Foreign Relations Committee of the Senate, and an expert stenographer, took verbatim notes of the whole examination.

When Judge Day had concluded he nodded to Senator Davis, who in turn asked a few questions. Senator Frye was then called on. It seemed to me that a good many of the questions involved repetitions of facts already well known. But I supposed their desire was to get all this in the form of recorded testimony from Gen. Merritt, which could be made available in a public document as justification for the course that might be taken by the Commission.

Judge Gray took up the examination on a nod from Judge Day after Senator Frye had finished. He presently developed a tendency to argue in favor of his well-known extremely conservative views [against acquiring territory] by the form in which he put the questions, and [by] the opinions on moral and humanitarian grounds which he attempted to extract from the General. It seemed to me that he was doing his best to entrap the General into admission which might be useful in support of his subsequent contentions. I began making a few notes in order to be prepared to draw out the argument on my side.

By the time I began my questions it was after 12 o'clock, and in response to my first one about maps, the secretary [Moore] interposed rather needlessly, with the assurance of the large number of maps we had, and immediately dispatched messengers to bring them. The examination was presently a good deal disturbed and interrupted by the arrival of bundles of maps and the activity of nearly everybody in un-

---

if for no other reason. See *For. Rels. 1898*, pp. 918–922; and *Treaty of Peace*, 319–330, 361–403.

rolling and looking at them. I finally suspended the examination until something like order was restored. It was evident that my line of questioning was gratifying to some of my associates. [It] rather tended to take my good friend Judge Gray aback, since it showed that two could play at the same game. After I had finished, Senator Davis in response to some whispered apology of mine for taking up so much time, said: "It was admirable; it could not have been improved; it was the very thing to do." Senator Frye said something of the same sort with equal emphasis. . . .

CHAPTER IV

Threats of Rupture: The Problem of the Cuban Debt

Friday, October 7th, 1898.

The first important question raised in the regular meeting of the Commission in my rooms this morning was the question of the protocol. Mr. Moore reported the arrival of the long-expected Spanish Secretary from Morocco, Mr. [Emilio de] Ojeda. . . .

Montero Ríos, it appeared, was the member of the Spanish Commission who had made the fight for the insertion of their papers in the protocols, his object being to secure a means of getting an official record and publication of the dismemberment of their country. Judge Gray and I both expressed some sympathy with their position, and a feeling that after all they were entitled to put in permanent form their protest against the various impending surrenders. The agreement Mr. Moore had reached with Mr. Ojeda was that in the case of any rejected proposition, the side making it would have the right to file one paper embodying their reasons, and the other side would have the right to file one reply. We first modified this, so as to insert the word "brief." Judge Day and others still feared that they would precipitate volumes upon us. . . .

Long cipher dispatches were received from the President and from Secretary Hay, which were sent immediately to the cipher clerk for translation. Meantime we proceeded with an elaborate paper on the Spanish debt prepared for us by Dr. Rodríguez. It gave elaborate details of the different issues and the purposes for which they were issued. . . . [There was] $600,000,000 of indebtedness, of which about $18,000,000 had been incurred for Spain's expenses in wars against Santo Domingo and Mexico, and the rest for her expenses in endeavoring to maintain her authority against insurrections in Cuba. The Spanish bond which I had procured for the Commission . . . was brought up, and its language studied with great care. The general conclusion [was] that it was an obligation of the Spanish nation [and] that the holders must appeal to Spain for payment. On doing so they would find that Spain had pledged for security of the loan a property over which she had lost control.[1]

A paper on the rules of international law with reference to responsibility for public debts as applicable to cases of conquest, annexation, or absorption was read. . . . While somewhat deficient in authorities, [it] was an interesting résumé of historical facts as to what had been done concerning the public debt in cases of transfer of territory within the past century. No case was cited, however, which seemed to be precisely parallel either with Cuba or the Philippines.

The cipher dispatches from the President and from Hay were next read. That from the President seemed to be rather a suggestion that the Peace Commissioners should do something to expedite the movements of the Spaniards in getting out of Cuba and Puerto Rico. Hay's dispatch on the other hand transmitted one from our commissioners in Cuba announcing irreconcilable differences between them and the Spaniards, and stating the inadmissible claims the Spaniards had made as to retention of sovereignty rights to machinery and navy yards and other immovable property, time for evacuation, etc. Hay also sent the President's reply approving the action of the American Commissioners in refusing assent to these claims, and urging upon them enforcement of the protocol and speedy evacuation.

Judge Day and Mr. Moore were disturbed at the preparation of the dispatch from our commissioners saying that they had disputed the Spanish claims as to the time when their sovereignty would cease in Cuba. [They] desired a dispatch sent objecting to [their] raising this discussion at all on the ground that it opened a door for endless talk in a direction in which we thought we had closed it finally by refusing as a peace commission to take up the demands of the Spanish government for the restoration of the *status quo* in Manila. A brief dispatch in this sense was prepared by Mr. Day and Mr. Moore, and with my assent (the other Commissioners having gone out) was forwarded. . . .[2]

---

[1] The exact amount of the so-called Cuban debt is impossible to determine. It was estimated at as little as $20,000,000 by the Spanish and as much as $200,000,000 by American sources.

[2] The United States Army and Navy were trying to evacuate Cuba and Puerto Rico of Spanish troops and equipment during the negotiations. With Latin slowness the Spanish were either unwilling or unable to do so according to the American government's wishes. The State Department urged the peace commissioners

In the afternoon we drove over to the Foreign Affairs Office and found that the Spaniards had arrived a moment before us. Mr. Montero Ríos presented their secretary, Mr. Ojeda, to each of us in turn. Ojeda had just arrived from Morocco, and undertaken the duties of the secretaryship.

The agreement as to the protocol was read [and] accepted by the Spaniards, and on its formal acceptance by our side there was apparent a sense of relief on their side and evident gratification all around.

Montero Ríos then presented the Spanish reply to our refusal to consider their demand for the *status quo*. It was read in Spanish and in English, and proved rather milder than we had expected. Secretary Day suggested that it should go on file and quietly remarked that we had no desire to make further reply.

The Spanish substitute for our proposed articles in the treaty, the cession of Puerto Rico and Cuba, was then read, first in Spanish and afterwards in English. It proved to be an insidious scheme, . . . ceding the sovereignty of Cuba to us [but providing] that after a suitable time we should turn it over to the Cuban people. [It also would] involve the United States in accepting [with] this cession a responsibility for the entire Cuban debt, including pensions and all sorts of Spanish obligations for running the government, even down to the very moment when the proposed treaty should be signed.

After brief consultation Judge Day expressed our sense of the proposals thus made, and our desire to study them carefully. He asked an adjournment therefore until Tuesday next, when we should present our conclusions, and we all parted with great amiability. The Spaniards were, I think, a little surprised and probably thought we were innocently swallowing the hook.

Mrs. Day left word before starting to the theatre in the evening that [her husband] hoped to see me upstairs, either in his own room or Mr. Moore's. When I went up I found that Mr. [John] Foreman, the author

---

to make clear to the Spanish that delay would not be tolerated. "There are still 3,500 Spanish troops in Puerto Rico," McKinley cabled on October 7. "No transports have been provided to carry them to Spain. Longer delay cannot [be] permitted. . . . Whatever help the American Peace Commission can give in this direction should be given . . ." (*For. Rels. 1898*, 922–923). The peace commissioners argued that if they could not interfere in Philippine matters they could not do so in Cuban or Puerto Rican matters. "It would open to them [the Spanish] a door which by our answer of Monday [concerning the Philippines] we hoped we had closed finally" (Day to McKinley, October 7, 1898; *For. Rels. 1898*, p. 923).

of the best book on the Philippines,[3] had arrived on our engagement
from London under an assumed name, and was in Mr. Moore's room.
We spent the evening with him asking questions as to his views on nearly
every point of interest to us concerning the Philippines. His talk revolu-
tionized our views about Mindanao, showing it to be a far less difficult
problem than had been supposed. He also spoke of Panay and Cebu as
[being] inhabited by a people who would be quite as easy to manage as
the inhabitants of Luzon itself. [He] described Negros as the richest sugar
island in the whole group, and said there would be no real difficulty with
its inhabitants either.

Saturday, October 8th, 1898.

The proceedings in the Commission were begun with reading the
translation of the Spanish proposals submitted on Friday concerning
Cuba and Puerto Rico. Members seemed more impressed than before
with the insinuating effrontery of the offer to [make us promise] Spain
that Cuba should be turned over to its own people, and that all the debt
incurred by Spain in attempting to subdue it should be settled upon it.

A summary of the proposition was prepared, carefully considered, and
sent to the cipher clerks for transmission.

A dispatch was next read from Secretary Hay approving our suggestions of the previous day, but implying that the commissioners in
Cuba were not attempting to discuss the question of Spain's sovereignty.
Secretary Day and Mr. Moore were strongly of [the] opinion that the
commissioners had raised this in the very first paragraph of their dispatch as recently transmitted to us by the President. A reply in this sense
was prepared, suggesting that the commission in Cuba should attend
solely to the question of military occupation and leave the question of
the transfer of sovereignty to us.

Mr. Foreman was then introduced, and an examination began with
[a] stenographic record. [It] continued until one o'clock, was resumed at
half past two, and continued until after four. His opinions were strongly
in favor of taking the entire group as the best thing, and in any case of

---

[3] The title of Foreman's book is *The Philippine Islands* (London, S. Low,
Marston, Searle and Rivington, Ltd. 1890). A second edition and the first American edition, published by Scribners, appeared in the United States in 1899. He
subsequently wrote *Will the United States Withdraw From the Philippines?*
(Chicago, American Anti-Imperialist League, 1900).

taking Luzon. His views of the value of the acquisition were so decided that Senator Gray remarked to me laughingly that he couldn't get a bit of comfort out of the examination even after he introduced such subjects as volcanoes and earthquakes. . . .

Sunday, October 9th, 1898.

. . . Secretary Day talked with a good deal of candor about the murder of [George] Saxton in Canton,[4] saying it was exactly what everybody expected, and . . . had been threatened long before. The circumstances had been concealed from Mrs. McKinley until now, and must therefore prove a great shock. The Secretary had thought it possible that the President might in consequence of this give up his western trip, but was not surprised that he did not.

Mr. [Henri Georges Stephane Adolph Opper de] Blowitz's dry and rather caustic comments in the *London Times* on Gen. Porter's proposal to have the American and Spanish Peace Commissioners at dinner together, led Secretary Day to repeat his concurrence in the hint I had given some days before, that we might better avoid the feasting of each other till we were sure that we should not soon go to fighting again.

After luncheon [I] took Mr. and Mrs. Day to the Invalides. They were immensely interested in everything, and it was delightful to see keen intelligence and historical knowledge and appreciation coupled with such absolute freshness of sensation and genuine candor and simplicity in expressing it. Mrs. Day was overcome by emotion at the tomb [of Napoleon I] itself, and actually shed tears for a moment. It was a striking illustration of the force with which stately and artistic surroundings cooperated with the historic associations in exciting a person of sensibility. . . .

Monday, October 10th, 1898.

Turned my London tailor over to Secretary Day, who wanted a heavy overcoat. Senator Fry wanted thereupon to know if we were American or English, and exhorted us to spend our money at home. . . . Secretary

---

[4] Mrs. McKinley's brother, George Saxton, had been shot in Canton, Ohio, by a jealous mistress, much to the family's distress and embarrassment.

Day inquired whether he should go without an overcoat this winter until peace negotiations were concluded and he got home to get one. Mrs. Frye has been impressing the same idea upon the ladies. She had bought all her own clothes at Lewiston, Me., and thought they would do better to do the same thing, rather than leave their money in Paris.[5]

Translation of the Spanish reply rejecting our proposed articles was read in the Commission this morning, and also a memorandum of questions as to its scope which had been prepared by Secretary Moore. A little discussion developed a general belief among the members that these questions would be unwise, since they invited a discussion on the subject of the Cuban debt, which we had made up our minds to refuse to discuss.

A memorandum of our rejoinder to this Spanish paper was then read. It had been prepared by Secretary Moore and was warmly praised by Senator Davis and Senator Gray, although a few verbal changes were suggested. After these were made Secretary Day said that he desired in part to recast it in cooperation with Mr. Moore, so as to base it more distinctly upon the Spanish agreements in the protocol, and finally took an adjournment till 2 o'clock for that purpose. . . .

Tuesday, October 11th, 1898.

The Commission made a further study this morning of the reply agreed on yesterday, striking out several clauses which seemed unnecessarily to broaden the issues, and changing phrases. By this time the manuscript had become pretty involved, so I took it and read it over consecutively, being able from newspaper practice with bad copy to make it a little clearer, and a few further changes were agreed upon. The main purpose of all the changes was to confine the reply to the exact limits of the protocol, refusing to raise the question of [the] United States' accepting the sovereignty because [it was] not in the protocol, and utterly rejecting the demands about the debt for the same reason. . . .

Archbishop [Placide Louis] Chappelle, formerly of New Mexico and now of Louisiana, appeared and presented his letters of appointment from the Pope to act as Papal Delegate in the newly acquired regions in the West Indies, with a view of explaining matters to the local clergy

[5] Senator Frye was, of course, a leading supporter of the high tariff and American-made goods. It is interesting to note how great a hold the idea had upon the people of the time.

and promoting an adjustment of the new relations without friction. He was most conciliatory in tone, and on minor matters it was evident that his instructions from the Vatican would lead him in every way to co-operate with the United States authorities.

He raised, however, the question of the Spanish seizure of the Church property coupled with a sort of agreement to make a certain, annual allowance in consequence of this seizure for the support of the Church. In answer to a question from me, he said that he thought it was sub-stantially an arrangement similar to the Concordat [of 1802] with Napoleon in France. He was unable as yet to give the details of the pay-ments made by Spain under this agreement, but he wished it brought early to our attention as an obligation for which the Church had given up its properties. While he recognized the difficulties from the American point of view, he was sure that we would also recognize the equity of the Church's expectation. He showed a letter from the Bishop of Havana asking that these facts be brought to the attention of the dele-gate from the Cuban Autonomic Government in the Peace Commission. [He] explained, of course, that this direction was through some misap-prehension in Cuba, and offered to give us a translation of the substance of the document. I suggested that it would save him trouble if he left the document with us to be put into English by our translator, and then re-turned to him, to which he at once assented. I thought it better that we should have the full document, and see exactly what the Church was aiming at.

The Archbishop evidently made a most agreeable impression upon the Commissioners. Senator Gray and some of the others [said] that the Church had acted with its usual worldly wisdom in selecting such a person for this work. [He was] an American by long residence, familiar with the French and Spanish languages, obviously conciliatory and naturally disposed, as far as possible, to aid the authorities in bringing the Cuban priests to a knowledge and acceptance of American ways.

A letter from the Secretary of State [Hay] was presented to the Com-mission announcing that the Spanish had taken away $40,000 from Puerto Rico, ostensibly for the payment of pensions to school teachers and others, without the knowledge or authority of the American Com-missioners, and suggesting that we might watch for some opportunity for a claim for reclamation.

In the afternoon [I] drove to the [Foreign Office] with Secretary Day and others. Immediately after the agreement on the protocol of the previous meeting, Secretary Day presented our paper rejecting the proposed Spanish substitute for our articles for the relinquishment of Cuba and cession of Puerto Rico.[6] To our surprise, after it had been read and translated, they immediately presented the reply, which they were authorized under the rule to file in explanation of their reasons for a rejected proposal. It could not, of course, be a reply to our paper, since they had not heard it when this was prepared. But it impressed us all, as the extemporary translation proceeded, as being an adroit and on the whole quite clever attempt to befog and shift the issue. At the close of this reading they said they were ready for oral discussion. After a moment's whispered conference, Secretary Day suggested that on our behalf we would retire for a few moments conference on the paper they had just presented. In this conference, after considerable scattering talk, I ventured to suggest that as the Spaniards had accepted the rejection of their proposal, and had filed their reason for it, under the rule we might assume that the question now before the conference would recur on our original proposal. [We] might ask that the oral discussion, which they proposed, should proceed upon that. This was agreed to, and we returned to the conference.

The moment the suggestion was made, however, Montero Ríos immediately replied that to his mind both the proposals before the conference stood on the same footing. The Americans had presented articles for a treaty, which the Spaniards had rejected. The Spaniards in turn had presented articles for a treaty, which the Americans had today rejected. Both were therefore rejected proposals, and if one came up for oral discussion the other should stand on the same footing. We did not think it worthwhile to combat this view. Montero Ríos then further suggested that since we had just given notice of our intention to avail ourselves of our right under the rule to file a response to their paper just read, the oral discussion would be more useful if [it was] held after they had had an opportunity to read our reply. [It] should therefore at present be deferred. He and others also said that it might simplify matters if they made an explanation at once on a point where they thought there was a misunderstanding. They had the impression that the

---

[6] A partial text of the correspondence between Cambon and the State Department at the time of the armistice protocol is found in *Treaty of Peace*, pp. 285–318; see also *For. Rels. 1898*, pp. 942–943, 955–957. The Spanish obviously wished to give both Cuba and her debts to the United States as a war indemnity, and apparently seriously thought America would annex the island. The war declaration of April, 1898, however, included a clause known as the Teller Amendment stating that under no circumstances would the United States annex Cuba. Puerto Rico, however, was taken as an indemnity.

American Commissioners objected to their proposal to transfer sovereignty to the United States, [so] that it might in turn transfer [sovereignty] to Cuba. They said they had only adopted this form because it was in the rules of Congress, but they would be just as well satisfied, if not better, to rest on the transfer of sovereignty to the United States, and if we desired it they would gladly amend their article in that particular. In further talk about the desirability of delaying the oral discussion, they suggested that the entertainment to be given to the Joint Commission by the Figaro [Theatre] on Wednesday might interfere with work on that day. . . .

Wednesday, October 12th, 1898.

There was an early meeting of the Commission over the question of a reply to the Spanish paper read yesterday. Some differences of opinion developed as to whether it was better to accept or reject their offer to transfer sovereignty directly to us. At first Secretary Day was a little inclined to accept it on the ground that it might make it easier in our subsequent dealings with the Cubans. The objection on the other hand was that the Spaniards thought it would strengthen them in their effort to saddle the Cuban debt upon us, since their contention was that a transfer of sovereignty carried with it a transfer of debts. Secretary Day, Senator Davis, and I finally declared strongly in favor of adhering to the exact language of the protocol, and merely requiring Spain to relinquish sovereignty. Senator Gray and Secretary Moore argued that this seemed to be equivalent to abandonment, and that a country could not thus become derelict. Sovereignty must reside somewhere; and if not in Spain and not in us, it must be in the Cuban people. Senator Gray thought we would be better situated with reference to the Cubans if they did not have this claim to sovereignty, though he insisted that ultimately we should turn it over to them provided they could fulfill the conditions in [resolutions] of Congress. Finally, a dispatch was sent to the State Department announcing the intention of the majority to adhere to the language of the protocol, but mentioning the fact of dissent, and asking for instructions.

Dr. Rodríguez sent up an extract from the great Spanish Law Dictionary, universally accepted as an authority, which completely upset the Spanish contention that there was a difference between abandonment and relinquishment. This was turned over to Secretary Moore, who was asked to prepare a tentative reply in line with the conclusions reached.

At five o'clock we took Senator and Mrs. Davis with us to the Figaro entertainment, and the other Commissioners followed. The Spaniards were given the right of the hall, and as the entry was on the left, it happened that our seats were so placed as to be in the direct thoroughfare between the entrance near the stage and the main aisle, and for half an hour we were constantly being brushed over and trodden on by the people passing to their seats, and by attendants arranging for the lights to illuminate and adorn Miss Loie Fuller. Madame Castillo was seated beside the Ambassador before we came in. She soon recognized us, and she and Mrs. Reid rose almost simultaneously to greet each other. The meeting was especially cordial on the part of the ladies. The other Spanish Commissioners took pains to be cordial. A great many members of the American colony were present, and a number of Frenchmen with American wives, like the Comte de Montsaulnin.

The entertainment was of the old Figaro type. The Coquelins, father and son, were perfect in old pieces, which they have been doing apparently ever since we left Paris in 1892, and certainly had been doing for years before that. There was some graceful and rather unusually risqué Spanish dancing. There were also Spanish songs, and the Spaniards had decidedly the best of it, so far as the entertainment went. When at last the American part of it came, it proved to be in the person of Miss Loie Fuller, who told in bad French, and subsequently in not very good English, one or two little anecdotes about on the intellectual level of a rather vulgar child's newspaper. Then the hall was darkened, the lights were thrown on her, and she gave her queer dance with "Star Spangled Banner" variations. Then the other national colors were from time to time thrown on her waving skirts, and again the "Star Spangled Banner" was introduced.

If it had stopped then it would probably have been considered by most of the audience a success. Unfortunately, as the people were on the point of leaving, she felt it incumbent upon her to ask them to wait a moment, and proceeded to make a sort of stilted, and yet childish stump speech about the beauties of peace, winding up, to the amazement of the Commissioners, with an appeal for having the questions at issue sent to arbitration. It was a gratuitous and incredible piece of folly and bad taste. Several of us had some difficulty in refraining from expressing our sentiments pretty candidly before we got out of the hall. Gen. Winslow, who was in a front seat, assured me, however, that she was a good woman, was always accompanied by her mother, meant well, and was really sustaining the Parisian theatre at which she is now appearing. . . .

We had little more than time to get back to the hotel and dress for the dinner given us at the German Embassy. . . . The Countess Marie [Münster] was rather quiet at the table, but took the opportunity to tell me that she had not sympathized with us during the war, and that she was in favor of the little dog. Recurring to the subject after dinner, in reply to my suggestion that the little dog ought not to have crowded the big one into fighting, she replied: "Well I wish he had taken a bite out of you any way."

In the smoking room Count Münster gradually approached the question of our negotiations and the Philippines. I took a tone of the utmost frankness, but really told him nothing he did not know. As to the question of Cuba, in answer to his remark that we were likely to treat it as England was treating Egypt, I said: "Yes, you have probably hit it. Our Congressional resolutions probably prove a counterpart to Lord Granville's famous letter, and it doesn't look as if we could get out much sooner than the English have."

In answer to his questions about the Philippines, I told him that Gen. Merritt reported the climate, while he had been there, as healthful, and every way admirable excepting for the torrential rains. [I] mentioned that our reports concerning the dry season represented it as one of the most delightful winter climates in the world. In answer to his talk about mineral wealth, I said we had no reason to believe there was anything of the sort there. The reports about coal were mistaken, there being nothing of the kind, so far as [was] known in the island, excepting lignite, which was not good enough to make steam by itself. I also mentioned incidentally that we were the chief consumers of their principal product, hemp. [I] added: "You know, in fact, the Philippines have always been American." This statement seemed to astonish him. Even when I explained that almost from the time of their first discovery down to the period in this century when Mexico gained her independence, they had been administered and controlled from Mexico, he seemed a little perplexed about it. . . .

Thursday, October 13th, 1898.

At the morning meeting of the Commission, we took up the tentative rejoinder prepared by Secretary Moore to the Spanish paper, giving their reasons for the proposal of their rejected articles for Cuba and Puerto Rico. It dealt in a conclusive way with the question of transfer of sovereignty, and used the authority from the Spanish [Law] Dictionary with telling effect to demolish Montero Ríos' effort to draw a distinction between abandonment and relinquishment. [It stood] on the protocol as excluding all consideration of debts, and showed that a transfer of sovereignty did not imply also an assumption of debts. It went on to say that under the circumstances of the claim advanced it seemed proper to make a few observations about these so-called Cuban debts. [It] then gave an analysis of them, showing how they were wholly incurred without Cuba's consent, [and were used] in the effort to enslave Cuba, and not in securing any communal benefits for Cuba. Various suggestions were made by way of developing some points of the argument a little farther, but the paper in general was highly approved and accepted. Secretary Moore retired with a few written suggestions from Senator Davis and myself for ideas that might be incorporated, and a revised draft was to be read at an adjourned meeting at 5 o'clock.

When the Commission reassembled, the revised paper was read, and a few more comparatively unimportant verbal changes were made. It was noticeable, however, that there was a strong difference of opinion in the Commission on the question of making a decided stand in refusing to accept the transfer of sovereignty. Senator Gray still believed that it was not a tenable position in morals or in international law; that the sovereignty of an island like Cuba could [not] be left "in the air." There were some signs that Senator Frye agreed with him. Secretary Day had said to me some days ago in one of our walks that this question also troubled him a good deal. Senator Davis's view was that we could not accept the sovereignty without thereby allowing Spain to impose upon us a trusteeship for the benefit of Cuba. If this trusteeship existed at all, he did not wish Spain to be a party to it. As to the sovereignty, he insisted that it would be left by the proposed Spanish relinquishment in the natural place, namely in the people of Cuba themselves. Senator Gray pointed out that that was precisely one of the difficulties in the case. The Cuban insurgents might say to the United States authorities: "We are the sovereigns here, and you are trespassers." Although the instructions [from President McKinley] seemed to make our duty clear on this point, the Senator was still apprehensive of trouble. . . .

Friday, October 14th, 1898.

Commander Bradford appeared before the Commission this morning, fairly filling my room up with the multitude of charts he had brought on from the Navy Department for use in his examination.

He had traced two big lines of division in the Philippine Archipelago, and began his statement by saying that he thought the best thing for the United States was to take the whole group. The next best [was] to take the island of Luzon, and all to the westward of a line drawn from the straits southeast of Luzon down to the northeastern extremity of Borneo. This would make an almost complete defensive line from Borneo to the northern end of Luzon facing westward on the China sea. The third possible division would be to draw a similar line from the little isthmus separating the attenuated southern end of Luzon from the main part of the island down to the same point on the north coast of Borneo and take all to the westward. The Commander was positive in his belief, however, that as a naval and strategic measure it would be better to take all the Philippines than a part, and thought it would be easier to defend the entire group than a part. He was also convinced that a division of the group would materially injure the commercial importance of Manila. He dwelt upon the fact that nowhere else on the face of the globe were islands crowded so closely together, saying that there was hardly one of them from the shore of which you could not bombard the coast of another.

Secretary Day attempted to draw out of him an admission that Luzon would be sufficient, but he was extremely outspoken and positive in opposition to this idea. Senator Gray drew him into a discussion of the questions whether first, the taking of the Philippines did not compel a great increase in our naval force, making us more exposed, and less easily defensible, and second whether we were under any moral or other obligation to remain in the Philippines at all. The latter point Senator Frye succeeded in setting straight by a question or two. I tried to help the Commander out as to the former by asking whether if Admiral Dewey had been defeated and the victorious Spanish fleet had entered the Pacific to threaten our Pacific coast, we would have found it easier with the same naval force at our disposal to defend the Pacific coast with or without the Sandwich Islands [Hawaii]. To this his reply was emphatic that it would have been easier with them. On the whole, the Commander proved a very strong witness in favor of the Philippines, and I even thought he impressed Secretary Day a little.

The afternoon proved altogether the most important and exciting day of the joint session so far. Immediately after the protocols were read, our rejoinder to the Spanish argument on sovereignty and the debt was presented. . . . On the whole, it did not seem to me that our paper, as it reached the minds of the Spanish Commissioners, gave them at first much idea of its real strength. They did seem, however, obviously disconcerted by the quotation from the Spanish Law Dictionary, which so completely upset their contention about the alleged differences between an abandonment and [a] relinquishment of sovereignty. They were obviously staggered by the array of figures we presented concerning the Spanish debt, [and were] impressed with the positive declination to accept responsibility for it.

These inferences were warranted not only by their appearance while the reading was in progress, but by the unusual heat which Montero Ríos, especially, showed in the oral discussion which followed.

He at once said that they were ready to discuss the first part of the paper which had just been read, dealing with the question of whether the United States should or should not accept the sovereignty of the island of Cuba from Spain. But not the second [part], relating to the question of whether sovereignty included responsibility for the debts. On that point they would need to study more carefully the arguments which had been presented.

Before beginning the discussion, however, he wished to make some comments (he apparently read them from a manuscript before him) on a part of the last paper we had filed. He was sure that the Commissioners should not desire to wound the susceptibilities of either side, and believed that in this regard the American Commissioners were animated by the same desire as they themselves. He believed, however, that there was a sentence in this reply which on its face seemed to attack the probity of Spain, and asked to have it read. The sentence in question was that this seemed to the American Commissioners to be a proposal to transfer a mass of Spanish obligations to the United States. He had no objection to the thought he believed the American Commissioners intended to convey, but wished the language modified so that there should be nothing in it that could be considered in a sense offensive to Spanish susceptibilities.

As it read, it would appear to the Spanish mind as equivalent to charging Spain with endeavoring to obtain money under false pretenses, an intimation which they repelled. They were perfectly willing to discuss the nature of these debts hereafter, but argued that an imputation like this should not be put upon them at the outset. Guarnica re-enforced Montero Ríos with the remark that such a charge ought not to be made at the outset because they would be easily able to show just what the Cuban debts were, and what justice in the premises called for.

Both of them spoke with considerable earnestness and feeling, but talked so long at a time that the translator was after all only able to give a condensed paraphrase in English.

Secretary Day in reply spoke in a singularly quiet and unimpassioned tone, saying briefly that the American Commissioners had said nothing, and intended to imply nothing, as to intent, but only as to the effect of the proposal. Montero Ríos immediately rejoined that he had not permitted himself to believe the intention could be otherwise, and therefore he had expected that the American Commissioners would say what Secretary Day had just said when their attention was called to it. But he still thought the language in the paper should be modified so that there should be nothing on the record tending to wound any one's susceptibilities. He referred to the readiness the Spaniards had shown at the last session to modify a phrase about transfer of sovereignty from the United States and from them to Cuba.

After a brief consultation among the American Commissioners without leaving the table, they agreed on my suggestion to insert the words "in effect" before "transfer," and on Moore's suggestion they left out the word "Spanish" before "obligations," and added the words "which in the opinion of the American Commissioners properly belong to Spain." When the sentence was read with these modifications the Spaniards agreed to it with a fairly good grace.

Montero Ríos then said they wanted it understood that whatever articles might be now agreed upon, this agreement [was] not to be considered final or binding if there was no agreement on the remaining articles in the treaty. In a word, nothing should be final till the final vote on the treaty as a whole. Secretary Day responded that it would be necessary to have a definite agreement on the first and second articles in the protocol.

Montero Ríos at once protested that they had no desire to resort to lawyers' quibbles or any device. They wanted everything above board. They were animated by an earnest desire to lay the foundations for an enduring peace. [They] wished to reach an agreement on one single treaty of peace, but if this were not agreed upon, all the articles that had been previously assented to must fall. To this Ojeda added that before the treaty was finally concluded it might be considered necessary to make mutual concessions on various points, which had previously been agreed to.

Secretary Day replied that our purpose was to arrive at a conclusion on the articles substantially fixed in the protocol before passing to others which had not been so fixed. The matters that were made plain in the protocol were to be understood as settled.

To this Montero Ríos replied with a great show of frankness that the minds of the Commissioners met perfectly on the question of Spain's yielding its sovereignty in the Spanish West Indies. On that the protocol stood as firm and undisputed as any instrument could. Still the question arose [as to] what sovereignty is, and precisely what Spain is to cede. She means to cede all, that is implied sovereignty.

Abarzuza, speaking in English with some difficulty, but with sufficient clearness, said that in his view the whole protocol, and all the subjects embraced in it, were open to discussion. The treaty made was to be a homogeneous document.

Senator Gray said that with reference to their proposal concerning sovereignty, instead of leaving the thing turned over as the protocol left it, or adding to it, it was a diminution or a taking away from the thing turned over. Senator Frye interposed that, so far as he could see, the only real point in discussion was what sovereignty really implied, whether it carried debts with it. To this there seemed to be a general and rather hearty Spanish assent. Finally, it was agreed to discuss the question whether Spain should in the language of the protocol simply relinquish its sovereignty, or whether it should in doing this turn it over to the United States. Montero Ríos thereupon made another long statement about his ideas of the necessity of having sovereignty lodged somewhere. Secretary Day replied at length, showing what was the specific purpose of the United States in using the word "relinquish" with reference to Cuba, while it used a totally different word, "cede," with reference to Puerto Rico.

At this point, Montero Ríos interposed what seemed to be a memorandum of conversation taking place between the French Ambassador M. Cambon and the President and [the] Secretary of State of the United States. In [it], when the subject of indemnity was mentioned, M. Cambon was made to ask: "Is not Cuba the richest indemnity possible?" To which he said that there was no reply. From this Montero Ríos inferred that there was no question at the time as to the United States receiving sovereignty over Cuba and as [to] its being counted in the indemnity for the war.

Secretary Day received this with obvious signs of disapproval if not contempt. [He] simply said in reply that there had been no proposal to turn Cuba over to the United States, but instead ultimately to the Cubans. Therefore, there could have been no serious thought anywhere of [using] Cuba as any indemnity to the United States. That, he remarked, was all he thought it needful or proper to say with reference to what had just been read. Montero Ríos had introduced this memorandum of conversation by saying that at this point the written correspondence [between Cambon and McKinley] had ended. Secretary Day thereupon read a letter subsequent to the date of the alleged conversation, which, he said, was included in the printed correspondence drawn from the files of the State Department and [was] in the possession of the Commission. Montero Ríos then said there certainly seemed to be some mistake; that this was a letter he had never heard of, and he would take time to investigate it. He then asked if, in the judgment of the American Commissioners, Spain was at liberty to turn Cuba over to the insurgents. Day replied that Spain had bound herself in the protocol to relinquish it, and that it would then be found in the military possession of the United States, which was amply responsible and able to protect persons and property. What might become of the sovereignty did not appear in the agreement. All Spain had to do was to relinquish it. That, in the judgment of the Americans, was all she had to do with it.

Montero Ríos replied with considerable heat, and at some length that that was a situation that could not be accepted by Spain. She had citizens and property in Cuba, and must have somebody responsible for damage to either. It was absolutely indispensable and imperative under the 4th article of the protocol that the sovereignty should be turned over primarily to the United States. Secretary Day replied that the 4th article did not deal with sovereignty at all. Montero Ríos said it showed that at any rate the United States was to take possession.

The discussion seemed to be developing more heat as it went on. The American Commissioners thought Montero Ríos had been considerably excited by the quotation of Spanish authorities against him in the paper that had been filed at the beginning of the meeting, as well as by the positive tone in which the Commissioners backed up its positions. Once or twice the suggestion had passed between us in whispers that the Span-

iards were getting ready to break off. It was agreed between Senator
Davis, Senator Gray, and myself that at any rate it would be a pity to
have the break come on an abstract question like that of the relinquishment of sovereignty. . . . We all believed it would be much better to have
it come on the question of the Cuban debt, which would be easily stated
and understood both at home and abroad; on which we were absolutely
united ourselves, and on which we believed our people to be.

Servants had been admitted for the first time since the sessions began,
to renew the fire and to bring in lamps. There [was] apparently no gas or
electricity in the room in spite of the gorgeous chandeliers and appliqués.
The discussion was so earnest that it went on without reference to them,
though it is doubtful whether they could have caught anything of its
meaning. Montero Ríos had said that the point concerning relinquishment of sovereignty was in some sense academical. But they showed no
disposition to stop talking. They had said two or three times that they
had adduced all the arguments they thought of at present on the question, but might possibly wish to add something at the next session. When
Secretary Day suggested that we might proceed to the discussion of the
second question involved in the paper, namely whether sovereignty carried the debts with it, Montero Ríos said there seemed to be no use in
this. If nobody took the sovereignty, he had no interest in what it included. This seemed to bring us tolerably close to a break; and not at the
exact point where any of us thought the break desirable.

Senator Gray had once or twice made the suggestion that a suitable
hour for an adjournment was already somewhat past, and now proposed
that we take an adjournment till two o'clock on Saturday. The Spaniards
thereupon objected. They were engaged to take luncheon at or near that
hour with the Spanish Ambassador [Castillo], and could not be in both
places at the same time. Accordingly at their request the adjournment
was made till Monday at 2 o'clock. The Commissioners of each country
collected in separate groups afterwards, and the talk among the Spaniards seemed to be earnest if not excited. We went home rather impressed with the idea that they were "riding for a fall."

Almost immediately on my entering the hotel I received confidentially,
through one of my trusted channels for information in Paris, news that
a dispatch had been received during the day by a certain Spanish duchess
(whose relations to the Queen Regent [Maria Christina] were close
enough to have the latter act as godmother for her children) from a private secretary to the Queen Regent, predicting the probable return of the
Spanish Commissioners to Madrid before the end of the following week.

At the same time I received some news of a peculiarly personal character concerning an intimate asssociate in a family in the [Spanish] Commission involving a Spanish effort to get news [of the Commission's work]. They had [apparently] learned early through this channel of our fixed attitude on the debt. A final piece of news was that a syndicate was believed to be making up, including some Paris bankers as well as some American capitalists (the Standard Oil Company or some member of it had been hinted at as one), for taking over a very large block of the Cuban bonds at one half their present selling value. The effect the Spaniards would expect this to be capable of having on some of the influences at Washington seemed plain.

Some of these points seemed so important that I felt bound immediately to communicate them to Secretary Day. I found him in his room, and explained to him that I should not mention them to anybody else, [and] should not mention them to him if I did not know him to be a veritable grave-yard for secrets. Under the circumstances, it seemed to be my duty to let him weigh the information in relation with other facts. He spoke of the first and second matters as of great importance, and promised implicitly the utmost reserve and discretion. We agreed that there was a strong probability of a rupture sometime next week. When I left him he was quite concerned as to the best means of avoiding it on the precise point we had reached in the oral discussion, and of tiding this over in some way so as to bring the break specifically and clearly on the debt. He was also impressed by the gravity of the situation in Cuba and the Philippines, as well as by the apparent political disadvantages at home, which our slow progress did nothing to relieve. Before dismissing the subject from my mind, I gave orders both in London and Paris that no reference to the Peace Commission should appear in the [New York] *Tribune*'s London cables, and also that its Madrid cable should not hint at the important news above referred to.

Saturday, October 15th, 1898.

The Commissioners began gathering in my room almost before we had finished breakfast. Senator Davis, who came first, was quite of opinion that a break was probable. When Secretary Day came in, he began with the remark that he had "held the subject under prayerful consideration through the night" and was feeling much better satisfied with our position. We had filed our full case, he said, on the question of sovereignty and the Cuban debt. The record was perfectly made, and the precise stage in the oral discussion at which the break might occur could not impair the force of the record.

The rest of us did not take this optimistic view. We all believed that it would be unfortunate if the Spaniards should have an opportunity to let it go out to Europe, or even to America, that we had broken off on what Montero Ríos called the academical question of the possibility of some-body's relinquishing sovereignty without somebody else accepting it. Sen-ator Frye expressed with some vigor the belief that on this contention the Spanish position was stronger than ours. Senator Gray was of the same mind, having all along favored our acceptance of the sovereignty both as the natural course under international law, and because of the advantage it might give us in subsequent dealings with troublesome Cubans.

I stated my belief that what the Spanish thought the trump card, which they held up their sleeve to play at the last moment, was a break on a question of this kind. [On such a question] they had a fair chance to defeat us in America, and get the sympathy of Europe. [They could fol-low this with] a declaration that there was no possibility of agreeing with us, but that they were ready to refer the matter to arbitration. The other members said that, of course, that could not be accepted (in which I fully concurred). I insisted that nevertheless it left us somewhat at a dis-advantage and thought it was far preferable to force the break, if con-vinced that it was near, and ourselves choose the ground on which it was to come. The debt seemed to me the clear thing. I proposed therefore to take advantage of Montero Ríos' remark that the question of transfer of sovereignty was at any rate more or less academical, and propose to them that it might be worth while to leave it for the time and proceed to the really vital question of whether sovereignty did or did not carry debts. Mr. Day and others predicted that they would be too smart to do that, though it was agreed that there would be no great harm in trying it. I then suggested that before a break finally came we ought to ask for a delay while we retired for consultation, and then present something in writing which could force the break on the debt question. Secretary Day jumped at this idea, and said: "Yes, let us have a paper ready for the emergency just as Montero Ríos had his the other day when we rejected their proposals." This idea took the fancy of all, and was hammered out at considerable length.

. . . [I] proposed to the Commissioners that the paper we were talking about drawing up should be composed substantially as follows: It should state first that the essential question in dispute was the question of the

Cuban debt. On this the American Commissioners felt it due to courtesy to say that after having given full weight to the arguments of the Spanish Commissioners they were constrained to the position they had first taken. These debts could not under any circumstances be recognized, and this position was final. Nevertheless, as both sides had proposed articles of a treaty intended to carry out the provisions of the first and second articles of the protocol, and as they appeared unable to agree upon these, the American Commissioners hereby withdrew the articles they had proposed and presented the following substitute (this substitute to be the exact language of the two articles in the protocol concerning Cuba and Puerto Rico).

Meantime, Mr. Moore had been jotting down a paper embodying these ideas. It was modified a little and thereupon generally agreed to, with the understanding that we should meet again at 5 o'clock to consider it further. Whatever was agreed to should be drawn up in ample time and our translator should have an opportunity to familiarize himself with it so thoroughly that he would be able to translate it accurately and exactly at sight when presented.

At the afternoon meeting the draft was again presented and discussed at some length. Secretary Day seemed curiously averse to a suggestion Senator Gray had urged that we might say also that in taking the military occupation of Cuba, we assumed all the responsibilities justly or legally attaching to that occupation both as to persons and property. Senator Gray wanted it inserted in the memorandum, and was even willing to put it in the treaty. I suggested that it would be better to present the assurance orally in the discussion. But even to this Secretary Day seemed at first averse. Finally, we separated with the closing suggestion from Secretary Day that we should all consider the question whether it was wise to allow our proposed memorandum to rest on the final refusal to consider the Cuban debt, or whether we should in addition withdraw our former articles, and propose instead new articles to be composed solely of the exact language of the two articles in the protocol relating to Cuba, Puerto Rico, and Guam. . . .

Monday, October 17th, 1898.

At the meeting today we had first several letters from the [State] Department. One of them transmitted a very long report by Gen. Greene embodying his observations at Manila, and what he had been able to gather concerning the Philippines. Another gave a detailed account of the effort of [Felipé] Agoncillo,[7] a representative of [Emilio] Aguinaldo, to get an interview with the President or some sort of recognition. It transmitted the extraordinary paper he had finally furnished when given permission to file an unofficial memorandum of what he wished to say as a private individual from the Philippines. In this [paper] he claimed an independent government for the Islands, asserted an alliance with the United States invited by us and accorded by [the Filipino insurgents], and quoted the language of the Declaration of Independence, which he requested Spain and the United States to make effective as to the Philippines.[8]

Discussion was then resumed after the plan of procedure agreed to on Saturday. Senator Gray did not want to retire for a consultation after the Spaniards should have closed their talk on our receiving sovereignty. [He] did want to embody in our formal paper, or even in the treaty, a substantial guarantee for Spanish citizens and property. Secretary Day objected strenuously to having such a guarantee in the treaty, though he had no objection to giving assurance in the oral debate. He thought the United States stood well enough to have something taken for granted. It ought not to be expected to put such guarantees in a treaty.

Davis and others suggested that merely declaratory stipulations of this sort were common in treaties. I prepared a little memorandum to be used as a basis for an oral statement to the effect that in taking military occupation, we accepted all the responsibility justly and legally attaching thereto for life and property. Secretary Day still evinced . . . a strong

---

[7] The Filipino rebels under Emilio Aguinaldo had established a provisional government during the course of their rebellion after 1896 and looked forward to American liberation. The McKinley administration at this time was in a delicate position in relation to them. No promise of independence could be made because American public opinion would not tolerate it. But the rebels could not be rebuffed completely lest they turn against the Americans, which they finally did on February 4, 1899, on the eve of the treaty's acceptance by the Senate. Felipé Agoncillo, Aguinaldo's diplomatic agent, had talked with McKinley in Washington, but received no assurances of any kind for the future. He then went to Paris and wished to testify before the Peace Commission, but was rebuffed, and returned to the Philippines with considerable bitterness toward the American government.

[8] As has been noted, Aguinaldo considered himself the rightful ruler of the Philippines and, until the treaty was concluded, had some hope of American recognition and assistance. In 1899 his rebels began the guerilla warfare against American troops that lasted until 1902, resulting in his own capture in 1901. The presence of the rebels and their paper government was an irritant to the peace negotiations and a taunt to those who claimed that all the Filipinos welcomed American rule.

desire to recast Saturday's paper himself. Finally he carried off the paper and memoranda and asked a meeting at 1:30. . . .

We thereupon proceeded to the Foreign Affairs [Ministry], arriving almost simultaneously with the Spaniards. Villa-Urrutia and Ojeda, however, were both absent, being ill in bed from colds. In an informal talk we agreed to proceed as if they were present, and at [the Spaniards'] request, the secretary of the Spanish Embassy in Paris was introduced to keep the record on their side.

Before proceeding to the regular business, Montero Ríos said he desired to call [the] attention of the American Commissioners to a telegram from Madrid advising them of the sailing of two United States war vessels for Manila, and also of their troubles with the natives in Luzon and elsewhere, who were holding large numbers of Spanish prisoners, special and military. He introduced this subject informally with the view of aiding in their efforts to secure an enduring peace, and in the hope [of] cooperation from the American Commissioners in avoiding causes of discord. Secretary Day asked for the reading of the telegram, but Montero Ríos, while willing enough, he said, to read it, did not wish to make its introduction quite so formal. His only object was to help bring about good relations. [He] did not desire to introduce the subject of the telegram by way of making a formal protest or raising any discussion. As to the prisoners, he would be quite willing to have them turned over to the Americans; in fact, would prefer it.

Secretary Day replied that it was no less our purpose to promote harmony and an enduring peace. The matters introduced in relation with his telegram properly belonged to the respective governments of the two countries. In the absence of instructions the American Commissioners would receive and note the oral communication made and its substance would be communicated to our government. Montero Ríos explained that he deprecated anything tending to exert an unfavorable effect on the public feeling in either country. [He] brought this up as a friendly communication in the common interest, not formal and not to be entered on the minutes, and therewith he said the incident [was] closed.

Secretary Day then said that if the Spanish Commissioners had anything more to present on the subject last under discussion, the American Commissioners would be pleased to give their best attention to it. Montero Ríos replied that it was at the suggestion of an American delegate that the discussion at the last meeting was carried over. If, however, the Americans now desired that Spain should again initiate the discussion, they were quite ready. Still, they had understood the American Commissioners to think that through the delay of the last adjournment some new light might be received. At present he could, if desired, only give a résumé, in somewhat different aspect, of views already presented.

Secretary Day responded that this should be exactly as the Spanish Commissioners desired. It was true that we had been quite willing to take time for the consideration of the views last presented in the hope that something new might develop that would bring the minds of the Commissioners closer together, but nothing of the kind had appeared on our side. Montero Ríos then said he had nothing additional to present now that was substantial. Nevertheless, he would be willing to present the subject in some other aspects in the hope of carrying conviction to the minds of the American Commissioners. He thought that article one in their draft, though not in the language of the protocol, had practically the same sense. But he would be ready to frame another entirely harmonious with the protocol, and with the dispatches which brought it about.

Gray incidentally whispered to me: "That is our opportunity," and hurried over to Secretary Day with the same suggestion. Day immediately began: "In view of the disposition thus shown by the Spanish Commissioners, we shall be glad to submit the following." He then read the document agreed upon as finally presented in my room just before we started for the Foreign Office. The effect of the reading was quite visible on the faces of all the Spaniards who knew English, and before the close Abarzuza was whispering very earnestly to Montero Ríos. It was then translated by our translator into Spanish, the Spanish Commissioners following it again most attentively, and, as I thought, giving considerable evidence of being disconcerted by it.

Montero Ríos began immediately, very courteously, but with manifest excitement. He said they would receive this document, reserving the right to examine and study the two articles submitted and see whether they could agree to them, or would need to offer others, and meantime he withdrew the draft they had formerly presented, reserving the right to offer others conforming to the spirit of the protocol as it appears to them.

Secretary Day replied that the American Commissioners fully recognized their right to examine it in detail, but added that this examination would develop the fact that the articles submitted merely embodied the exact language of the protocol already agreed to between the two countries. He then read a phrase, which Gray had written out at my side and shown me during the recent translation, and had then handed to Secretary Day, to the effect that the American Commissioners suggest that if we adopt the exact language of the protocol, to which both nations agreed, then whatever responsibility attaches to either nation by the terms of their protocol cannot be avoided. When the interpreter came to read this over, Abarzuza tried to have him include in it not merely the words "language of the protocol," but "also in conformity with the language of the dispatches leading to the protocol." Day replied that he had referred to exactly what the protocol said. They then asked for a copy of the memorandum of this sentence, not for [the] record, but merely for their convenience. It was to be received merely as a verbal communication.

Secretary Day then asked what was now their desire; Montero Ríos replied that as the American Commissioner General to the exposition had invited them to this reception on Tuesday afternoon, and the American Ambassador to a dinner on Tuesday evening, it would seem impossible to have a meeting before Wednesday afternoon. To which the American Commissioners assented. As we parted, the Spaniards evinced even more than their usual cordiality. . . .

The Grand Duchess of Vladimir has arrived to get a trousseau for her daughter.[9] We are in possession of her old rooms, and so the Hotel Continental people have established her in rooms farther up the Rue de Rivoli at the corner nearest the Place de la Concord. There has been a great bustle in clearing up the private staircase [to] which we have heretofore had practically the exclusive use, placing palms and flowers in the corners, etc. Some of the Commissioners and their wives seemed a little restrained by the multitudinous rush of servants in the corridors, as well as by the careful closing of the doors across them at our end, and wondered whether we were to be excluded from the pathway reserved for royalty. It was left to "Eddie," the faithful colored doorkeeper for so many years at the State Department, who has been guarding our doors during all the sessions, to solve the difficulty for them by explaining that "we still had some rights."

---

[9] Reid's reference here is not clear. The title Grand Duke Vladimir was accorded one of the Russian czar's uncles. Reid may mean here either an aunt or great-aunt of Nicholas II.

Tuesday, October 18, 1898.

The Commissioners met at 10 o'clock, Senator Davis declaring that he was still up in the skies with his recollections of last night [at the opera]. He read us a letter from Senator William E. Chandler introducing Agoncillo, the so-called representative of Aguinaldo, and gave an account of a little interview he had with this half-Malay this morning. He wants to appear before the Commission, and it was finally agreed that if he made a written application to that effect we should reply giving the permission, but explaining that he could only be received unofficially.

The substance of the letter filed with us some days ago by Archbishop Chapelle, the representative of the Pope for Church matters in our new possessions, was read. It asks that the treaty should include specific agreements by Spain to return to the Catholic Church a large amount of property seized under some sort of "Concordat" arrangements many years ago. Included in this is even the present custom house. We have generally agreed that this was not a subject for us to touch at all. Finally, on my motion, the secretary was instructed to prepare a dispatch to the [State] Department reciting the appearance before us of Archbishop Chapelle, the exhibition of his credentials from the Pope, his statements, and the favorable impression he had made upon us, and then the substance of the letter which he presented from the Bishop of Havana. [I would also include] our conclusion that unless otherwise instructed we should advise him that these were entirely questions for the home government, and not matters with which, under our present authority, we would be at liberty to deal in the treaty of peace.

In the afternoon Secretary Day and I went to the rather elaborate headquarters of our Commissioner-General of the Paris Exposition for 1900, Mr. [Ferdinand] Peck, at No. 20 Avenue Rapp, to which we had been invited some days before. We had intended not to go, but on finding that the Spaniards were going, felt that it would not be decorous in us to be absent. The Senators, however, all stayed away. . . . Secretary Day and I made our way through the various rooms, and were preparing to beat a hasty retreat, when two or three of the Spaniards came in. We spent a few moments in conversation with them, and got away, agreeing that we would have been better content if we had been able to escape it altogether.

In the evening, the Days went with us in our carriage to the big dinner given by the Ambassador [Horace Porter] to the Joint Peace Commission, and the representatives of the French Government. Four of the

Spaniards were present, Montero Ríos, Abarzuza, Guarnica, and Cerero, besides the Spanish Ambassador and his wife. From the French Government there were Brisson, the Premier, Delcassé, the Minister of Foreign Affairs, and Cambon, Ambassador to the United States, and his wife. . . .

In the smoking room [after dinner] fate or possibly some design on the part of the others landed me with Montero Ríos and through two cigars on his part, two cigarettes on mine and two glasses of cognac apiece, I was compelled to make conversation with him. The talk began about the house, objects of art, and the French artists, and soon drifted to Madrid, the gallery, Velásquez, and the glories of Spanish art. The old gentleman seemed keenly alive to these, but not very proud of modern Spanish art. . . . The talk, however, soon drifted on the condition of Spain, the necessity for peace, and above all the necessity for means for internal development. The whole tone of his talk indicated a readiness to be rid of the colonies, but a feeling that they ought to get money enough for them to be able to prosecute internal improvements and develop their own country. His talk was very earnest, and, at times, almost pathetic. I was scarcely able to bring it to an end before we were all moving out to join the ladies.

On the way, the Spanish Ambassador Castillo intercepted me, and began (with his much better command of French) a vigorous argument on the necessity of magnanimity to the fallen nation, in the form of a recognition of the Cuban debt. He argued that a large part of this debt had been incurred for purposes of internal development of Cuba, railroads and the like. [He] repeated several times that speaking unofficially, and as one old friend to another, he gave me his word of honor that if he were in the place of the United States he would gladly take the Cuban debt. Otherwise we should surely have trouble with the Cubans. If we assumed this debt, we had absolute control of Cuba in the eyes of the world. I told him there was not the remotest possibility of our doing it; that if we did we could not return to our own country. He protested against this view. When I added that paying this debt would really be paying them for carrying on the war against the Cubans, whom we had freed, he said: "No, but for preserving order in an island which otherwise would have been a prey to the worst of disorders."

These two talks convinced me that the Spaniards were by no means ready to accept our final statement concerning the debt given them yesterday. This conviction was confirmed when a little later they appealed to Secretary Day for the postponement of the meeting tomorrow until

Friday at the same hour on the ground that they could not possibly be ready sooner. It is more and more clear that they mean to insist on payment of the Cuban debts and watch for some opportunity to ask an arbitration on it.

Wednesday, October 19th, 1898.

Archbishop Chappelle called at the office this morning wishing to see Mr. Day with reference to his recent communication. After he had waited an hour or two, [Day] sent down word that we were waiting for a reply from the government to our communication on the subject, and should hope to see him as soon after that as possible. The Archbishop, meantime, having gone, the secretary [Moore] was instructed to write him in this sense.

I gave to the Commission the Philippine bond, which, by their authority, I had taken steps to procure in Madrid, together with a translation of it prepared for me by Dr. Rodríguez. It was read and a long and desultory talk on both the Cuban and Philippine debts resulted. It reached no precise conclusion excepting that we must stand firm in our refusal to recognize them, and wait to see what trick the Spaniards had next up their sleeve. Senator Gray, however, evinced a considerable desire to do something in the nature of concession by way of displaying magnanimity to the Spaniards. If any of these bonds were clearly for internal improvements, he thought that proportion of the debt might be recognized.

Senator Frye in deploring the delay until Friday, which the Spaniards had requested, urged that there ought to be a meeting at any rate on the day fixed in the adjournment, even though no quorum should be present, in order to preserve the continuity of the proceedings. Judge Day took the ground that this could be arranged between the two secretaries in the daily protocol, and it was left at that.

Afterwards we drifted into a talk about the necessity of soon reaching a positive conclusion as to the Philippines, which finally ended in Secretary Day's calling on Senator Frye to state his position. He thereupon pulled out a paper, which he had written the other day, and read a couple of pages strongly urging the retention of the whole archipelago. The meeting seemed about to break up, when I asked why we should not hear an equally explicit statement from Secretary Day. He at first laughingly avoided the question. But presently [he] took it up seriously, and avowed that he had regarded the retention of anything beyond Manila with great disfavor, but had felt himself gradually driven to the belief that we must hold a much larger part of the archipelago than he had at first contemplated. His language almost implied that we must have to hold the whole of it as indemnity. He ended by calling on me for my views. I replied in a single sentence that I was, since the evidence we had received here, more than ever inclined to hold the whole of it by right of conquest. The war, in the unexpected turn it had taken, left us the masters of the capital and of the army and navy that had occupied the country. [We were] thus practically the masters of the whole country.

Senator Gray then expressed with great frankness his opposition to the retention of any part of the Philippines. He referred to the resolutions of Congress under which the war had begun, thought the ground there taken was a high one, and had been proud of his country's position. [He] was unwilling now to let it degenerate into a war of conquest, and did not believe that we were under such obligations to the Malay rebels as to prevent us from getting out and leaving the country to itself.[10] He believed it would be a very unfortunate possession for the United States, and one that we could not govern in conformity with our old theories of our form of government.[11] Secretary Day drew him into a keen discussion as to the nature of our obligations to the rebels, the one maintaining and the other denying that these were of such a nature that we could not now honorably leave them.

Senator Frye, after the others had gone, renewed his suggestion that he, Senator Davis, and myself should have a meeting to agree upon a form of statement of our views to the President.

In the afternoon Senator Frye came in again and told me that he and

---

[10] The injection of the Philippine question into the Spanish-American War was a twist of fate for many Americans. It was one thing to free Cuba, and quite another by apparent accident to acquire territory as a result. Thus many Democrats and Republicans who fervently urged war for Cuba between 1895 and 1898, bitterly opposed acquiring the Philippines. Senator Gray is a prime example of this split thinking. He thought he could cite the Teller Amendment as proof that the United States could not take territory after the war, though that statement dealt only with Cuba. And, of course, his own objections, as the Diary shows, went much deeper, involving his idea of constitutional government.

[11] The chief legal opposition voiced in America against expansion in general and the Treaty of Paris in particular by opponents in 1898 and 1899 was that the Constitution did not permit the acquisition of territory not intended to be formed into states to be admitted to the union. The historic American principles of democratic rule and personal liberty, these people argued, could not exist in a ruler-ruled situation. Hence the United States could not legally or morally acquire possessions.

Senator Davis had both put their views in writing. He wished I would look through them, to see to what extent I could agree with them, and, so far as we held views in common, he would like to have me put them in shape so that all three could sign them.

In the evening, shortly after our return from a drive in the Bois, M. and Madame [Alexandre Félix Joseph] Ribot called. After a little general talk, Ribot asked me about the other members of the Commission, saying that Senator Davis had sent him a letter of introduction, and he wished to call on him. I accordingly piloted him upstairs and presented him to the Senator, returning myself to talk with Madame Ribot.

She soon touched upon the Dreyfus case and became very earnest.[12] She was not the wife of a Minister at present, she said, and had a right to her opinions; besides she was an American and had a right to talk. She had no doubt of the innocence of Dreyfus, considered the whole persecution monstrous, and the present intense and proscriptive excitement through the country on the question as disgraceful. The whole motive, she said, was a reckless determination to force Jews out of the army, and especially out of the État-Major [the general staff office]. It began in Dreyfus's case at the military school. In spite of his standing second in point of scholarship in the class, they had marked him zero. It was not until a general officer with some self-respect had told them this was too

[12] The Dreyfus Affair was one of the most controversial and famous events in recent French history. The number of times it is mentioned in Reid's diary shows something of its complexity and importance. Captain Alfred Dreyfus, son of a prosperous middle-class Jewish family, had begun a promising career in the War Ministry when he was suspected of passing official secrets to the Germans in 1893. On October 15, 1894, he was arrested, subjected to a secret court martial, and sentenced to degradation and exile to Devils' Island for life. Not everyone was convinced of his guilt, however, and Colonel Georges Picquart, a fellow staff officer, unearthed evidence that Dreyfus had been framed. He in turn was dismissed, indicating that the convicted man's opposition was powerful. Radical politicians like Georges Clemenceau seized upon the issue to embarrass the government and added impetus to the growing public demand for an inquiry. In January, 1898, the famous novelist Emile Zola published his open letter to the President of the Republic, titled "J'accuse," so sensational that it sold 200,000 copies in one day. Zola was prosecuted for libel and convicted, but his action had the desired result. In September, 1898, the case was reopened and a year later Dreyfus was returned to France for retrial. He was found guilty by a vote of 5–2, but the new President, Emile Loubet, remitted the sentence. In 1906, after protracted efforts on his own behalf, Dreyfus was cleared of charges and reinstated in the army by act of Parliament. He had been the scapegoat for one Major Esterhazy and a group of highly placed spies. As Reid indicates here, the Dreyfus case focused attention on many strains in French society and politics. Virulent anti-Semitism, the question of freedom of the press, and the character of the government and the upper classes were brought into debate.

monstrous that they had changed the grading a little, so as to let him get in at all. There had never been a time when they did not intend to drive him out, and they meant to stop at nothing to accomplish their purpose.

Before she had finished this talk her husband had returned. We walked into the adjoining parlor to look at the map of the Philippines, but she instantly returned to the Dreyfus subject and finished her statement with some vehemence. Ribot, himself, said little on the subject. He thought the conditions of the French Government at present were very much as he described them to me in his letter last autumn, explaining why he had declined to take the Presidency of the Council again on M. Faure's invitation, and had left it to Brisson. I suggested that he might have the opportunity to decline again very soon. He obviously thought the downfall of the present government merely a question of weeks, but was clearly of opinion that the same conditions existed and would render the success of any new government equally precarious. Before they left they had fixed a day when we were to dine with them.

Dined with the Comte and Comtesse Montsaulnin at the Cercle Agricole at the foot of the Boulevard St. Germain. . . . Here the talk ran on the same lines. Montsaulnin said the government might fall in three days after the Chambre met next week. If it were not toppled over so soon it would be only because its enemies were resolved to compel it to submit to the humiliation of defeat by the English on the Fashoda question rather than leave that uncomfortable legacy to the next Government.[13] The French had no conceivable right in Fashoda but the press had so worked the people up that the public men connected with the necessary surrender would make themselves odious.

[13] Fashoda was a city on the White Nile in the Sudan, some 375 miles south of Khartoum. Controlled by Egypt until 1884–1885, it was coveted by both the French and the English. In 1896 the French dispatched to the Congo and then to Fashoda an expedition under the explorer Jean Marchand. In July, 1898, he and a small garrison reached the city and raised the tricolor. Unwilling to allow the French to possess territory athwart the proposed Cairo-Capetown railway, the English dispatched General H. H. Kitchener, victor of the recent Battle of Omdurman, to meet the French at Fashoda on September 19, 1898. The result was an acute diplomatic crisis that was the talk of European chancelleries and newspapers for weeks. War between the two countries seemed imminent, and the whole crisis threw into sharp relief the larger questions of African power politics and European diplomacy. The English government was unwilling to go to war, but maintained pressure against the French. On December 11, 1898, Marchand and his garrison withdrew and ended the crisis. An international convention later awarded the area to England, but suspicion deepened between the two countries. Only in 1904, with the first efforts at a *rapprochement* ending in the treaty arrangements that created the Entente Cordiale, did the two countries sink their mutual differences to stand against Germany.

As to the [Dreyfus] "Affair" neither he nor his wife dared talk with any one, the feeling was so intense and general. Even his own kinsfolk, among them a cousin who was a distinguished general in the army, could not bear to hear them express their views about it. Yet no good person out of the army could doubt that Dreyfus was horribly persecuted, and that the attitude of the government and the army was disgraceful. They evinced a lively interest in small details about the *modus operandi* of the Peace Commission, how the Americans got on without either Spanish or French, the ladies of the Commission, etc., etc. Considerable curiosity was also expressed as to the nature of the dinner at the [American] Ambassador's as well as to its motif.

Montsaulnin gave some amusing accounts of his relations to the anarchists and communists in his department, who had at last succeeded in defeating him for the Chambre des Deputés. The most notorious of them had come to him scores of times in the Chambre to borrow twenty francs to get dinner for himself and a friend or two, and had not scrupled to give receipts for such petty loans of which Montsaulnin said he had scores laid away in his safe. He had even offered to get his anarchist opponent in the last campaign "removed" so as to give him a clear electoral field, asking only 5000 francs for the job. Once in a previous campaign he had given this fellow 500 francs and had required him to preside at one of his own (Montsaulnin's) meetings, which the fellow had done with fairly good grace, thereby insuring his election that time. In the last campaign, when the crowds were howling in the streets "Au mort Montsaulnin!" this fellow, at the head of the worst of the rioters, had shouted in a very angry and defiant tone: "There is the citizen Montsaulnin! I have a few words to say to him." [He] approached Montsaulnin, asking if there was anything he could do to help him, and then reassuming at once his defiant and angry tone had shouted: "Now Citizen Montsaulnin, I hope you understand me once and for all, and know what you have to expect at the hands of myself and my friends." The Comte seemed to take the situation cheerfully, though he declared that the hostility to birth and property was on the increase, and the condition of his region was really very disturbing.

Thursday, October 20th, 1898.

The talk at our meeting this morning turned first on the hostile attitude of the Paris press. . . . The talk then turned on the protocol and on
Montero Ríos' change of front. He had expressly said when he introduced the Madrid telegram about disorder in the Philippines the other
day that he did not do it officially, and did not wish it mentioned in the
protocol. The secretary [Moore] now reported that it had been inserted
in the protocol by the Spaniards at Montero Ríos' special direction. He
was instructed to make the protocol conform to the fact with the understanding that some mention would be made of the incident when it came
up for approval.

The talk turning on the Philippines, Frye remarked that he had
written out his views and handed them to me. Davis had done the same,
and they had asked me to put them in shape along with my own, provided we all concurred in practically the same views. They [wanted]
these telegraphed to the [State] Department with a request for an extension of our instructions. Day at once asked for the reading of them. I
told him that I had only received the memorandum last night. [I] had
barely time to make a rough draft of the proposed dispatch on my return from dinner, and had not had an opportunity to show it to either of
the gentlemen concerned, to see whether it expressed their views as well
as mine. So far as their views went, I thought I had incorporated them.
Day still insisted that it might as well be read, and the others making no
objection it was read. There was a curious silence excepting on one
point. Day inquired specially as to the alternative proposition I had mentioned of a division of the Philippines by a line running from the Straits
of Bernardino to the northeast corner of Borneo, so as to leave all to the
westward including Luzon, Mindoro and Palawan to the United States.
He asked to have Commander Bradford come in with his maps and
charts with reference to this dividing line. Frye then took my draft and
apparently studied it over very critically line by line.

Meantime, Secretary Day asked for the reading of our instructions,
which Senator Gray began. During the reading Commander Bradford
came in. Gray asked whether the reading should continue and Frye said
rather hastily: "Yes." No one else objected, and so, for the first time, the
instructions were openly referred to in the presence of an outsider. As
soon as the reading was finished, Secretary Day had the big map un-
rolled to examine Commander Bradford's line of division. I had attempted to indicate it in my dispatch, but had made it run below the

island of Maspate instead of north. Commander Bradford said on the whole he thought that would be a better line than the one he had traced. Senator Frye thought differently, and the matter was dropped. Secretary Day then produced Gen. Greene's report and read a number of interesting statements from Gen. Greene about our relations to the insurgents. He then asked Com. Bradford a number of questions about the size of the different islands embraced in this division, population, etc., and Bradford read a quantity of statistics and other information from a late English book on the subject. The session of the Commission lasted till about half past one o'clock, but it took no action of any sort.

The dinner at the Spanish Ambassador's this evening was, as Madame Castillo told me, intended solely as *un dîner intime*. The other guests were Señor Abarzuza of the Spanish Commission, Madame Candamo, our old neighbor on Avenue Hoche, the wife of the Peruvian Minister of that day, Mr. and Mrs. Santo Suárez, Spanish residents in the American Colony (who have property in New York, and who sent Mrs. Reid a handsome Red Cross contribution), the Marquis Villanova, who seems to be connected with the [Spanish] Embassy, and a young man also connected with the [Spanish] Embassy who told me he had met me in America during the Columbian Exposition [of 1893] and subsequently, and reminded me that he was a nephew of the Duke de Veragua. Besides these were the two for whom, as I subsequently suspected, the dinner had been really arranged, the Marquis and Marquise Comillas. The Ambassador took out Mrs. Reid, I took out Madame Castillo and found Madame Candamo at my right. The Comillases were given the other places of honor. The talk at the table ran chiefly on Paris gossip, reminiscences of acquaintances in Madrid, London, etc., with a few inquiries about [Queen Victoria's Diamond] Jubilee last year.

After coffee we were summoned back to the smoking room. In a few moments Castillo introduced the conversation he had evidently determined to have with the question "What is going to happen tomorrow?" He added that he dreaded it, and wished the meeting were well over. "You are in danger," he exclaimed, "of an impasse. You are the only diplomat there. It is the duty of a diplomat to find some middle way, to avoid the absolute failure of negotiations, to accomplish something."

By this time, when I looked around, I found that the smoking room had been suddenly cleared. The only one left to share the conversation with the Spanish Ambassador was the Marquis Comillas, who, from time to time, interjected observations quite as energetic as those of the Ambassador. Castillo repeated again the declaration he had made to me at the American Embassy. "If I were a citizen of the United States, I should think it to her interest to hold this debt as a means of holding Cuba. You are sure to have trouble with the Cubans. The island is immensely rich, it might be the richest colony in the world. If you take this debt you have an absolute grasp on Cuba, and can do with it what you like. Besides you ought to take it. It was incurred in obedience to your demands. We were merely doing our best to carry out your wishes; to abate the disorders of which you complain and restore order, the first and highest duty of a government. We tried every means you suggested, coming even at last to autonomy; but all failed. The revenues of the island are pledged for this debt. How can you take the revenue now without incurring the obligation."

To this I replied, from time to time, questioning some of his statements. [I assured] him that there was no possibility of the United States assuming the debt. [I declared] that a large part of it did not represent legitimate obligations any way, but sums seized by Governor Generals and other officials. The rest of it was spent not in conferring permanent benefits upon the Cubans, but in efforts to compel them to submit to a rule which was so intolerable that we finally aided them to throw it off. I pointed out besides that the first $18,000,000 of the debt had no relation to Cuba, but concerned their wars with Santo Domingo and Mexico. A very large part of the remainder actually represented the cost of the war they had been waging against the United States, and even the present pay and pension list of their imprisoned soldiers.

Both replied that there was not the least reason for taking into account the first $18,000,000, which was trifling any way, nor would they think of urging any part of the debt incurred during the last insurrection, or during the war against the United States. The cost, however, of subduing the nine years' insurrection, which they had fairly subdued, clearly rested on the island since it was distinctly an expenditure in discharge of Spain's successful effort to do her highest duty in restoring order. This debt, they argued, thus reduced at both ends would amount to nothing to the United States, would be so small as to be trivial and could be refunded at a very low figure, 2½%, 2% or less. All the Spanish South American States, they said, had assumed the debts incurred by Spain during their wars of independence.[14] International law, exclaimed Castillo, and the opinion of the civilized world are uniform on this subject.

---

[14] It is true, as the Spanish argued here and subsequently at great and detailed length, that some of the Spanish colonies in the New World accepted debts upon separation from the mother country. Such debts were generally connected with

This proposition I disputed. Castillo at once brought forward the declaration again that we even paid to Great Britain a part of the expenses of our Revolutionary War. I assured him that this was utterly unfounded and ridiculed the idea that a colony which had gained its independence should turn around and pay debts incurred in hiring Hessians to attempt to subdue it. They alluded then to Texas, and I explained to them that the debts we had paid for Texas were not debts held by Mexico, but debts incurred by the [Texan] insurgents in their successful efforts to secure their independence from Mexico. They claimed also that we had paid the debts of Louisiana and Florida when we annexed them. Though I pointed out the fact that we did nothing of the sort, but simply purchased these regions as we might have purchased any other commodity in the market, they still seemed to believe that the cases were parallel with the present situation.

All the time I was convinced that Castillo had up his sleeve some trump card, which he wanted to play. Presently he led up to it by renewing his declaration that it was the duty of a diplomat to bring negotiations to a successful result, not to lead them into an impasse. It was especially my duty to seek some middle way that gave Spain some opportunity and would not be offensive to the United States. "Were I in your place," he said at last, "let me tell you what I would do. I would agree upon a mixed commission of experts with reference to debts that might fairly be chargeable to the island, Spain choosing experts on her side, and the United States choosing experts on hers. It should be the duty of this commission to study the origin of these debts and report what portion of them is fairly chargeable to Spain, and what portion chargeable to Cuba." He did not renew his previous talk about their having debts incurred for building railroads, but did talk vaguely about permanent improvements and permanent betterments of the island.

When I told him that the plan of such a commission would not be entertained by the United States, the countenances of both the Ambassador and the Marquis de Comillas could not conceal their feeling of disappointment and chagrin. I said there was absolutely no considerable body of opinion in the United States that would sustain such a scheme, and that we would scarcely dare to go home if we accepted it. I explained the view in the United States that these debts were incurred by

---

internal improvements. It was a specious precedent, since payments by a newly independent country to its former mother country are far different from payments by a conqueror to the conquered. The United States did finally pay for some internal improvements in the Philippines.

Spain in its effort to hold the island in subjection, and that it would be monstrous after the island were freed to load it down with debts incurred for its enslavement. "But," exclaimed Comillas, "the bonds pledge the revenues of the island, what are the bondholders to do?" I replied that the bondholders must reflect on the old common law maxim "caveat emptor." They knew perfectly what the object of the loan was. They knew that if that object were defeated, the so-called security was gone, and that Spain had no longer the power to pledge it. They gambled on Spain's success, and must pay the penalty of having gambled on the wrong side.

Comillas looked as if he were being robbed of his last penny, while I made these explanations. He protested that it would make a great commotion throughout Europe, and in reply to my suggestion that most of the bonds were held in Spain, [he] insisted that nearly a third of them were held in France. He was himself president of the bank (at Barcelona, I think he said) through which he said the coupons of these bonds were paid. Speaking from memory only, he was pretty sure that something like one third was the proportion held abroad, principally in France.

The conversation had by this time become almost dramatic in its intensity. All three of us were standing. Castillo was frequently touching my shoulder, or grasping my coat lapel in the earnestness of his gesticulations. Once or twice, when I hesitated for the French words Comillas said: "Speak in English, I can understand it, although I do not venture to speak it." After I had spoken in English, he rapidly translated in Spanish what I said to Castillo.

In answer to Castillo's urgent appeals to do something, I finally assured him of my earnest desire to do anything for him personally that could be done. But [I] assured him that, in this case, what he asked was quite impossible, and then warned him that at any rate the Cuban debt was not the chief difficulty. This seemed to surprise him still more. He said: "You don't refer to the Philippines." I replied: "Yes, that, I fancy, would be a much more difficult question for you than the Cuban debt." He still insisted that he thought the big question was the Cuban debt. By this time it was long after 11 o'clock, and the ladies had long been impatient. When I tried to start from the smoking room, however, Castillo still delayed me for a final appeal for my best efforts. [He] urged that I was the only diplomat in the Commission, the only one known to them, and they were sure of my fairmindedness, etc.

. . . Mrs. Reid [later] told me that during the conversation at the table Castillo had been excessively earnest in trying to conciliate her good will by singing my praises, declaring that if I had gone to Spain [as Minister] when the President suggested it [in 1897] instead of [Stewart] Woodford, they could have escaped the war. He complained of Woodford's inability to communicate with them, make acquaintances, negotiate or in any way smooth the way for Spain's complying with our request, etc., etc. It was obvious that he had determined to make a tremendous effort to gain a foothold in some way in the American Commission.

Friday, October 21st, 1898.

Senator Frye handed back to me this morning the draft in which I had undertaken to express my views on the question of the Philippines, embracing also the few points contained in the written memorandum he and Senator Davis had given me. The only statement to which they objected was that Spain could not restore her power in the rest of the Philippines outside of Luzon. This was a statement to which Secretary Day had also objected when it was first read. It seemed to me unimportant in view of the well-known facts that the Spanish navy was destroyed, the Spanish army prisoners in Manila, and that the Visayas were already in revolt, and so I agreed to take it out. Fresh copies were accordingly made in a little while. When Secretary Day came in I handed him the paper, saying that we hoped he would read it, and, if possible, concur. He said he wished to have it before him in writing his own, and wished to see how far he could agree with us.

I then mentioned the dinner at Castillo's last night, and gave a rather detailed account of the conversation in the smoking room. The Commissioners listened with the greatest interest. Day and Gray both expressed the opinion that it was of the utmost importance. [They agreed] with me in my belief as to Castillo's having disclosed what the Spanish proposition was likely to be, and [were gratified] at the nature of my replies on the subject of debt. Senator Davis was also very complimentary as to this. I understood the Commissioners at this time to be unanimous in the belief that the proposed mixed commission to consider the debts could not be considered.

Some desultory discussion occurred concerning the probable reply of the Spanish Commissioners to our proposal of the terms of the protocol pure and simple. The belief was still general that they meant to break off the negotiations, and it was agreed that we should try to force this breach, if it must come, on the Cuban question, on which we were all of the belief that the purpose of the American people was practically unanimous.

On the reassembling of the Joint Commission in the afternoon Montero Ríos first raised a question about the protocol. Where it mentioned the dispatch he had communicated concerning the United States troops sent to Manila, he wished the protocol to use the exact words of the dispatch; namely that they were "re-enforcements for the garrison of Manila."

After this was arranged to their liking, Montero Ríos continued that he was sorry to state that the American offer of a substitute for its former proposals could not be accepted. He was ready, however, in like manner to withdraw their former propositions and offer a substitute, re-enforced by a memorandum of the reasons therefor. This memorandum was long, and it might be inconvenient to the Americans to undertake the translation of it at this session. The Spaniards had therefore no objection to our taking time to consider it at some future day. Senator Frye thought their proposition should be read; also that they should understand that there was no reply about their telegram, probably on account of the absence of the President from Washington. For this statement Montero Ríos expressed his thanks, and said the Spanish Commissioners would await the pleasure of the President.

The Spanish substitute was read. The first article relinquished sovereignty which the United States accepted for the purpose of turning over to Cuba after pacification. The second provided a commission to examine and apportion the debts, thus fulfilling my prediction based on Castillo's talk. The third provided for relinquishing under previous conditions the buildings, wharves, barracks, and other public property, but excepted property owned by ecclesiastical and other civil corporations and other associations having equal capacity to acquire property.

It was now found that the memorandum they submitted contained sixty pages (Foreign Office size) [of] closely written matter. Some consideration for the translator was at once expressed. Montero Ríos said that if the American Commissioners thought they could give this memorandum sufficient attention from listening to such a free off-hand translation, as was then practicable, they would not feel that they had the right to object. All they would ask was to have it affixed to the protocol. Secretary Day said he would prefer to have a careful translation and suggested an adjournment till Monday for that purpose. Montero Ríos explained that this was a reply to our paper and under strict rules he thought that closed the power of filing papers on that subject. He had no objection to our responding, however, if they had the same privilege afterwards, repeating many times over that he only wanted to have the two Commissions placed on an equal footing in this respect.

A long and confused discussion ensued about rights for filing papers under the rules. Montero Ríos speaking on the Spanish side and Day, Davis, Gray and Frye on ours, not being always clearly in accord. I thought it best not to [add to] the confusion, on what seemed to me, after all, a comparatively trivial subject. Montero Ríos kept replying in turn to each of our Commissioners, saying the same thing over and over again in different words. The other Spanish Commissioners in the meantime were sketching on the pads lying before them with colored pencils, producing leaves, trees, designs for "chiffres," etc., with indifferent success but considerable industry. At last it was stated by Montero Ríos that the long paper, which they had submitted with their broad proposals was only furnished now for the convenience of the American Commissioners, and was not to be considered as filed unless the American Commissioners should reject their articles. Meantime it might be a convenience to the American Commissioners to examine it. If, unhappily, after the oral discussion which they hoped for, these articles should effectually be rejected, they might then wish to make some additions or modifications to this document suggested by the oral discussion before they filed it with the protocol, as their reasons for a rejected proposition.

At this point Senator Davis gave the talk an interesting turn by suggesting that as the American Commissioners had already expressed their final opinion concerning the debt, it might expedite the matter if these articles should be rejected now. Montero Ríos expressed the earnest hope that if rejected at all, it should only be after full consideration of the arguments presented in the written memorandum, as well as after full oral discussion.

Senator Davis then waived the suggestion, but said to me afterwards on my way home that he was afraid he had made a mistake. He was convinced "that that old devil" had been very much frightened at the idea of immediate rejection, and for that reason he (Davis) inclined to think it might have been better to do what Montero didn't want. . . .[15]

---

[15] As the Diary shows, Davis was a rather crusty individual. He had considerable seniority in the U.S. Senate, was a man of power in his state and party, and was very outspoken on foreign affairs. He disliked Spanish deviousness and long-winded discussions. "We are having a most practical ordeal here with the dilatory and meretricious diplomacy of Spain," he wrote a fellow senator at about this time. "I can appreciate the force of that passage in Genesis (as I recollect it), 'now the Serpent was more subtile than any beast of the field which the Lord

Saturday, October 22nd, 1898.

At the meeting this morning, Secretary Day first submitted the draft of a proposed telegram to the State Department summarizing yesterday's Spanish proposals. I insisted that we ought to go farther, and explain the rather positive line of procedure we thought of taking so that if the government wished to give instructions on the subject it could do so. Senator Gray seemed quite averse to this, arguing that it might be desirable to make some concessions to them on the subject of a commission and that it would be better not to hurry them too much. I finally wrote the following, and made a rather aggressive little speech in favor of having it appended to the dispatch. "Our probable line of procedure, if you do not disapprove, and if we think emergency has arisen, will be to repeat that our position on Cuban debt is final, and that, if now again rejected nothing is left to us excepting to give notice of only one more meeting, to close the protocol." The other Commissioners were all in favor of this, and Senator Gray finally abandoned his proposal and the dispatch was sent.

Mr. Moore presented a translation of the first half of the Spanish paper filed in connection with their substitute articles. It was read slowly and accompanied by a running debate by the Commissioners. Senator Gray continued to express the belief that we were greatly embarrassed by refusing to accept the sovereignty for the island of Cuba, and trying to leave it in the air. The Spanish statements about precedents in the payment of debts were thought plausibly presented, but a number of them were curiously inaccurate.

In the afternoon the translation of the rest of the Spanish paper was read, and after a little further interchange of views by the Commissioners, Secretary Moore was instructed to prepare a tentative draft for a reply. The opinion was generally expressed that the paper was an adroit and able one, not very difficult to answer, but imperatively requiring that an answer to it should be made and spread upon the protocol. . . .

God had made.' Our Commissioners have yielded nothing and will yield nothing. But I am getting tired of this ———— toil of dropping buckets into empty wells, and growing old in drawing nothing up, and so are all my associates" (Davis to J. B. Foraker, October 25, 1898, Foraker Papers, Library of Congress).

Day, a more patient man, was more charitable, or more diplomatic. "Personally we are on very agreeable terms with the Spanish Commissioners," he wrote his friend the President, "and our meetings are conducted without friction. Indeed, I think you would be interested, often amused, by the extraordinary exhibition of politeness which accompanies our meetings" (Day to McKinley, October 23, 1898, McKinley Papers, Library of Congress).

Monday, October 24th, 1898.

This morning Judge Day, almost before the Commissioners had all assembled, took from his pocket and read his proposed dispatch on the Philippines. He has made a considerable advance. In Washington he was against anything but Manila itself. Here he has, of course, accepted the President's instructions for Luzon, but long maintained that the less we could get out with, the better off we should be. He has seemed at times a good deal impressed by our arguments as to the danger of taking Luzon alone, and has obviously been influenced also by the cabled reports of the President's speeches and of the popular temper.[16] In this paper he argued in favor of taking all to the north and west of Commander Bradford's proposed line of division beginning at the Straits of San Bernardino and going north of the island of Maspate. He preferred this to the line we had recommended going south of Maspate. The strongest point in his paper was the one with which he concluded, that the adoption of this line besides accomplishing our main purpose would relieve us from the imputation of proposing at Washington to negotiate on the subject of the Philippines, and then when Spain came to Paris to negotiate simply saying that there was nothing to negotiate about, since we intended to take the whole thing. He also would require that Spain should not alienate any of the rest without our consent, preferring this last form to requiring them not to alienate excepting to us.

Senator Frye and others then expressed with some eagerness that Senator Gray should immediately prepare his views. He seemed reluctant to begin, said there was no hurry yet, and thought we need not be in such haste to attack this subject until we had disposed of the Cuban debt. Under renewed representations of the unfairness of leaving the President without knowledge of our recommendations, and also of the probability that we might very soon be face to face with the question,

[16] Representative Joseph G. Cannon, of Illinois, an associate of McKinley's, once said the President's ear was so close to the ground it was full of grasshoppers. McKinley was intent upon fulfilling this epigram in the fall of 1898 while the peace negotiations were in progress. On a "swing around the circle" as far west as Omaha, he spoke to enthusiastic crowds who cheered his evident purpose to acquire the Philippines. The standard historical explanation of McKinley's action has been that he was sounding public opinion in order to follow it. In point of fact, he was far more subtle. Much evidence indicates that after Dewey's victory at Manila Bay on May 1 he was committed to retaining the Philippines. He was in fact creating support for this policy through his tour, his careful public attitude, his instructions to the Peace Commission, and within his own party and Administration.

he agreed to prepare his views within the next day and carried off the paper I had prepared, as well as Secretary Day's, for that purpose.

Judge Day presented a letter from Dewey. It merely transmitted a letter from the Belgian Consul at Manila giving some personal details about the quarrels among the natives and expressing strong views as to their unfitness for government and as to the wisdom of thus taking possession.

Senator Gray read a memorandum for use in our reply to the Spanish claim that the word relinquishment in the protocol necessarily involved the debts. (He subsequently used it in the oral discussion in the afternoon.)

A letter from Archbishop Chapelle was read enclosing such an article as the Catholic authorities desire in the treaty with relation to their church. Some of its provisions were obviously inadmissible, and it was particularly noticeable that the good Archbishop took pains to stipulate for the Catholic Church *eo nomine*.

[A] dispatch was read from the State Department fully approving our proposed course as outlined in our dispatch of Saturday. This was important, since it committed the government to approval of the proposal I had caused to be inserted, that if we thought the emergency arose, we should give notice of only one more meeting to end the protocol, and so break up the armistice.[17]

A long discussion sprang up on the form of rejecting the Spanish articles. Senator Frye finally wrote a memorandum distinctly rejecting their articles, so far as they involved our acceptance either of sovereignty or of debt. Senator Gray stood out for an offer to consider some of their stipulations, taking the ground as he has done nearly all along that at some point or another we must make concessions to them.

In the afternoon there were the usual friendly but ceremonious greetings at the Foreign Office, and business began immediately with the curious discovery that the protocol had failed to mention the Spanish rejection of our articles at the last meeting.

When this business was ended, Secretary Day began making the state-

---

[17] "Under the circumstances we deem it important, while refusing to assume Cuban debt, to express readiness to incorporate in [a] treaty properly guarded stipulations, acknowledging and assuming any legal responsibility to which we are by our own declarations and course of conduct committed. We meet Spaniards Monday 2 P.M., and desire instructions" (Day to Hay, October 22, 1898; *For. Rels. 1898*, p. 930). "Your position as to Cuban debt and your proposed procedure in accordance with engagements of note of July 30 are fully approved" (Hay to Day, October 23, 1898, *ibid*).

ment, which we had agreed upon, in reply to the Spanish articles and memorandum. It had been reduced to writing during the morning session, but finally Secretary Day had carried it off to make some changes, so that in the precise form in which it was presented none of us had read it. He kept the manuscript before him and followed it pretty closely in his oral statement. [He introduced] for the first time the wise policy of pausing after each sentence to give the translator opportunity to interpret it to the Spaniards at once. The essential point in it was that we naturally and of course assumed all the responsibility attaching to military occupation.

Montero Ríos at once wanted to know whether the subject to be considered as thus included would involve the commission on debts, which they had proposed. Abarzuza here interrupted him for an "aside" and they consulted in a low tone for a moment. Montero Ríos then continued that the only purpose they had was to ascertain whether the United States accepted the principle that debt went with sovereignty. The transfer of one included the transfer of the other, whether, therefore, the United States would assume control with all its elements. They raised now no question of any principal, concrete debt. It was only the principle they wished established.

Secretary Day replied at once that we accepted whatever responsibility properly attached to military occupation. We would not accept the Cuban debt in whole or in part. Montero Ríos then asked as to Puerto Rico. Secretary Day replied [that] we accepted the cession of Puerto Rico without any debt, if such debts exist. Montero Ríos then referred to article four of their proposals. Secretary Day said we had not considered it because of the apparently irreconcilable difference on articles one and two.

Montero Ríos then attempted to have the articles taken up *seriatim,* sentence by sentence and clause by clause, inviting the American Commissioners to point out at each step the clause or word to which they objected. [He] began by asking whether we accepted the principle of the first clause in their first article.

Secretary Day objected to taking up the articles in this way by sentences. "We are here," he said, "to say to the Spanish Commissioners that we cannot accept *anything* which attaches the sovereignty or the debt of Cuba to the United States. It is not a question of phrase that divides us. It is, as you have said in your paper, a question of the Cuban debt." Montero Ríos persisted that he wanted to know precisely where the difference existed as it appeared in the minds of the Commissioners on each side. Day replied that we rejected the articles absolutely because of the Cuban debt. There was no good in the discussion of a part of them, or in dwelling upon particular phrases in these rejected articles. We had already tendered to the Spanish Commissioners the exact language of the protocol. He was willing to add to that a provision for the protection of life and property while Cuba remained in our military occupation. Montero Ríos repeated that they were very desirous to enter upon the discussion of the principles involved, but reserved the right to have the fact of the rejection of each article entered upon the protocol together with the reasons for the rejection of each. Secretary Day replied that they had already reserved the right to modify or add to their argument in favor of these rejected articles, which had been furnished in advance on Friday. He was ready to consider these arguments when put on record, and to enter in full our reply to them, which had not been brought today because of their reservation.

Montero Ríos then apparently abandoned the idea that he could draw us into any petty verbal discussion of the article sentence by sentence, and remarked that they had not asked that any certain amount of debt should be paid. Spain did not look for re-imbursement for what she had spent, but did ask for assumption of unpaid debts on public works.

Senator Frye herein interrupted to ask what was the amount of these debts, and for what they were contracted. Montero replied that he could not answer in detail to that question, because Spain was an interested party. What he asked was that an impartial commission should examine as to these claims. Such examination was not the province of this Peace Commission. The only point in the question which concerned the Peace Commission was that it should recognize the principle that the debt goes with sovereignty. Spain would abide by any decision then arrived at by a commission appointed under that declaration. Secretary Day asked Senator Frye if he wished to reply, but Senator Frye said he did not.

Secretary Day quoted the protocol, saying it did not provide that Spain would relinquish sovereignty to the United States with the debts. As to the equities of the case, he said that if we did not stand on this contract in the protocol—or even waiving any consideration of that, for the moment— . . . the United States was deriving no profit from the present relinquishment of Cuba. For fifty years Cuba had been a source of constant loss to the United States. Over and over again the burning of property and general destruction had entailed immense losses upon American citizens. As far back as Gen. Grant's administration and

again under Cleveland, the United States had protested that this condition entailed loss and disturbance to its citizens, which could not longer
be endured. These repeated declarations of past administrations had
been again extorted from the United States under McKinley by the continued provocations. In spite of all remonstrances, the condition in Cuba
went from bad to worse, and the intervention of the United States was
compelled. In this intervention great loss of life and property had been
sustained in order to abate what had become an intolerable nuisance.
Now the Spanish Commissioners were here asking that besides paying
the cost of abating this nuisance, the United States should pay the previous cost to Spain of maintaining it.

Mr. Day made these declarations with more than his usual clearness
and force. They were obviously received by his colleagues with favor. It
was equally obvious that they produced a marked impression upon the
Spanish Commissioners.

Montero Ríos interposed in his blandest way the declaration that he
had supposed that all damages inflicted upon the United States up to
those caused by the last insurrection had already been paid for by Spain,
except where it had legitimate offsets. As to the damages inflicted in the
last war, was not Spain paying for them by giving up Cuba, Puerto Rico,
and Guam? Ever since its discovery, Cuba had been a constant drain
upon Spain, the thorn in its side, the cause of hundreds of millions [of]
loss to the mother country. Besides, he was not aware of a single transfer
of sovereignty since the middle of the eighteenth century [which was
not] accompanied by a proportionate part of the debt. Belgium took a
part of the debt of the Netherlands. Napoleon took part of the debt of
Lombardy and afterwards a part of the debt of Venice. The United
States paid the claims of various foreign countries against Texas. He
did not know of a single case to the contrary.

Senator Gray explained that Texas had gained its independence before there was any question of the payment of this debt, and that it was
not until its peaceful admission to the United States that the debt was
assumed. This statement seeming to me to leave the case not quite clear,
I interposed to explain that the debt of Texas was not a debt imposed
upon Texas by the mother country in attempting to subdue it or maintain sovereignty over it, as was the case with Cuba. On the contrary it
was a debt incurred by the Texans themselves in fighting against Mexico, a contest in which they successfully established their independence.
Sometime after that, on their admission to the United States and volun-
tary surrender of sovereignty to the United States, the latter assumed

their debts. A parallel case, I explained to the Spaniards, would be found
if the Cubans had succeeded in gaining their independence; if then
they had sought and been granted admission to the United States, surrendering to it their sovereignty; and if then the United States had paid
these debts incurred by the insurgents in fighting against Spain. Instead
of this, what the Spanish Commissioners were asking was that the
United States should pay the Spanish debts incurred in their unsuccessful attempts to maintain their sovereignty over Cuba. But Mexico in
its similar unsuccessful attempt had never thought of similar requests
nor would they have been entertained for a moment.

Montero Ríos was evidently staggered by this crumbling away under
his feet of the ground on which he had planted himself with so much
confidence. He began talking about other subjects while getting his second wind on this. He referred first to the case of Denmark in its struggle
against Prussia and Austria for Schleswig-Holstein, and the assumption
of a part of Denmark's debt. The case of Alsace and Lorraine was even
more eloquent in support of his contention. There they had actually
paid France 325,000,000 francs for her railroad. Coming then to Texas,
he merely said that it had been assisted by the United States in its strug-
gles against Mexico. Out of this ultimately grew the war between the
United States and Mexico. The first thing the United States demanded
was the independence of Texas, then it paid Mexico $15,000,000 for
California, etc., and released Mexico from the claims of those citizens.
The United States, he maintained, then treated Mexico fairly and gen-
erously. He could not now see why Spain should not be treated in the
same way.

Senator Davis here began what was obviously a carefully prepared
statement of which he had notes before him, and which he delivered
with much clearness, pausing at the end of each sentence for the translator to interpret it in Spanish, and declining to be interrupted. Our two
nations, he said, were in a state of war, merely suspended for the moment
by an armistice. We were here to try to end this war. We had for a basis
the solemn compact of Spain to relinquish Cuba and cede Puerto Rico.
That relinquishment, we claimed, did not lead to any assumption of
sovereignty by the United States, and with our refusal of sovereignty,
their whole discussion as to the debt, even on the ground on which they
place it themselves, must fall.

Waiving that, he denied that there was any principle in international
law compelling the payment of debts piled on a distant colony by the
mother country, which loses it in war. The case of Denmark and others

cited have been cases of public agreement between the parties. There were other cases of a different nature, which he cited in answer to their challenge for examples. About the middle of the last century England deprived France of all her colonial possessions in America. France had previously expended much money in those colonies, and incurred enormous debts in wars to defend them. In the treaty no allowance was made for those debts or expenditures, nor was there ever the slightest pretension of a claim for such an allowance. In the Revolutionary War, Great Britain had more than doubled her existing national debt, and she had previously spent much money in improvements, in defending the American colonies against Indian wars, etc. It was an error into which the Spanish Commissioners had fallen to suppose that any proportion of this debt was assumed by the United States; such an assumption was not even asked. Montero Ríos had not been accurate either in his statements as to Mexico. But he [Davis] would content himself on that point by saying that Mexico never claimed that any portion of her bonded debt, which might pertain to Arizona, New Mexico, or California should be assumed by the United States. For reasons of public policy, not dictated by any canon of international law, the United States had agreed to pay for those territories a certain sum. In the present case it was absurd to ask a nation which does not acquire, and protests that it will not have, sovereignty to take upon itself colonial debts, and there was no canon of international law requiring it to do so.

Montero Ríos said he understood that if pecuniary obligations ensued from carrying out the protocol, the United States was ready to assume them. Now, the object of a treaty was simply to develop the protocol. He referred to the quotations from the President's message, and said he was not only familiar with them, but had actually copied them in the Spanish memorandum, and that the idea of them was carried out in the Spanish proposals. But the words of the President had nothing "near or far" to do with this question. They were limited to indemnity, while the question of the meaning of sovereignty was within the purview of this Commission. Mr. Davis' second point, that the United States did not make war for the purpose of annexing Cuba, was quite distant from the question under consideration this afternoon. The only question now is whether the individual debts of Cuba and Puerto Rico should go with them wherever they go. They were burdens resting on the sovereignty of those islands. The sovereignty of Puerto Rico must go to the United States. There was no mystery about his words. Any debt, great or small, as to Puerto Rico must rest there; the Cuban debt must go with the territory. If the United States doesn't take the territory, then it doesn't take the debt. While it holds the territory it must have it with the debt upon it. If it assumes a protectorate it must assume the obligations.

As to Mr. Davis's third point, that international law did not embody these principles, he was aware that the idea that burdens upon a territory only pass where the whole sovereignty is swallowed up is supported by one English authority, but it was not by others. The three cases cited by Mr. Davis were not to the point. The reason no debt passed with Canada was because Canada had no debts; the same happened in the case of Spain when she transferred Florida. As to the Revolutionary War through which the United States gained their independence, assisted by France and by Spain, it was true that the United States did not assume any proportion of the British indebtedness. But it was well known in the chancelleries of Europe that in 1783 a secret treaty was negotiated in Paris by which the United States gave England 15,000,000 pounds for these debts. In the treaty of Guadalupe Hidalgo [that ended the war with Mexico], the United States paid 15,000,000 dollars and assumed debts to the amount of three millions held by American citizens. The United States seemed far harsher now in its disposition with Spain than it had been then with Mexico. It must be admitted that there was no written code in international law embodying the principles illustrated by these transfers of obligation with the territory, but one was being framed by an eminent United States authority, Mr. David Dudley Field. It would be well established, since the principle had been followed from the latter part of the eighteenth century to the present day. He referred to Bulgaria, Servia, Montenegro, etc., and inquired whether Spain was not entitled to as much consideration from other civilized nations under international law as Turkey had been.

Secretary Day replied that their whole argument now seemed to turn on the question whether the United States accepted the sovereignty which Spain relinquished. They had admitted that without sovereignty there was nothing on which to base the claim for the debt. In every case they had cited, the country had assumed the sovereignty. If the United States were here for itself acquiring the sovereignty of Cuba, it might be necessary at least to consider the examples they had cited. He thought, however, the learned Spanish Commissioner would be troubled to find any case where a nation had interfered to end intolerable conditions in a neighboring colony controlled by a distant power and was thereupon held for its debts. He regretted to observe that the learned President of the Spanish Commission thought that the United States practiced a different rule towards Spain from that employed towards other nations. Now, in the case he had cited of Mexico, we were acquiring for ourselves vast domains, for which we could well afford to pay. In the course of a settlement with that country we had purchased this territory, which had not been involved in the war. There was not the least similarity to the present case of Cuba. Two answers might be made to his whole contention: (1) We did not contract to take but carefully abstained from taking sovereignty; and (2) No equity had now been urged requiring the United States to enlarge the obligation it had assumed.

Montero Ríos said that in reply to the challenge for a case where a nation had intervened and did not take the sovereignty, although assuming the debts, he named Schleswig-Holstein, which was not incorporated with the intervening state. For a second example he named Austria and France. In the controversy concerning Lombardy, where France assumed a part of the debt, and for a third he cited Venice, where Austria demanded the assumption of a part of the debt by a country not taking the sovereignty. In like manner he referred to Romania, Bulgaria, Servia, etc. The great point, he concluded, was not whether the debt should go to the United States, but whether it should go with Cuba and Puerto Rico wherever they went.

Mr. Day said he did not understand that in any of the cases just cited the intervening nation took upon itself the debt. As to Puerto Rico, he simply stood on the protocol, though he did not understand that there was any debt in Puerto Rico. He had the high authority of the Spanish government itself for that statement. The whole argument so far had been that the United States must take this debt. The Spanish Commissioners now changed and wanted to fasten it to the island wherever [possible]. What right would the United States have thus to bind a government not yet in existence? When that government [was] formed would it not have a right to present its equities in its answer to such demands?

Montero Ríos said that Lombardy and Venice were the only cases he recalled of countries whose independence had been demanded for the purpose of passing sovereignty over them to another nation. In that case Italy was not represented. There had been frequent occurrences, however, of the same sort. He repeated that he did not ask the United States to assume the obligations of Cuba, which would be undoubtedly unjust, but he did ask that the debt should follow the property.

Senator Davis said such results had never followed mere military occupation. Secretary Day said it would be unjust to force Cuba to assume this great mass of indebtedness. Montero Ríos said Cuba [was] here represented by the United States. Day said we interfered largely on our own account, not as representatives of Cuba, interfering for ourselves to end conditions which we could no longer endure. We had incurred heavy expenses for a long time in patrolling our own coasts to prevent filibustering expeditions induced by these very conditions. We were not agents of the Cuban people. There was no government there. We had refused, in obedience to Spain's desire, even to recognize a state of belligerency in Cuba. We were here now, therefore, on our own account, and all we asked was that Spain should carry out her contract. We were not undertaking to enlarge that contract; but we were insisting on its execution.

Montero Ríos said: "When the United States appears here espousing the cause of the Cubans, we naturally consider it as coming in a representative capacity. If the American Commissioners think that the treaty ought only to contain the words of the protocol, there is hardly any need for these negotiations. Our desire is to carry out the sense of the negotiations, which preceded and interpreted the protocol."

Senator Gray said: "That protocol is in itself an executory contract. It promises to relinquish all sovereignty and title over Cuba. We ask Spain to do that now."

Montero Ríos said: "That is my idea exactly. The Joint Commission is here to determine the details of this execution. We have submitted them twice."

Senator Gray responded that the protocol promises a certain definite thing. [It is] not incomplete; it carried its own meaning with it. On the part of Spain it is interpreted one way; on the part of the American Commissioners another way. If both sides insist, we are at an impasse. The only thing we have been able to do is to fall back upon the exact language of the protocol.

Abarzuza here interrupted in English: "But we are here to make a treaty of peace not to get two protocols."

Senator Gray replied: "You can do what you promised to do. If any such responsibility as you think thereby attaches to us, so be it. We cannot avoid just responsibilities, and do not wish to."

Montero Ríos said: "We would be glad to arrive at some agreement. We are willing to have the exact words of the protocol in the treaty provided you embody it in the sense in which those words are to be interpreted."

Secretary Day here interrupted, speaking with singular precision and quietness, to ask if the American Commissioners were to understand that the Spanish Commissioners would not consent to any articles relating to Cuba and Puerto Rico which did not embody or carry with them in some form an assumption of the Cuban debt, either by the United States or by Cuba or by both. It was instantly felt in the Commission that the turning point in the negotiations had come. The Spanish Commissioners raised up involuntarily as it seemed, and all clustered about Montero Ríos, whispering excitedly but quietly. Montero Ríos asked to have the question repeated, obviously for the purpose of gaining time. He then replied that it was one of vital importance. They would either delay their reply for a day or two, or ask leave to withdraw to consider it now. Villa-Urrutia asked to have it written down for their consideration. This was done by Mr. Moore and Secretary Day and it was then read twice.

After some more excited whispering with his colleagues Montero Ríos broke out rather impetuously: "No matter where the debt comes in, in the first article, or in the second, or in the last, but we want it somewhere, or else we want the question left open for both sides. It might be wise to go on discussing other points in the treaty. That discussion might then suggest some other solution."

Secretary Day said that we agreed at the first on the order of discussion. The American Commissioners must now persist in their desire to dispose of this question in its proper order now. Montero Ríos recalled nothing in the minutes to that effect. What was adopted was that if any point were agreed upon today, it would nevertheless fall if the whole treaty were not agreed upon.

Secretary Day then said he would like to ask if the Spanish Commissioners were now prepared to say that they would not agree to a treaty which did not contain in some of its articles an assumption of the Cuban debt. Two or three of the Spanish Commissioners almost simultaneously said: "We must consult."

Senator Frye here inquired if their paper on the rejected articles was ready to file now. Montero Ríos said he would like to examine it, to be brought back at the next session, that they might meantime see whether they wished to make any changes or not. Secretary Day here promised to furnish the question he had asked in more concise form, and inquired when we could meet again. Montero Ríos said Wednesday would be difficult because they had a luncheon on that day, and suggested Thursday. Secretary Day said: "Why not tomorrow?" Montero Ríos said the memorandum was too long for consideration in that time. Secretary

Day said: "Is Wednesday quite impossible?" Montero Ríos said it was a question of ladies. Frye suggested a morning meeting. Montero Ríos said that if a Wednesday meeting were necessary, he would rather have it at four in the afternoon. Secretary Day asked if they would kindly advise him of any changes made in the memorandum so that the American reply could be made to take note of them if necessary and thus save time. Montero Ríos promised to let the American secretary know tomorrow night. We parted with the usual ceremonious courtesy, and with the general belief among the American Commissioners that the Spaniards would yield. . . .

Tuesday, October 25th, 1898.

There were two sessions of the Commission in my rooms today. . . . Senator Gray had not yet finished his paper on the Philippines. Senator Frye and others urged the necessity of getting it done at once, and finally the Senator withdrew, promising to let us have it in the afternoon, in order that the several opinions of the Commissioners might be transmitted to the President at once. All agreed that if we passed the present crisis about the Cuban debt in safety, we should be face to face with the Philippines at once, and must have our final instructions.

Finally, rather late in the afternoon, Senator Gray came in with his paper. It was a precise and forcible presentation of the conservative Democratic grounds for opposing any annexation whatever. Senator Frye and others complimented him on its force and lucidity. I immediately said that it led me to desire to make a short addition to the paper which I had prepared for the signatures of those of the three Commissioners who were able to agree upon it. With the assent of Frye and Davis I modified the first paragraph, so as to point out distinctly that we considered the question of retaining a foot-hold in the Philippines at all as closed by our instructions, and had not therefore argued from that point of view. This seemed to me necessary because Senator Gray was arguing the general question of the policy of having possessions in the extreme East, as if we had no instructions. I made the desired changes at the table, and the three dispatches were immediately sent off to be put in cipher. It was supposed that they might be in time to catch the cabinet meeting the next day on the President's return.[18]

[18] See Appendix III.

Was just starting in the evening to dinner . . . when a letter was handed me from the Spanish Embassy marked "Très Urgent." It proved to be a note from Castillo asking to see me on a matter of great importance before half past eleven tomorrow. He added in a postscript that he was free that evening and would be glad to call if I were not engaged. I waited long enough to concoct a brief French letter in reply explaining that I was just going out to dinner as his note came but would return at half past ten, and be glad to see him then if he wished, or at any hour before eleven that he liked in the morning. . . .

We reached our rooms in the hotel again at half past ten, and two minutes later Señor Castillo was announced.

The conversation which followed left me somewhat puzzled as to whether it was to be considered as an adroit and painstaking piece of Spanish diplomacy, or as an honest and sincere effort to avert a rupture. He began by telling me that he greatly dreaded the next meeting of the Joint Commission. He feared a rupture; Montero Ríos considered it inevitable. He had spent a good part of the day talking with him and remonstrating against his views [but] Montero Ríos seemed ready to go back to Madrid at once. Finally, in response to his (Castillo's) appeals to try to do something, he [Montero Ríos] had said: "Very well, go and see Mr. Whitelaw Reid, and see whether it is possible to arrange anything to avoid a rupture." Castillo insisted that there ought to be some concession with regard to the debt in order to make it possible to continue negotiations.

On this point I took very positive ground in reply, assuring him that there was absolutely no possibility of any concession; that the [American] Commissioners were unanimous on the subject; and that the sentiment of the American people was equally unanimous absolutely without distinction of party. I tried to explain to him our point of view. The debt was purely and simply a debt created by Spain for the purpose of maintaining a rule in Cuba which we found so bad and tyrannical that we had been at last compelled to intervene to upset it. It was not a Cuban debt at all, since the Cubans had had no voice in the creation of it, and had derived no benefit from it. Now they had been freed from the rule this debt was created to maintain and perpetuate, it would be monstrous to saddle the debt upon them.

He insisted in return that the sovereignty was passing either to us or to Cuba, and that according to all rules of international law in cases of transfer of territory the power receiving the transfer assumed either the whole debts of the territory transferred or a portion of them, and he made some reference to the case of Great Britain in our Revolutionary War, and of Texas after the Mexican War. . . . I pointed out to him how completely he was mistaken in both cases. In the case of our Revolutionary War we never paid anything to Great Britain, and were never asked to. In the case of Texas what we had paid was not a claim of Mexico, but a debt contracted by Texas in fighting against Mexico in the war in which she gained her independence. I pointed out also that not long before our Revolutionary War, France had been compelled to cede her enormous possessions in North America to England, colonies for which she had incurred large expenses in public works, public defense, maintenance of order, etc., and that in the transfer there had been no talk of transferring debts.

He insisted that in that case there had been no debts to transfer. I asked him what then had become of the enormous national debt of France incurred in part in these colonial enterprises beginning with Louis XIV and continuing on down to this. He had no reply excepting to say that some errors had possibly been made in their statements.

[He] then suggested that it might be wise, at any rate, to leave this whole question of a public debt in order to see whether they could not get concessions in the Philippines, which would justify them in abandoning it. Otherwise, he said, it would be practically impossible for them to make a treaty and go home. Montero Ríos would be hooted in the streets of Madrid if he secured no abatement whatever of our terms. To this I told him that we were in the same difficulty. We would hardly dare to show ourselves at home if we had made the slightest concession on a point on which the American people were united in favor of a demand which they considered not only unjust but monstrous. Again and again he returned to the consideration that this left them powerless, that they must break off, that it was the ruin of Spain.

I regretfully admitted that this might be so in part, but insisted that the consequence ought to have been considered before they forced us into war. [I] told him I hardly thought he realized the American point of view with reference to the war. In trying to explain this I referred to the case of the *Maine*. He at once insisted that he had sought for full information on that subject, and was absolutely convinced that the *Maine* had not been blown up by any Spanish agency or connivance. I replied that our experts and whole people were morally convinced that it had been blown up by a [Spanish] government torpedo. Not necessarily exploded by an officer of the Spanish Government, but in all probability by someone who had been under the command of [General Valeriano]

Weyler. I tried to impress upon him the nature of the feeling such a barbarous crime had aroused in the United States, and the impossibility of pleading conditions growing out of their loss of Cuba as a means of softening the American demands. They should absolutely [have to] leave the western hemisphere unburdened either with their government or their debts.[19]

All this I tried to put with civility but with extreme distinctness, and it evidently distressed him. In further justification of our attitude I said that he knew if there were debts incurred for public works as yet unpaid for, we were perfectly ready to assume these, and that all private debts, municipal obligations and the like would be safe. To this, however, I added that in my belief there were no public works of that character; at least none to speak of. [I] suggested that if there had been, they would have named them the other day when the subject was mentioned. In answer to his further incidents on the law of nations, and the sense of justice calling for a transfer of debts, I asked him to consider what such a doctrine led to. What [was] there to prevent a tyrannical government from piling debts on a discontented colony until it could never get its independence, or get any other nation to accept it?

Castillo kept returning to the point that we must find some way to avoid a rupture; that it was the duty of a diplomat; that it was absurd to have negotiations which merely consisted in laying down an unprecedented requirement. [He] said he thought never before had a vanquished nation been treated so cruelly.

At last I said to him [that] it seemed to me the best policy for Spain would be to accept the inevitable in the case of Cuba, in the hope that possibly there might be something to negotiate about in the greater question that was coming. He repeated what he had said to me at his own house, that he thought Cuba was the great question. I repeated to

---

[19] The Spanish were still touchy over the destruction of the U.S.S. *Maine*, a direct cause of the war. The American commission which investigated the wrecked ship in Havana harbor after February 15, 1898, decided that it was destroyed by an external explosion, assigning no responsibility but leaving the impression that agents of Spain sank the vessel. President McKinley mentioned the ship's destruction in reviewing the causes of the war during his annual message to Congress of December 5, 1898, while the peace conference was in progress. His intimation that the Spanish were responsible especially nettled Montero-Ríos. As Reid notes, most Americans assumed that the Spanish blew up the ship, not stopping to realize that Spain, of all parties, had least to gain from such an incident. A later investigation of the wreck left divided opinions as to the cause of the explosion. Many subsequent historians and naval experts believe the explosion was entirely accidental, due to a fault of construction in the ship's magazines.

him what I said there, that it seemed to me the Philippines presented greater difficulties. At last I held out a vague hope to him that it was possible, repeating carefully, "I say possible not probable, that there might be some concession there from the present American attitude either as to territory or as to debt." I explained that certainly the American people had not desired the Philippines [before the war]. But it was conceded on all hands that they must retain what they now occupy; and that during the past few months there had been a rapid growth of a desire [in America] to hold the whole archipelago. At the same time I said [that,] unlike the Cuban question, there is on this question of the Philippines a decided difference of opinion. There is a respectable and important minority [of people in America] holding different views. They are not sufficient to control the policy of the government, but it might be that here would be Spain's best chance to negotiate.

He repeated that he thought this doubtful, and that he feared the negotiations would have to be broken off. By this time he had reached the door, and was obviously greatly depressed. He said in saying good-by: "My dear friend, it is cruel, most cruel; pray God that you may never be likewise vanquished." In return I expressed the most earnest conviction that it would only be adding to their misfortunes to break off the negotiations. [I] assured him that he could hardly conceive what an unhappiness they would be bringing down upon Spain, if they should persist in so unwise a course. Shaking hands again at the door, for perhaps a second or third time, I closed with the words: "Do not break off." And with every expression of cordiality, but obviously with great sadness, the Ambassador disappeared in the corridors of the hotel.[20]

Wednesday, October 26th, 1898.

As soon as the Commissioners gathered in my room this morning, I communicated the details of Castillo's call substantially as recorded above. Secretary Day immediately stated that he had received a call from the American Ambassador advising him of a briefer, but similar

[20] As is only human, perhaps, Reid assigned too much importance to his conferences with Castillo, though his firm talk did doubtless impress the Spaniards that the Americans were not bluffing. Secretary Hay himself considered the conversations important. "Your talk with the Spanish ambassador was to my mind the turning point of the negotiations" (Hay to Reid, November 3, 1898, Reid Papers, Library of Congress). This judgment seems excessive. The Spanish would doubtless have capitulated on the Cuban debt question in any event.

conversation Castillo had sought with him. All agreed in considering the communication as of the utmost importance. Secretary Day called attention immediately to my parting suggestion to Castillo concerning possibility of some concession, either territorial or financial in the Philippines, and said "Possibly that may return to trouble us." I reminded the Commissioners of the suggestion which I received before leaving America in a private letter from John Bigelow to the effect that we had a wolf by the ears, which we could not let go of with dignity, and which it would take us a long time to tame. [He thought] that probably our easiest and cheapest plan would be to imitate our course with Mexico and reconcile them to the inevitable by a money payment.

Senator Gray developed a strong desire for the appointment of a mixed commission to consider any just claims the Spaniards might have for public works in Cuba. Secretary Day and the rest of us opposed the appointment of such a commission at present. [We were] perfectly willing to recognize any just claims for such improvements, when the Spaniards should present them.[21]

Secretary Day presented a strong dispatch from Col. Hay, in answer to ours of yesterday. It approved our purpose to stand by the protocol, and

---

[21] In a dispatch of October 25, 1898, Day asked:

Would you approve an article in [a] treaty which should provide that the United States, while not contracting any independent liability of its own, would use its good offices with any people or government possessing sovereignty in Cuba for acknowledgement of any debts incurred by Spain for existing internal improvements of a pacific character in the island? A mixed commission to be appointed to ascertain whether any such debts exist, and if so, their amount. This would necessarily be a precedent for Puerto Rico, Guam, and [the] Philippine Islands. [The American Peace] Commissioners may feel inclined to make this concession on [the] strength of precedents and statements of publicists, as to passing of local debts or debts incurred specifically for benefits of transferred territory." (Day to Hay, October 25, 1898, *For. Rels. 1898*, pp. 931–932.)

To which Hay responded, indicating that the Administration did not want to set such a precedent:

. . . the President directs me to say that under no circumstances will the Government of the United States assume any part of what is known as the Cuban debt. . . . It is not believed here that there are any debts outstanding incurred by Spain for existing improvements of a pacific character. It should be made clear what is meant by such improvements and what is included. The President regards it as most desirable that in the present negotiations you should adhere strictly to the terms of the protocol. If this proves impossible you will ascertain as definitely as you can the exact meaning of their suggestions as to local Cuban debt and the evidence thereof and report to the President with your recommendations." (Hay to Day, October 25, 1898, *ibid.*)

authorized us, in case of necessity, to call on the Spaniards for a bill of particulars as to any public improvements of a pacific character. Its most notable feature, however, was the requirement that we should not lose sight of our right to hold Manila by conquest, as well as by the protocol.

Senator Gray was a good deal troubled by the dispatch, and made earnest repetition of the desirability of delay before finally committing ourselves. He referred impressively to the fact that there was a strong minority in the country, eminently respectable by reason of its intelligence and conscientious convictions, which was strenuously opposed to staying in the Philippines at all. He did not believe in being carried off our feet by temporary popular excitement. [He] thought it our duty to act on our best judgment as to our real rights and duties, and assumed that [by] the time the [American] people were as fully informed of the facts as we were they would come to the conclusions to which we were driven. He spoke of the embarrassment of his own position. He had tried to make the President understand it. But after reading this dispatch [he] felt as if he had made a mistake in coming. . . .

In the afternoon meeting at the Foreign Office, after the protocols were approved, Montero Ríos finally filed their memorandum defending their rejected articles. The few changes they had made in it were comparatively unimportant, and had already been explained in detail to our secretary. Senator Frye, however, asked for the reading of the changes. One of them maintained that Spain would necessarily be free from the liability for the Cuban debt if deprived of the revenues which were devoted to its payment. Another denied that they had anywhere said there was no Puerto Rican debt. As soon as this was concluded, Secretary Day filed our response.

Montero Ríos then said that they had considered the question asked at the last meeting and offered a written answer to go upon the protocol. Secretary Day said that the disposal of it could not be properly determined till it had been heard. Montero Ríos said the answer must necessarily be recorded anyway, since the question had been. Day insisted that we ought, at any rate, first to hear it before deciding that point, and that we must reserve any rights we might have about it. Montero Ríos explained that, as the question had finally been submitted to them in writing at the last session, he had brought his answer in the same way, and then handed it to the translator.

Abarzuza now offered a suggestion that Mr. Ferguson, the translator, should take the time to read the reply over to himself, before making his translation aloud. There was rather a dramatic pause now for this purpose. The Commissioners on both sides [talked] with each other for a few minutes in low tones, and then [lapsed] into silence.

Finally the reply was read. Its purport was that the Spanish Commissioners, having studied the question in its full scope; considering that in the meeting on the 14th it was agreed settled that no agreement reached should be binding unless the whole treaty were adopted; considering therefore that an acceptance of the principle in the American articles now would not imply their definite and final approval; considering that this treaty is not to be finally constructed on the strictest ideas of their just rights, which may be held by either side, but on some necessary modifications for the sake of reaching an accord; considering all this, the Spanish Commissioners believed that strict law favored their contention, but were disposed to moderate it in the hope of other concessions. Retaining their convictions as to the law, they would not decline to take into consideration other articles not containing their view but would reserve their rights. [They] asked now to proceed to the consideration of the Philippines, and would like the American Commissioners to propose what they wanted.

So the danger of an immediate rupture was passed. Senator Gray pressed my elbow as the meaning of the document finally was disclosed and whispered: "There is the result of your conversation with the Spanish Ambassador." He then asked if we should not have a private conference. Day, however, interposed with the question whether we were to understand that the Spanish Commissioners now accept the American articles subject to their reservations as to a final agreement on a treaty. Montero Ríos said to the secretaries that he would like both of them to take note of his reply for entry on the protocol. He then said in the sense just set forth, [that the Spaniards] would accept the American articles and pass to the consideration of other questions. Secretary Day immediately replied that in that sense the American articles would therefore now stand as approved. Montero Ríos responded: "In the sense of our paper, we accept the proposals of the American Commissioners as to Cuba and Puerto Rico, or would accept any articles on those subjects they might choose to present subject to the final decision on the whole treaty. . . ."

In the evening there was a long call from Count Münster, the German Ambassador. He asked many questions about details of the Commission. How we conducted the discussion, what oral dispute occurred? How the remarks were translated, etc.? Then he said: "They want you to pay the Cuban debt; but you won't do it." I replied: "Why should we?"

"But," he said, "you will pay for public improvements." "Possibly," I said, "if there were any; but there are none. The debt was incurred in trying to maintain the cruel and despotic rule we have just overthrown." He seemed rather to assent to this view, and then said: "You want the Philippines too." To this I replied that when we took the capital [Manila], sank the Spanish fleet, and captured the Spanish army we had practically taken the Philippines. They were certainly at our mercy to do with as we liked. He asked many questions then about the misconduct of the friars and other features of Spanish rule, but made no hint as to German expectations. The general impression he left on my mind was that Germany was eagerly watchful, but had no thought of interfering with us. Referring to the young Emperor's [William II's] trip to Jerusalem, he said: "He is coming home sooner than he first planned and I am glad of it; he travels too much. . . ." As he left, I promised to dine with him again, he saying laughingly: "I am glad to perceive that you will be here a long time yet." It was the longest conversation I have had with him during this visit. He impresses me as having grown old rather rapidly, and as being more nervous than formerly. But his head is as clear as ever, and he has the old, rather direct and masterful way of putting questions, which go just to the edge of what even friendly intercourse between colleagues would permit. He spoke pityingly of France and of the Dreyfus case, again saying very explicitly that so far as Germany was concerned there was absolutely nothing in it.

A message came down from Secretary Day that he wished to see me about nine. Misunderstanding it, I went up to his room but found him absent. Eddie [the doorkeeper] told me that he was in Senator Gray's room, whither I followed him; but found that he had been intending to come down. After a brief call he made an excuse of a desire to talk with me, and we took our leave, going to his room. He showed me a long dispatch he had written to [the] President about my conversation with Castillo. Part of it he had put considerably stronger than I thought warranted, but he at once offered to change it in any way I desired. Finally [he] handed me the dispatch asking me to rewrite it, and promising to come down to my rooms in half an hour or so to get it, and have it put in cipher for transmission tonight. I accordingly re-wrote it, trying to bring out the exact spirit of the conversation and the extent of the hint I had given Castillo at the close. The rest of the Secretary's [Day's] dispatch I left unchanged. It ended with an expression of his opinion that a rupture today had been averted by my talk, and of the need for immediate instructions on the Philippines.

CHAPTER V

Taking the Philippines

Thursday, October 27th, 1898.

. . . We were all eagerly expecting a dispatch from Washington, but none had been received.[1] Secretary Day revived my old suggestion about the possibility of an adjournment to Nice, and said we should evidently find something of that sort a great relief if the negotiations should be much prolonged. He wanted some scheme by which the Spanish Commissioners might be induced to propose it.

Senator Gray wanted to offer an article for the treaty, in which the United States should give definite guarantees for life and property during our occupation of Cuba. It was finally agreed to submit such a proposition first to Washington. It was also agreed that it would be better to adopt the articles we had first proposed to Spain rather than the shorter ones merely reproducing the protocol, which were afterwards merely put in as a substitute provided Spain would agree to the first ones. . . .

At the meeting of the Joint Commission at the Foreign Office this afternoon nearly everybody seemed to be half an hour late. Four of us arrived first. Some little time later three of the Spaniards came in; later two others. And at last, just as we were beginning to think of sitting down, Senator Gray hurriedly came in. He had been caught on a shopping excursion with his younger daughter, had forgotten the time, and had finally rushed away . . . just in time to get to the Foreign Office by sacrificing his breakfast.

We began at once with the offer by Secretary Day of the first and second articles for a treaty in the form originally proposed. Montero Ríos at once said that the acceptance filed yesterday by the Spanish

[1] See Appendix III for the various Commissioners' views as they began to discuss the Philippine problem in earnest.

Commissioners referred not to these but to the last articles we proposed, and was, of course, conditional upon the final acceptance of the treaty. The paper filed yesterday did not in any way prevent them from again presenting the second article of their own draft. The same remark might be made as to others, which they might be compelled to present again if we did not reach an agreement on the later parts of the treaty.

Secretary Day at once responded that the Americans were content to take their acceptance as already answered on their protocol in their own language. Montero Ríos then said that although their answer as filed yesterday referred to the last (or substitute) articles we had filed, they were quite willing to take up and discuss the first articles we had filed to which reference had just been made. Secretary Day closed the question with the simple remark that we were quite content to let their acceptance apply to the articles last filed.

Montero Ríos then asked, premising that he made no demand, whether it would be acceptable to the American Commissioners to incorporate in the text of the American article relating to Puerto Rico the words that it was ceded as indemnity for the war and payment for damage to American citizens.

Secretary Day said we would prefer to stand on the articles accepted. Montero Ríos asked to have the question and this reply spread upon the protocol. Senator Frye asked him if he would permit the insertion before the word "indemnity" of the word "partial," to which Montero Ríos replied: "I only request that the question as already asked, and the reply given, be spread upon the protocol. I make no great point of it, but desire the fact that the question was asked be recorded, together with the reply."

Senator Gray interposed that what Montero Ríos asked was already embodied in the President's message.

Montero Ríos resumed, saying he wanted to know if there was any objection to having incorporated somewhere in the treaty the fact that this cession of Puerto Rico is by way of indemnity. Secretary Day replied that the United States would make no objection to that in some proper form when it came up. But he preferred not to confuse the acceptance of the present articles.

Montero Ríos once more repeated that if the American Commissioners did not feel disposed to answer, or did not wish to answer, he did not insist. But, in any case, he wanted his question placed on the daily protocol. Senator Frye interjected the remark [that] in the treaty somewhere there will undoubtedly appear the fact that the territory ceded

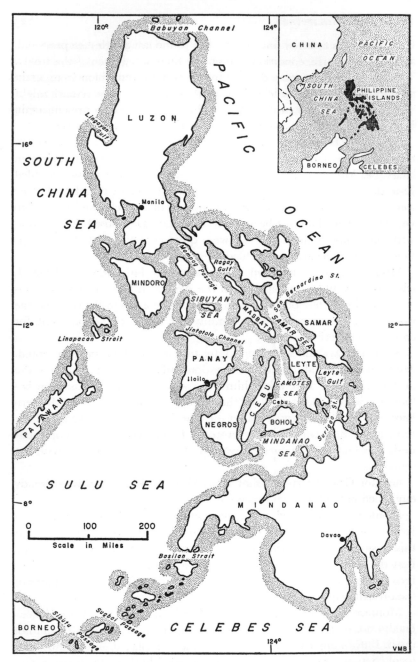

The Philippines

is by way of indemnity and as payment for damages to American citizens. Montero Ríos instantly rejoined: "What I want to know is whether that is the individual opinion of the Commissioner, or is the position of the Commission." Secretary Day said: "The cession of Puerto Rico is on account of indemnity and claims of American citizens. We do not intend to take any territory on other grounds."

Montero Ríos said then: "The two commissions are agreed. In view of the last remark we can proceed to other business. Before taking up other subjects in the first proposals of the American Commissioners, however, on which our differences are perhaps not very substantial," he said, "I would like some explanation as to the last remark in your written reply yesterday as to the Philippines. I do not mean to be understood as pressing, but only want some answer."

Secretary Day replied that in view of the importance of that subject, we must take some time to prepare and submit articles. We had not already formulated such articles, did not have them here now with us ready to present. Montero Ríos replied: "Very well, then; we can now take up other matters in the first American draft, and I think it will be easy to reach an agreement." Secretary Day then said: "What subjects does the Commissioner wish to take up first?" Montero Ríos replied: "I understood the President of the American Commission to ask if our acceptance could be entered as referring to the first American draft. We have no objection, in view of what has been said, to take up now the points in that first draft relating to the preservation of records, etc."

Secretary Day whispered to me an inquiry as to whether it might not be better to let the two secretaries formulate an article on this subject. I replied at once that this seemed to me simplest and wisest and that it would be well to take a recess for that purpose, and let the secretaries, on our reassembling, present their draft.

Secretary Day thereupon proposed this plan. Montero Ríos at once said it was a very good idea. Day said the only question was, how long should the recess be. Ojeda protested that they were the hardest-worked persons in the Commission, and must have some time. Thereupon Montero Ríos said that it might be left to the secretaries to report whenever they were ready. Secretary Day said the American Commissioners had no doubt these gentlemen could agree upon an article mutually satisfactory. [Then] at the next time we met, we should be prepared to take up and give undivided attention to the question of the Philippines. The only question was how much time should be taken to prepare and formulate proposals on that subject.

Montero Ríos said that the Spanish Commissioners were entirely at the disposal of the American Commissioners on that subject. If they were not ready now to fix the day when they felt sure that they would be prepared, a further adjournment could be arranged in advance at any time on twenty-four hours' notice. Or the two secretaries could give an even shorter notice to their respective Commissioners. Secretary Day proposed an adjournment until Tuesday. Montero Ríos said that was All Saint's Day, and that the following day was also a holiday. Secretary Day then proposed Monday, with the understanding that if [we] were not ready, we might avail ourselves of their courteous offer of further delay. It was so agreed.

At Secretary Day's suggestion I sat down with him to frame a dispatch for [Secretary of State] Hay reporting results.[2] Secretary Moore had already begun one, and so when mine was finished the two were read. The Secretary [Day] and Senator Gray [took] mine, as embracing somewhat more, and being shorter. The Secretary [Day] was at first inclined to give the Associated Press an announcement of the result, but both Senators Frye and Gray objected to this. It was believed that the result would undoubtedly be announced through Spanish sources. But, in the judgment of our friends, it was not advisable for us to give it out, at least [not] without consulting with the Spaniards and having their consent. . . .

---

[2] In his dispatches Day explained the outcome of Reid's talk with Castillo and the importance of realizing that the Spanish could not go home empty-handed. A break in the negotiations seemed imminent unless something could be given them in return for whatever portion of the Philippines the U.S. finally took.

To-day [the] Spanish Commissioners presented [a] document (now being translated) which, we understand, accepts articles proposed by us, subject to agreement in final treaty, and invites proposals as to the Philippine Islands from us. After [the] meeting, [the] Spanish secretary said to me that they accepted our articles in the hope of liberal treatment in [the] Philippine Islands; [he] said no government in Spain could sign [a] treaty giving up everything and live, and that such a surrender without some relief would mean national bankruptcy. . . . We deem it proper that you should know [the] exact situation before sending conventional instructions on Philippine Islands. We are inclined now to believe that rupture to-day [was] only averted because [the] Spaniards grasped at a hint thrown out in the conversation of Mr. Reid Thursday night with Ambassador [Castillo]. (Day to McKinley, October 27, 1898, *For. Rels. 1898,* pp. 936–937.)

Friday, October 28th, 1898.

No news yet from Washington, excepting a dispatch that the President is in Philadelphia, and promising instructions sometime today.

At our morning meeting, Mr. Parnow, a German merchant long resident in the Philippines, appeared. He had presented letters of introduction to Secretary Day and myself from Andrew D. White of Berlin, who commended him highly. [He] had been put off for a day or two on account of our engagements with the Spaniards. His testimony was not taken quite so formally as that of previous witnesses about the Philippines. It proved confirmatory of much that had already been told, and developed one or two interesting new points. One was that the Philippines, according to a financial statement which he had presented, had paid the expenses of their own administration and also the cost of the entire consular and diplomatic service of Spain in the East, as well as of the Department of Colonies at Madrid, pensions to soldiers and civilians, who had been in the Philippine service, pensions paid the Duke of Veragua and others on account of their relationship to Columbus, etc. He said only a small proportion of the Philippine loan had been taken by the individuals and this was in the nature of a forced loan. He spoke well of the natives, both in Luzon and in the Visayas, and was distinctly of opinion that it would be a mistake to divide the archipelago. . . .

All the talk among people one meets and in the newspapers is about the possibility of war with Great Britain over the ridiculous Fashoda incident. . . .

Saturday, October 29th, 1898.

Secretary Day came in rather early this morning with a dispatch in his hand from Washington.[3] I read it, and as each of the other Commissioners came in it was handed to them. Senator Gray came last, and it was then read aloud for his benefit. Up to that time we had all received

[3] Historians almost always cite a dispatch from John Hay to Day, October 26, 1898 (*For. Rels. 1898*, p. 935) as the instructions upon which the Commissioners acted in demanding all of the Philippines from Spain. Careful detective work by Professor Richard W. Leopold has recently proved that this dispatch was never sent, and that the Commissioners acted upon the instructions of October 28, 1898, as Reid's entries confirm. See Leopold's article, "The *Foreign Relations* Series: A Centennial Estimate," *Mississippi Valley Historical Review*, 49 (March, 1963), 598–599, n. 12.

it rather silently, although Secretary Day had been somewhat sarcastic and amusing concerning our new fellow citizens [the Filipinos]. It was curious to notice Senator Gray's face as he heard the precise instructions for claiming the whole of the Philippines. The rest of us preserved a decorous attitude and avoided any signs of gratification or the reverse. Senator Gray expressed some regret, but intimated, as he had done before, that while he should not conceal his individual opinions at home, he felt bound to be governed by the instructions of the President and the action of the Commission.

There was some discussion of the best form to adopt in carrying out the President's instruction. Finally, Senator Frye made a motion that tentative articles be prepared claiming the whole of the Philippines and offering to consider any legitimate debt for internal improvements or other pacific purposes, and Secretary Moore retired to prepare it. . . .

Monday, October 31st, 1898.

. . . There was some speculation as to the attitude the Spaniards were likely to take when our Philippine demands were presented. Secretary Day was full of eagerness to study all the French dictionaries I could lay my hands on as to the meaning of the words "disposition," "government," and "control" as transferred from the English to the French text in the protocol. The rest of the Commissioners generally held the view expressed by Senator Gray that these words were so plain that it would be of little use to cite definitions or permit much merely verbal dispute about them.

A dispatch from Secretary Hay was read acknowledging our last dispatches concerning our intentions and approving them. It contained, however, a specific instruction not to lose sight of the fact that we held Manila by right of conquest as well as by the protocol.[4] Secretary Day

---

[4] Dewey destroyed the Spanish fleet in the Battle of Manila Bay on May 1, 1898. Lacking troops, however, he could not occupy the city, which was ringed by Filipino insurgents. On August 13 the city finally fell to General Merritt's newly arrived army, one day *after* the armistice was signed in Washington, due to a lag in communications. The Spanish held that this invalidated claims to the Islands by right of conquest, when combined with the fact that the Americans had never possessed more than the city of Manila and its immediate environs. To the Spanish, the most the Americans could claim was the island of Luzon, and not that by right of conquest. The State Department, however, insisting that the capture of Manila was in effect the capture of all the Islands, since it was their prin-

disputed this emphatically, and cited the resolution passed in the Pan-American Congress [in 1889–1890] on the motion of Secretary [of State James G.] Blaine committing our government against any territorial acquisitions by conquest. [He] maintained also that this was the tendency of civilization, and of the best writers on international law. [He thought] it would never do for the United States government to take Luzon or any other territory by conquest. It must be rather in the nature of indemnity for the war, which had been forced upon us or in payment of damages to American citizens. He also referred to the various authorities on international law holding that places captured after an armistice had been agreed upon, but before the news of it had reached the spot, must revert. This is the precise point to which I had called his attention weeks ago. I now reminded him that I had then pointed out the tendency of the authorities that way, and he had entertained an opposite

---

cipal city and controlled the diffuse archipelago, never surrendered the right of claim by conquest. Hay's dispatch on the subject, mentioned here, made this very clear, but also showed that the United States government would entertain a reasonable proposition to relieve Spain's embarrassment.

The formal instructions upon which the Commissioners acted in demanding all of the Philippines read as follows:

While the Philippines can be justly claimed by conquest, which position must not be yielded, yet their disposition, control, and government the President prefers should be the subject of negotiation, as provided in the protocol. It is imperative upon us that as victors we should be governed only by motives which exalt our nation. Territorial expansion should be our last concern; that we shall not shirk the moral obligations of our victory is of the greatest [concern]. It is undisputed that Spain's authority is permanently destroyed in every part of the Philippines. To leave any part in her feeble control now would increase our difficulties and be opposed to the interests of humanity. The sentiment in the United States is almost universal that the people of the Philippines, whatever else is done, must be liberated from Spanish domination. In this sentiment the President fully concurs. Nor can we permit Spain to transfer any of the islands to another power. Nor can we invite another power or powers to join the United States in governing them. We must either hold them or turn them back to Spain.

Consequently, grave as are the responsibilities and unforeseen as are the difficulties which are before us, the President can see but one plain path of duty—the acceptance of the archipelago. . . . The terms upon which the full cession of the Philippines shall be made must be left largely with the Commission. But as its negotiations shall proceed it will develop the Spanish position, and if any new phase of the situation arise, the Commission can further communicate with the President. How these instructions shall be carried out and whether to be presented as a peremptory demand, the President leaves to the judgment and discretion of the Commissioners. (Hay to Day, October 28, 1898, *For Rels. 1898*, pp. 937–938.)

The language of this telegram can be only McKinley's.

view. He frankly admitted it. [He said that] on investigation, he found that my view was absolutely right, and that there was not a single respectable authority on international law which did not sustain it. He had been having Secretary Moore and others in the office collate these authorities, and a long series of extracts was read. . . .

The Commissioners seemed to be unanimously of the opinion that we could not claim Manila by conquest. Senator Frye went so far as to declare that we had no right to the Spanish prisoners we were now holding in Manila. Others combated this view on the ground that we could not have released them, since then they would have inevitably proceeded to make war upon the insurgents in other parts of the Philippines. [This] we could not be justified in permitting, after the co-operation the natives had rendered us.

When we encountered the Spaniards in the ante-room at the Foreign Office in the afternoon, they were obviously under a little constraint and excitement, though, as usual, ceremoniously polite. Our proposal was handed to the interpreter. I fancy that they had not expected it to be ready so promptly, and were a little disappointed at seeing it turned over; but this may have been mere imagination. Abarzuza asked to have it first read in English before the translator put it into Spanish. It seemed to me he wanted to break its force a little in reaching Montero. Ferguson read it first in English, and then made a rather fluent translation. The attitude of the Spaniards while this reading was going on seemed to be one of despairing resignation.[5] Guarnica once or twice whispered some proposal to Montero, who said "No," rather positively. Villa-Urrutia also whispered some suggestion, which was received in the same way; and then the two whispered together with Cerero. Abarzuza's resigned attention to the reading was almost plaintive.

The instant it was finished, Montero said quietly that the proposals were of such gravity and importance, as would require the most careful attention and considerable time. He therefore suggested a postponement

[5] The Spanish reaction to the demand for all the Philippines may be imagined; its tense drama is well described in the Diary with an economy of words. Montero Ríos cabled home that the demand "causes amazement" and lay outside the protocol. The Spanish Foreign Minister characterized it as "the greatest extreme imaginable in the claims of the United States. . . ." Castillo himself told Madrid: "The intention of the Americans is to deny the Cuban debt and purchase the Philippines for the least sum possible." In the days that followed the demand, the Spanish government bravely counselled its Commissioners to resist, fortifying their notable tendency to delay and extend debate. See *Spanish Diplomatic Correspondence and Documents 1896–1900: Presented to the Córtes by the Minister of State* (Washington: 1905), pp. 309, 320.

until Friday, with the possibility of their even then finding it necessary to ask a still longer delay. We at once agreed, and the Commission arose.

The members, however, lingered much longer than usual. In fact it seemed to me at one time as if the Spaniards were trying to out-stay the Americans. They walked up and down in the ante-room in groups, talking sometimes in an earnest and somewhat animated way. Gray and Day continued at the table writing.

Day finally asked me to detain Frye and Davis, since he wanted to telegraph the government reporting what we had done, and reply to the instructions requiring us to hold Manila by conquest, as well as by the protocol. So far as the mere question of Manila was concerned, the Commissioners might possibly have agreed. But Secretary Day had written his dispatch so as to embody a sweeping declaration that there were no circumstances under which the United States could hold territory by conquest. I was inclined to object to this, but was fortunately saved the necessity of antagonizing the Secretary [Day] by the outspoken opposition of Senator Davis. He would not, he said, sign any such proposition, because he did not believe it to be good international law or good sense. He did not consider that we were bound by Secretary Blaine's rather gushing resolution in the Pan-American Congress. He would have to take in hand the work of carrying this treaty through the Foreign Relations Committee and the Senate. He did not propose to have his hands tied by a declaration of this sort, which he might have to repudiate. Judge Day was little inclined to argue the question, but Senator Davis was positive. He then said that there would be no object in sending his dispatch unless the Commission could be unanimous about it. He would not argue in favor of the right of conquest, himself, but if other members of the Commission wished to do so in the joint session, there was no reason why they should not. He would also reserve to himself the liberty of writing to the President expressing his individual views, and asking for a revision of the opinion expressed in the dispatch.

[Day] and one or two of the other Commissioners continued at work at the table. The Spanish Commissioners had sometime before taken their leave of us and gone home, and Davis and I finally left our colleagues and drove home. . . .

Tuesday, November 1st, 1898.

. . . Judge Day was a good deal troubled [today] by the statement in
one of the papers that the French yellow book contained a declaration
that our occupation of Manila was only provisional.[6] He had procured a
copy of the yellow book, and found that while the protocol and the correspondence relating to it were all right, the French Foreign Office in
drawing up a summary of the negotiation for the information of its
ambassadors at other courts, had carelessly overlooked the clause relating to the subsequent decision by the Joint Commission as to the
control, disposition and government of the Philippines. We discussed
the best means of setting this right, and finally agreed that our Ambassador should call M. Delcassé's attention to it, believing that he would
then set it right, and recognize that it had probably been the oversight of
one of the Foreign Office clerks. He accordingly left me to consult Gen.
Porter about it. Frye and Gray subsequently came in and spent the
morning in chat about the situation. Gray inclined to the belief that
the Spaniards would break off rather than surrender the Philippines.
Frye like myself thought it rather more probable, though by no means
certain that the money bait would hold them. . . .

Wednesday, November 2nd, 1898.

Dispatch from the President to Senator Frye read this morning together with Frye's previous dispatch to the President which had called it
out.[7] Frye expressed the belief that we should get no treaty. The Presi-

---

[6] Books of documents relating to foreign affairs issued by governments are often
known by the color of their cover. The French had just published such a collec-
tion relating to the Spanish-American crisis. See France, Ministére des affaires
étrangères, *Documents Diplomatiques: Negociations pour la Paix entre l'Espagne
et les États-Unis* (Paris, 1898).

[7] Frye took the lead in suggesting a way out of the impasse by holding that the
United States could legally and honorably pay Spain for pacific internal improvements in the Philippines, which she was acquiring, while she could not con-
sistently do so in Cuba, which she was not acquiring. On October 30 he wrote
the President at length.

It seems to me that the most undesirable happening would be our return without a treaty of peace, and yet that is probable in my opinion. If the Spanish
Commissioners should accede to our demands as at present outlined they could
not return home, while our country, it may be, would not justify us in tender-

President William McKinley

Drawn by T. de Thulstrup
Harper's Weekly, August 29, 1898

The American Peace Commission at a conference in their council room at the Continental Hotel, Paris: left to right—Whitelaw Reid, George Gray, John Bassett Moore, William Rufus Day, William P. Frye, Cushman Kellogg Davis.

William Rufus Day, president of the American Peace Commission.

Whitelaw Reid in later years.

William P. Frye, United States senator from Maine, member of the
American Commission.

Cushman Kellogg Davis, United States senator from Minnesota, member of the American Commission.

George Gray, United States senator from Delaware, member of the
American Commission.

John Bassett Moore, secretary to the American Commission.

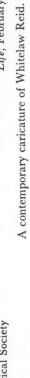

Life, February 3, 1898

A contemporary caricature of Whitelaw Reid.

Ohio Historical Society

The Young Whitelaw Reid

United States Department of State

Eugenio Montero Ríos, president of the Spanish Peace Commission.

Buenaventura de Abarzuza y Ferrer, member of the Spanish Commission.

United States Department of State

General Rafael Cerero, member of the Spanish Commission.

José de Guarnica, member of the Spanish Commission.

Wenceslao Ramírez de Villa-Urrutia, member of the Spanish Commission.

Emilio de Ojeda, secretary to the Spanish Commission.

dent gave us pretty large powers in the way of concessions and almost
turned the whole question of what we should give for the Philippines
over to us, subject, of course, to his final revision. . . .

---

ing any more liberal terms. Spain made a determined fight to secure concessions as to the Cuban debt, while we were persistent in our refusal to yield anything. Our articles were accepted, but provisionally, for if no final agreement is
reached they too fail. It seemed to me that we might have agreed to use our
good offices with any government hereafter established in Cuba to secure the
assumption by it of any indebtedness incurred [in] internal improvements
there, and ourselves assume any like indebtedness in the territories finally ceded
to us. The amount could not be large. Might we not go further, and agree to
pay Spain from $10,000,000 to $20,000,000 if thus a treaty could be secured?
If [there is] no treaty, then [there will be] war, a continued disturbance of business, an expenditure of a million dollars a day, and further loss of life. Would
not our people prefer to pay Spain one half of war expenditures rather than in-
dulge in its costly luxury? Europe sympathizes with Spain in this regard
exactly. The correspondent of the London *Times*, in his yesterday's letter, criticized severely our attitude. The precedents for the last century are antagonistic
to our position. Of course we will not pay debts incurred in the suppression of
colonial rebellions. I do not forget that we demand no money indemnity for
[the] cost of war to us. It may be because our enemy is bankrupt. I am sorry the
Carolines were not taken by us as they are infinitely more valuable than the
Ladrones. If war is resumed I hope orders will be given Dewey to seize at once
all of the Philippine Islands, also the Carolines.

You may be sure I should not make these suggestions if I did not regard a
treaty of peace of vital importance to our country and the danger of failure to
secure it gravely imminent. (*For. Rels. 1898*, p. 939.)

The President fully understood the Spanish attitude, and while he could not
judge the Spanish disposition to break off the conference too accurately, he was
unwilling to run the risk if the Commissioners on the spot thought such a rupture
imminent. Speaking through Hay, he therefore agreed to Frye's suggestion on
November 1, 1898.

The President directs me to say that no one would more deeply regret than
himself a failure to make a treaty of peace, and is surprised to hear from you
that that result is not improbable. He hopes and believes that your negotiations
can be so conducted as to prevent so undesirable a happening. He desires the
Commissioners to be generous in all matters which do not require a disregard of
principle or duty, and whatever the Commissioners may deem wise and best in
the matter of the debts for internal improvements and public works of a pacific
character in the Philippines will receive his favorable consideration; nor does
he desire the Commission to dis-regard well-established precedents or make any
conditions which will not be worthy of ourselves and merit the approval of the
best judgment of mankind. If it should be the opinion of the Commissioners
that there should be paid a reasonable sum of money to cover peaceful improvements which are fairly chargeable to us under established precedents, he
will give cheerful consent. The money payments, if any is determined upon,
should rest solely upon the considerations suggested in your message of Sunday
night. He desires that you may read this to the Commission with your message
to him. (*Ibid.*)

Thursday, November 3rd, 1898.

Secretary Day read this morning a long letter he had sent to the President arguing against the right to hold the Philippines by conquest.[8] In this he took distinctly the ground I had suggested to him weeks ago as to the tendency of the text writers on international law, as to our conquest of Manila. But [he] went much farther in objecting to our acquiring any territory now by that title. I told him it would not do to argue against the validity of such a title, since we had no other to the United States; and that, in fact, hardly any civilized nation had any other. He was strenuous, however, in the belief that we never ought to consent to receive such a title now. I maintained that title by conquest was absolutely recognized by all international law, and that there was nothing approaching a formal utterance against it that could be called binding unless it was Secretary Blaine's resolution in the Pan-American [Congress]. . . .

Friday, November 4th, 1898.

Considerable time was spent this morning in translating to the other Commissioners the articles in the *Figaro* and *Gaulois,* which had obviously been inspired, if not actually written, at the Spanish Embassy. We at once accepted [them] as certainly outlining the course the Spaniards would take at the joint session this afternoon. I had also some information gathered last night at a dinner at the Duchess of————[*sic*] (for whose children the Queen Regent has stood godmother, and with whom she appears to be in frequent correspondence). This confirmed our views as to the newspaper forecast, and also to the reasonable probability that the Spaniards were rather agreed to get rid of the Philippines. [They] wanted, of course, to make the best terms possible. It seemed also clear that they were "sparring for time" at present, in the hope of an administration reverse in the elections next Tuesday in America, which might weaken our attitude.

    [8] Day remained somewhat squeamish about the whole question, and as Reid notes here, wrote the President, an old and close personal friend, his doubts about the legality and morality of claiming all the islands by right of conquest. He cited for support the well-known facts about the delays caused in capturing Manila, and the question of whether or not this was in fact the capture of the Islands or even of Luzon proper. The letter is very lengthy, and is dated November 2, 1898 (McKinley Papers, Library of Congress).

Secretary Day recurred to the subject of Hay's recent dispatch warning us against yielding our claim to Manila by conquest, as well as through the protocol, and saying that we practically conquered Manila when Admiral Dewey sank the fleet. The Secretary [Day] vigorously rejected this view; declared it had not a leg to stand on in international law. [He] said he was sure the President had not given it full consideration; but that he knew the member of the cabinet who was constantly bringing forward that idea. He seemed strongly inclined to contest the ground, and had prepared a dispatch to the President about it, which he said he had revised carefully in order to avoid seeming impatient or insubordinate. He had prepared it so as to insert in the body of it the names of the Commissioners who had concurred with him in his view. I saw at once that Senator Davis would certainly disagree, and thought on a question of this sort it was undesirable to seem to be arguing about our own instructions with the State Department, and arraying the Commission pro and con on the question whether we approved the instructions we had received. I also thought it undesirable to meet the new Secretary of State [Hay] so early in our official intercourse with an intimation that he didn't understand the subject as well as we did.

Part of these views I hinted at, but with sufficient distinctness to induce the Secretary [Day] to make some modifications. Senator Gray and Senator Frye had at once concurred with the doctrine of his dispatch. I suggested that on this he might, instead of inserting the names of those who agreed with him, simply say that a majority of the Commission concurred in his views, and this he accepted. [He accepted] also a few verbal changes, which I made tending to make the difference less pronounced. He also wrote one or two of the sentences himself and added some, and in the form his dispatch finally took I said I believed Senator Davis would consent to it. The Senator being absent, we sent for him. He was reluctant to agree to it even in the modified form, and suggested one or two slight verbal changes, which were made. Then he said he had no objection to it as far as it went. To which I replied with the inquiry whether it was necessary to go any farther, whether we might not leave further bridges to be crossed only when we reached them.

Finally, this general view was accepted. [However], Senator Davis prepared a dispatch of his own, explaining that in his judgment the ground of mere conquest was too natural, and explaining that indemnity, damages, obligations to the natives, dangers from the vicinity, imperilled commercial interests, etc., might also enter into it. It was finally understood, though not very definitely or formally agreed to, that both dispatches should be sent. The one being signed by Secretary Day, and the other by Senator Davis. . . .

The Spaniards were a few minutes before us at the Foreign Office, and the slight stiffness, which I fancied observable in their greetings at the last meeting, had entirely disappeared. In fact, they seemed rather more cordial than usual.[9] The moment the protocols were approved, Montero Ríos made a little statement to the effect that they had been greatly surprised and pained at the nature of the proposal submitted by the American Commissioners at the last session. While they found themselves unable to accept [the American proposition, they had prepared a paper setting forth a counter] proposition. Instead of handing this over as heretofore, he passed it with a word or two in Spanish to their Secretary Ojeda, who in turn ceremoniously delivered it to Secretary Moore with the remark that he was instructed to do so by the President of the Spanish Commission. The procedure seemed a little stilted, and I wondered whether they had any special motive for it. Moore passed it to Secretary Day, who in turn handed it to the translator. The Spaniards seemed rather to expect that we would immediately ask an adjournment in order to have it translated. Two or three of the American Commissioners suggested that even if the translation, which could be made at sight, had to be a little rough, it would be better to have the document read at once. Montero Ríos assented with a shrug of the shoulders, and Mr. Ferguson began at once the translation.

It was soon apparent that the forecast of the *Figaro* and *Gaulois* had been semi-official. When the translation reached the point where they referred to the French yellow book, and then began quoting from the dispatches of M. Cambon, Secretary Day interrupted to inquire as to the date which they gave to a certain dispatch, in order to make sure that they were referring to a dispatch which in our documents bore a date one day earlier. Montero Ríos explained that the discrepancy was probably due to the fact that all communications had been sent by Cambon to the French Minister of Foreign Affairs, and had been by him transmitted to Spain. The date he had given was that marked on

[9] Despite the tension in the air of the conference, Reid always felt that the Spanish delegates were courteous and polite. "The Spanish Commissioners continue to show the utmost courtesy," he wrote McKinley, "but the talk of old Montero is endless and their capacity for producing long documents apparently increases" (Reid to McKinley, October 28, 1898, McKinley Papers, Library of Congress).

the dispatch indicating the date of its receipt, which they supposed to be also the date on which it was sent.

Secretary Day inquired whether the dispatch was transmitted from the French Foreign Office in the language in which it was received or whether it was there translated into Spanish, to which Montero Ríos replied that he was not certain. He professed the greatest willingness, however, if the American Commissioners desired, to verify dates or text or for any other reason [wished], to procure the originals as received and filed in the Foreign Office in Madrid. The Secretary thanked him, but said he had only desired to clear up the little perplexity from the discrepancy in dates.

When the end of the argument on this point was reached in the translation of the Spanish paper, Montero Ríos interrupted the translation to recur to this subject and explain it more in detail. He said that when the good offices of Mr. Cambon were employed in the negotiation, the Spaniards had requested of the French Foreign Office that they might communicate directly with Mr. Cambon from Madrid. The French Foreign Office had not assented to this suggestion, but had required that all communications with the French Ambassador in Washington should pass through the French Foreign Office. The Spaniards therefore were not responsible for this mode of transmission, but had, of course, no choice excepting to assent to it.

The translation was closed at twenty minutes before four o'clock. After a brief consultation among the American Commissioners, Judge Day remarked that he understood the paper to amount to a rejection of our last proposal, and an offer of other proposals in their place. In view of the time required for writing out a careful translation and considering the nature and scope of the document, it did not seem probable that the American Commissioners could be ready with their written reply before Tuesday next. Montero Ríos replied that under the rules, the American proposal not having been accepted, the American Commissioners had a right to file a memorandum. As the paper presented today also set forth Spanish proposals, if these were rejected, the Spanish Commissioners would have the right to file a similar memorandum. He then agreed to the proposed adjournment till Tuesday....

Judge Day whispered to me that he was anxious to see our Ambassador [Horace Porter] at once in order to challenge the explanations already given us by the French Foreign Office of their accidental omission from their summary of the protocol in their circular sent to their ambassadors of the clause relating to the control, disposition, and government of the Philippines. I promised to drive him up to the [American] Embassy. Being detained, however, for two or three minutes in taking leave of the Spanish Commissioners, I found on getting to the door that the Judge [Day] in his eagerness had already rushed off. Supposing that we could catch him at the cab stand or on the way to the Continental Hotel, I instructed my carriage to follow. Missing him, [I] went on to the Embassy, and thence to Gen. Porter's house. At the latter place I found that he had already been there, and having missed the Ambassador had returned. On getting back to the hotel I found him in his room, where he gave me an amusing account of his getting along with the French cabbies without my knowledge of French. He seemed to have made a success of it so far as getting over the ground quickly was concerned. His great anxiety was to get hold of Porter at once, so as to have him immediately see Delcassé and explain to him the use the Spaniards had attempted to make of this accidental omission in a French document. He believed that it would irritate Delcassé, and cause him not only to sustain our contention on this point, but to throw his influence a little against the Spaniards because of their obviously tricky and unfair effort to draw him into the controversy.

On our return the Spanish document was placed in the hands of the translator and typewriters with instructions to have the translation completed at the earliest moment for consideration at Saturday's meeting. We were all agreed that the first reading had impressed us with a sense that it was a document requiring great care in the answer. We also thought the answer on most points would not be difficult, and on some points would need to be made somewhat positive if not aggressive. Judge Day was very clear in his conviction that he never had an easier task than to upset their contentions about the scope of the protocol. Senator Frye was a good deal disturbed about the claim that Manila ought to be returned under international law, and expressed the belief that this part of the answer would have to be treated by the legal method of conviction and avoidance. Senator Davis inclined to dissent from this, but preferred to wait for the full translation, and also to give the subject mature consideration. Senator Gray was quite impressed with the ability of the document, and repeated his old wish that we were well out of the Philippines with nothing but a coaling station. . . .

Saturday, November 5th, 1898.

The Commissioners began early this morning on the translation as far as it had advanced, reading and pausing, from time to time, for discussion. Judge Day was more than ever convinced of the ease with which he could dispose of the whole Spanish contention as to the protocol, and indignant over the improper use they had made of the obvious lapse in the yellow book. The effort to drag in the Cuban debt again so soon after having waived that question seemed to all of us extraordinary, if not offensive, and I finally said I would like to write something on that subject. The arguments from international law and otherwise concerning Manila troubled some of the Commissioners somewhat. Senator Frye repeated his belief that we seemed to have no right to hold the Spanish army there as prisoners. I dissented from this on the ground that we owed it to the insurgents not to turn the Spaniards loose upon them. Senator Davis [dissented] on the ground that since the protocol made no exemption of the soldiers, it was a fair inference that they were to be held with the city. Senator Davis finally said he believed he could make a good argument on the ground that the doctrine of military occupancy under an armistice would fully warrant everything we had done at Manila, and expressed his intention of writing a reply to that part of the paper.

A summary of the Spanish document had been prepared by Mr. Moore to be telegraphed to the State Department; but we all felt that it was too brief, and I insisted especially that it gave no adequate idea of the offensive tone the Spaniards had assumed both with reference to the debt, and with reference to Merritt and Dewey in connection with the capture of Manila. I took out several of the most offensive sentences and insisted on incorporating them in the dispatch. Senator Gray at first protested, claiming that it was not fair to the Spaniards to single out the worst things they said, as if these fairly indicated the tone of the whole document. But after my additions had been incorporated and the dispatch was read to him, he professed entire satisfaction with it, and it was accordingly hurried off.

Sunday, November 6th, 1898.

Drives both forenoon and afternoon and a quiet evening at home.
Tried in the morning to take several of the Senators out; but Senator
Davis was hard at work in his shirt sleeves with a cigar in his mouth and
a typewriter[10] at hand, over his doctrine of military occupation. . . . He
thought he must spend the whole day on it. Judge Day was even harder
at work with his typewriter, and gave promise of making his response
pretty long, however easy it might be to make. Frye had gone to church,
and Gray had made some social engagement. In the evening I made a
few notes myself as to the debt question and as to Manila, but wrote
nothing out, preferring to see first whether the others covered all the
ground.

Monday, November 7th, 1898.

. . . When the Commissioners assembled in my rooms, Judge Day produced a dispatch from Washington in answer to those which he and
Senator Davis and others had sent intended to bring out final instructions on the Philippines.[11] The dispatch was a compound of injunctions
to make a settlement just and honorable to the nation, characterized by
humanity, etc., with confidence in the Commissioners, desire for a treaty,
and disposition to give the greatest weight to any course we should

[10] This does not mean that the Senator was typing. The term "typewriter" in
this era referred to a person, not a machine.
[11] The Secretary of State wrote in part:

The President has no purpose to question the Commission's judgment as to
the grounds upon which the cession of the archipelago is to be claimed. His only
wish in that respect is to hold all the grounds upon which we can fairly and
justly make the claim. He recognizes fully the soundness of putting forward indemnity as the chief ground, but conquest is a consideration which ought not
to be ignored. How our demand shall be presented and the grounds upon
which you will rest it he confidently leaves with the Commissioners. His great
concern is that a treaty shall be effected in terms which will not only satisfy
the present generation, but, what is more important, be justified in the judgement of posterity. The argument which shall result in such a consummation he
confides to the Commission. He appreciates the difficulties and embarrassments and realizes the delicate work before you, but that the Commissioners
will be able to conclude a treaty of peace satisfactorily to the country, justified
by humanity and by precedent, is the belief of the President and your countrymen generally. (Hay to Day, November 5, 1898, *For. Rels. 1898*, p. 941.)

finally resolve to recommend. As it was concluded Senator Davis said: "If that isn't equal to Jack Bunsby I am mistaken," whereupon Judge Day broke out with the quotation: "If not, why not?" The Judge [Day] seemed quite desirous of addressing further inquiries and insisting upon having the President take the responsibility of the course to be finally attempted. . . .

Tuesday, November 8th, 1898.

We began quite early this morning the further consideration of our reply to the Spanish Commissioners, really intending only to read for slight verbal corrections, and finish as rapidly as read to the type-writers. Senator Gray protested strongly against a phrase which Judge Day had used in a part of his response, where he spoke of "this per-version of facts." Both Davis and Frye sustained the language as exactly justified by what the Spaniards had said; but it was finally agreed to use a softer phrase.

By this time it was evident that the typewriters would find it impossi-ble to complete the paper in time for a meeting by two o'clock, and the secretary [Moore] accordingly sent a note to Ojeda of the Spanish Com-mission referring to their offer at the last adjournment of as much more time as we wanted, and explaining that as the copyists could not com-plete the fair copy of our paper in time, we should be glad to hold the meeting . . . at 4 o'clock in the afternoon instead of two. Their reply was to the effect that expecting only a short meeting at two, they had made engagements for the rest of the afternoon, and would therefore prefer to have the meeting postponed until two on the following day. Their ex-cuse seemed to us improbable, but there was nothing to be done but to accept the delay which they obviously desired for the purpose of hear-ing the election news [from the United States, which they expected to be] unfavorable to the administration. . . .

Count Münster made a long call in the evening. He began by asking about the reported explosion under the Supreme Court rooms in Wash-ington.[12] [He] then referred to the newspaper announcements that we were to meet today [and] inquired whether we had done anything very important. It was evident that this was the purpose of his call, and that

[12] An explosion, caused by leaking gas or steam pressure, had occurred in the Capitol building, injuring several people. Though accidental, some hasty jingoes attributed it to a Spanish plot to blow up the government.

he probably considered that the expected meeting today would be the turning point in the negotiations on the Philippines. I explained the delay, and he then talked about the protocol, which he said he had read. He was inclined to believe that it sustained the Spanish view. I thereupon got our official copy of it, and called his attention to both the English and [the] French text. He then fastened on the word "disposition," saying that it would have been better to leave the original word "possession," since it was best in diplomacy, and especially in precise matters like treaties and protocols, to say the exact thing that was meant. He predicted that we would have a good deal of trouble out of it. He was evidently curious about the Philippines, and I finally thought it best to talk with some frankness. I showed him the map and explained why any division of the Philippines was difficult and unnatural. [I] dwelt on the duty which the fortunes of war had unexpectedly imposed upon us with regard to these Philippine insurgents. [I] said that it was evident now that it would make less trouble for the rest of the world, and involve us in little more, to take the whole group instead of leaving a part of it as a fire brand for Europe. The Count said on this part of the subject: "We certainly don't want them; at least I don't want them, and I hope my government does not."

Wednesday, November 9th, 1898.

My first greeting this morning was a dispatch . . . announcing Republican victories.[13] Before the Commission met, the Associated Press agent, Mr. Mack [a reporter] had rushed in with a request for a sentence or two from each of the Commissioners indicating their feelings over the result. I was alone at the time, and gave him a single sentence to the effect that I was greatly delighted over it, even more delighted than I could possibly have been if at home. He at once began asking what in my view would be its effect on the work of the Commission. I replied that I did not wish to say anything on that subject, and would be quite unwilling to admit that any party divisions or successes or defeats at home could interfere with the united work of any body of commissioners

---

[13] As Reid noted, the Spanish were obviously playing for time in discussing the Cuban debt in the hope that the Republican expansionists would be defeated in the November congressional elections. Though not a sweeping victory, the election presumably endorsed the Republican stand on expansion by giving the Party control of both houses in the new Congress.

abroad fairly representing their country in an effort to secure its just rights. A moment later Senator Davis entered the room, and in reply to Mr. Mack's question was ready to plunge at once into a statement of the great advantages he thought the Commission would derive from the result of the elections. I ventured, however, to check him, and suggest the view I had taken. He at once accepted it and told Mack he would write out something for him. When he returned half an hour later, he amused me by relating that he had taken the very caution I have given him and elaborated it into a statement of his views.

When the Commission met, Senator Davis said that, while he was not wholly convinced, he was disposed to accept the views of his brother Commissioners and withdraw the final pages of his paper to which exceptions had been taken. I thereupon took what I had written about Manila, Merritt, and Dewey and fitted it in at the close of what was left of his paper, and the completed document was immediately sent to the typewriters to be put in shape for the afternoon meeting. Senator Gray arrived about this time, seeming a good deal depressed and abstracted. Very general sympathy was felt for his defeat at yesterday's elections, but not a word of reference to the subject was uttered by any Commissioner.[14]

Commander Bradford was then introduced. He wished to file with the Commissioners his statement of the relative importance of the Caroline and [the] Ladrone Islands. He left a formal statement about the different harbors in the Ladrones and repeated his declaration that the Carolines had far better harbors and were almost in every way more important to us. The question was raised whether, as the Commander was to sail for home on Saturday, any of us wished to send by him any messages to the President. I took this opportunity to ask him whether, in his judgment, the Carolines together with the Canaries and Ceuta would be a fair equivalent for that portion of the Philippines left outside of the line of division, which he had recommended to us. He hesitated about the reply, saying that it involved political considerations which he did not feel competent to discuss. He was sure, however, the Canaries would be valuable. At his request I made a memorandum of the question. I then asked him whether, if a division of the Philippines had to be made,

---

[14] Senator Gray's Democratic Party in Delaware was defeated, which resulted in his failure to be re-elected to the Senate. McKinley, however, appointed him a federal circuit judge, at which post he served from 1899 to 1914. Many Democrats charged that this was payment for his work on the Commission. In view of his steadfast opposition to the President's policy this seems untrue.

he would not consider a division which I had proposed [as] more natural and more advantageous to us than his. My proposed line was north of Mindanao through Surigos Strait and thence to the Northeast end of Borneo. It left out solely the Mohammedan portion of the archipelago, i.e., Mindanao and the Sulu group. He had once said that he would consider this a more natural line, and a much more advantageous one. I was rather struck by the fact that for the first time Judge Day seemed also impressed by the advantages of this division. . . .

Judge Day was curiously insistent before the Commissioners separated on having Secretary Moore read editorials which had been sent him (Day) from the *New York Evangelist* and the *London Observer*, dwelling on the dangerous experiment of taking the Philippines. It occurred to me that if we were going into this business, we might do it a little more thoroughly, and so I embraced the opportunity to read aloud a strong and very friendly article from the *London Standard* taking a different view. . . .

At two o'clock we drove over to the Foreign Affairs [Ministry] where the Spaniards were just arriving. Their greetings were rather more cordial than usual, and as soon as we were seated at the table, Montero Ríos asked the translator to express to the American Commissioners the regret with which they had heard of the explosion in the Capitol, and the sympathy they felt for this misfortune together with their hope that the accident might not prove so serious as the first reports indicated. Judge Day immediately replied thanking them and saying that the American Commissioners would highly appreciate this expression of sympathy. They had not yet received details, but hoped the reports had been exaggerated. The protocols were then read, and the American answer to the last Spanish paper was immediately presented. It made 50 typewritten pages large foolscap size. Montero Ríos looked at it doubtfully for a moment, turned over to the end to notice the number of pages, and then said that obviously this document would require great study. They would begin on it at once—this very evening—but would like to have some idea as to the date of the next meeting. They would prefer, in fact, to leave it unsettled till tonight, when they would send us word after a preliminary reading, which might enable them to fix a date for the next meeting. If another course were preferred, they would be willing to name a date now, reserving the privilege of changing it in case of necessity. Judge Day said he thought it would be more convenient if a day should be named at once. Thereupon, after a moment's consultation Montero

Ríos said he would name next Saturday, at 2 o'clock, reserving, as before stated, the privilege of changing in case of need.[15]

Thursday, November 10th, 1898.

At the beginning of our meeting this morning, Secretary Day presented a dispatch just received from Bellamy Storer, our Minister in Belgium. It was a copy of the dispatch he was sending to the State Department reporting a very confidential message brought to him from the palace by the legal advisor of King Leopold to the effect that the Spanish government had offered to cede to him the entire Philippines. The dispatch was a little confused (apparently owing to some blunder in transmission or deciphering) as to the conditions. But it seemed to read as if they had proposed to do this provided the United States would make no objection.

It was at once noted that such a cession would naturally be expected to carry an obligation for the amount of the Philippine debt. I commented on this as a deliberate effort on the part of a bankrupt power to dispose of its property before settling with its creditors. Judge Day now raised very seriously and persistently the question whether we could not get together on some definite agreement as to any final concessions we

[15] During these tense days and weeks, Reid and the other American Commissioners could not decide whether the Spanish would really break or were bluffing. Reid wrote McKinley that he felt at one point Montero Ríos was ready to go home. Castillo remarked to him that "neither Sagasta nor Montero nor anybody could consent to take the Cuban debt." Reid himself noted on October 28: "I have some doubt as to whether these people will ever sign any treaty we can afford to make. They reason that they can be no worse off if they fail to sign; and that there is always the possibility of our arousing so much sympathy for them by pushing them to extremes, that there might be a strong appeal for arbitration." The Spanish were misinformed if they seriously thought the United States government would consent to arbitration. Nor could Madrid likely have begun the war again. As Reid noted on November 15, "I think I know from inside news from Madrid, from the court, that the Queen Regent is now convinced that nothing can be gained by contending either for the debt or for the Philippines, and that she is anxious to accept the inevitable and end the agony." What would have happened had the United States made no money payment for the Philippines cannot be known, but it is quite possible that Spanish pride would have compelled a resumption of the war, however futile. They preferred utter defeat on the field to negotiated defeat at the conference table. See Reid's two letters to McKinley, dated October 28, and November 15, 1898, in McKinley Papers, Library of Congress.

should make, whether as to money payment or in territory to secure a treaty and avoid a rupture. Senator Gray again expressed himself against taking anything beyond a coaling station. Senator Frye intimated a willingness to accept the old Bradford division line of the archipelago, leaving to Spain everything south of it. This would abandon the Visayas as well as Mindanao. Senator Davis expressed himself strongly in favor of taking the whole archipelago and giving no money.

I had declined to express myself when Judge Day first asked me, "in advance of the grave and reverend Senators." But now [I] said I would be willing to give them some money, possibly twelve to fifteen millions for the whole of the archipelago, together with the dependencies governed from it, including the whole of the Carolines and [the] Ladrones. [I] then said that as a last resort I would be willing to leave them the Mohammedan part of the archipelago and take the rest without any money payment. Judge Day named substantially the same amount of money, and was willing to make the division on Bradford's line. Finally, it was agreed that we should have a meeting in the afternoon at four and each present in writing his views for transmission to the State Department.[16]

After a drive with my wife in the Bois, and a long walk in the Avenue des Accacias, I sat down to write out mine. At the afternoon meeting the

[16] Reid's private estimate of his colleagues is interesting, all the more so since he presumed to write of them to the President:

We have had a singularly harmonious and agreeable Commission. All my colleagues have distinctly risen in my estimate of them during these six weeks; and Judge Day, in particular, has shown great clearness, precision of view, and well-balanced judgement. There has been the freest expression of all divergencies of opinion; but from first to last there has not been a personal jar. Senators Davis and Frye have agreed so well with me that when I had written out my views some weeks ago on the Philippines, they joined me in signing them, almost without the change of a word. Judge Day has gradually advanced, under the testimony and arguments here and the reports from home, till he does not seem very uncomfortable on our platform. And even Senator Gray, who generally starts out on every question by stating the Spanish side of it, generally lands on ours,—though often with many a protest and reservation. But, considering his politics and position, he is really doing wonderfully well and personally he is most delightful, while nobody can help admiring his honest effort to be fair-minded and judicial (Reid to McKinley, November 15, 1898, McKinley Papers, Library of Congress).

The tone of condescension is probably unconscious; it was a fixture in Reid's makeup. The assumption that he and the President are very close, and that he himself is the pacifier of the Commission is much overstated. McKinley was inured to Reid's long letters of self-praise, and while grateful for the information they contained, was adept at reading between their lines.

others presented their dispatches all written out at some length. Senator Frye went into a great many details about religious liberty, trade regulations, harbor restrictions, etc. Senator Gray had compressed into effective form his objections to taking any Asiatic territory, and Senator Davis had taken much the same ground as in the morning meeting. My proposition was elaborated a little so as to give two alternatives. When I finished reading it Senator Gray asked me whether if I were a Spaniard and heard such a proposition, I would not think it very hard and unreasonable. I replied that if I were a Spaniard I would try to remember that people who insisted upon dancing must pay the piper. I added that it seemed to me our first duty was not to consider what the Spaniards would think, but what our duty to our own country required, and what our own countrymen would think. Secretary Moore thought my statements as to general agreement on the doctrine that the successful nation had a right to exact an indemnity for the full cost of the war might be too sweeping. Judge Day afterwards said to me privately that he also inclined to think it a little too strong, and so I shaded this part of it down. At last about six o'clock all the dispatches were ready and placed in the hands of the secretary [Moore] to be put in cipher and transmitted.

Judge Day did not leave the room till about half past six. I still had to put my dispatch in shape and hand it to the secretary. On returning [I] had barely time to dress for dinner, when I was interrupted with the report that Judge Day had been taken suddenly ill, had had a violent chill and had been sent to bed. . . .

Friday, November 11th, 1898.

Dr. Clarke turned up early this morning, and said that Judge Day was in no danger, but must certainly keep his bed today and probably tomorrow. Senator Frye was the only Commissioner who appeared in my room. After a half hour's chat I proposed to him that we should get the ladies and go to the flower show in the Garden of the Tuileries. After he had wandered through the extraordinary display of fruits, chrysanthemums, etc., he broke out with the declaration [that] for once he was willing to lower the American flag, and admit that this was better than anything we did. True to her colors, Mrs. Frye after a rather reluctant assent added: "Yes, but we could do it as well if we tried." Comte and Comtesse Kergorlay ran against me as I was studying a fruit display at the farther end of the tent, and were naturally very cordial. They had just returned to town, and gave rather bad news of the Comtesse's sister Madame Lagrange. While we were chatting the President of the Republic passed, and when I broke away from them for a minute to tell Mrs. Frye who it was, she was as interested and eager to see him as a school girl. . . .

Saturday, November 12, 1898.

The *Temps* announced last night that it was doubtful whether there would be a meeting of the Joint Commission today, and this morning this news is confirmed by a message reported by Mr. Moore as reaching him from Ojeda to the effect that they are delayed by waiting for documents from Madrid, with which they expect completely to overcome Judge Day's contentions about the scope of the protocol. Senator Frye and Senator Gray came in for an hour's gossip, but no business was taken up. Judge Day is reported as better but still required to keep his bed; and we are all glad therefore that the Spaniards had already decided to ask for delay since otherwise they would surely have thrown the responsibility for it upon us. . . .

Sunday, November 13th, 1898.

Church in the morning with a little drive afterwards. Long chat in the afternoon with Judge Day about the prospects of the conference. He is nearly over his illness, though still weak. I gave him the results of various reports reaching me from Paris, Madrid and elsewhere to the effect that the Spanish Commissioners were talking about breaking off. While we were considering the probability of this, Beriah Wilkins, proprietor of the *Washington Post*, came in. He had spent some time this afternoon at the headquarters of the Spanish Commissioners talking with Ojeda, to [whom] the others referred him, and having a little conversation also with some of the Spanish Commissioners themselves. He described them as bitter, resentful, and above all not willing to make themselves martyrs by signing a treaty which would ruin them at home. . . .

Dinner in the evening at Sir Campbell Clarke's and fine amateur music afterwards. The German Ambassador, our own, and the German military attaché almost the only guests. . . . Count Münster evinced a great curiosity to know the present status of our negotiations and said:

"The Spaniards will not give up the Philippines. Do you still insist upon them, or will you waive that?" When I told him that the attitude of the United States on this subject would be uncompromising, he said: "Well then they won't sign the treaty. You may be sure of it, they are not going to sign." This in various phrases he repeated several times. His idea, as I gathered it, was that none of the Spanish Commissioners were willing to make martyrs of themselves at home for the sake of getting a treaty. He seemed to think that we would thereupon immediately take possession of the whole group, but said: "You will have a hard nut to crack." I explained how without the remotest intention originally of acquiring territory in that quarter, we had been forced into the attack on the Spanish fleet at Manila, and had become responsible for the present situation there. He seemed to agree with me that we could not honorably turn over again to Spain the government over a region where we had broken her rule down. I then dwelt on the difficulty of making any other disposition of the Islands. [I pointed] out that if we gave them to England or Japan, or Russia, or any other power, we were immediately provoking international difficulties. He rather assented to the proposition that the best thing possible for all concerned was that the United States should retain them. [He] repeated, however: "You will find it a hard nut to crack. We don't want them, however," he repeated, "and my government doesn't.". . .

Monday, November 14th, 1898.

As the members straggled in this morning Judge Day explained that a long cipher dispatch had come, and was being translated. While awaiting it we discussed the probability that the Spaniards would refuse to agree to anything we could propose, and the general judgment tended this way. When the translated dispatch was brought up it proved to follow tolerably closely in its reasoning the lines of my dispatch sent last week, and in one place it referred to Senator Frye's and my suggestions by name. It provided for the retention of the whole Philippines and an effort to procure the most eastern of the Carolines. It disclosed an apprehension that either Judge Day or Secretary Moore might have made some commitment to the German Ambassador in Washington, which would interfere with this.

The dispatch was listened to in profound silence, but after a few moments Senator Gray broke out in the most earnest and vehement expression he has yet made. [He deplored] the whole attitude and [declared] that the government was in a hypocritical position, really striving for the utmost conquest possible, while professing to be controlled solely by motives of duty and humanity. He ended with the exclamation: "If you do get such a treaty you won't get it ratified." No one made the slightest reply. In a few moments he was as placid as the rest of us and joined in the discussion as to the wisdom of drawing up a proposal in which we should now embody our ultimatum.

Gen. Porter was announced in the midst of this, and came in with a story of an interview which some unnamed friend of his had had with Castillo. It was substantially to the same effect with what we had already heard; that they [the Spanish] declared they could not and would not make martyrs of themselves at home by signing such a treaty. If the United States resumed hostilities they could not be much worse off, and would at least preserve their honor, yielding only to superior force. [They thought] it was possible that the United States might not resume active hostilities, although they assumed, of course, that she would take whatever she wanted of the Philippines. Castillo had admitted that they would consider a large payment in return for the Philippines, but would not think of $40,000,000. Five or six hundred million francs was the least sum they would consider. He had expressed some apprehension about the probable loss of the Canaries [sic Carolines?]. [He] thought, however, in the end it might be possible for the two governments in some way to come together and make a treaty direct, which would not involve the ruin of commissioners negotiating it. Senator Gray volunteered the suggestion that we might have to send word to Castillo soon as to just what the Spanish Commissioners could depend on, and proposed that Gen. Porter should be the medium of such a communication. Judge Day rather assented to this idea.

After Gen. Porter retired, Senator Frye was anxious that each member should prepare a draft of the articles which he considered indispensable in a treaty. Gray objected to this, saying that with five separate drafts we would have great trouble. Judge Day proposed that the secretary [Moore] should draw up a tentative draft, and this was finally agreed to. Senator Frye still [said] that he should have one of his own in order to know whether anything which he considered essential was left out. The meeting lasted till half past one. . . .

Tuesday, November 15th, 1898.

. . . I had made a little memorandum the night before of the sort of paper I was inclined soon to suggest filing. It was in the nature of a statement as to the extra delays over matters which we had supposed settled in the protocol [concerning] the two questions of the Cuban debt and the annexation of the Philippines, on which the position of the American Commissioners was fixed. [I also referred] to the uselessness of spending more time unless those proposals were accepted. [I ended] with a statement that if they were ready [we should] proceed to details, [and if not we should] move for a final adjournment. I read these rough notes, and the members were generally inclined to think that something of that sort must come soon.

Mr. Moore now appeared with his memorandum. It also proved to take the form of a practical ultimatum. In the Philippine article it embodied a distinct offer of $20,000,000, thus going to the extreme limit the President had authorized. Senator Frye and I demurred almost simultaneously on the ground that with this we ought to secure also the island for cable purposes and a naval station in the Carolines, as well as guarantees for religious freedom, liberation of political prisoners, etc. On this a lively dispute sprang up, Senator Davis siding with us. Senator Gray and Judge Day insisted that it would be better to leave these matters out of the ultimatum altogether, confining it strictly to subjects embraced in the protocol. I pointed out that in my belief it would be far better for the popular reception of the treaty at home, as well as for its chances in the Senate, if this large payment of money were not conditioned solely upon acquiring what the American people thought we were already entitled to in the Philippines. I was quite willing that the offer should go into the proposal, but thought it ought to come at the close. I would leave the taking of the Philippines to rest primarily on the ground of the necessary indemnity. [I] would then ask for the Caroline island, for the liberation of political prisoners, religious freedom, etc. [I would] say in consideration of all these things, and of pacific improvements made in the Philippines, [that] the United States would be willing to pay, etc.

Judge Day, however, was even more than usually tenacious [about] confining the ultimatum absolutely to the questions in the protocol. [He wished to have] the acquisition of the Caroline Islands . . . subsequently negotiated for and made the subject of a separate payment. We all pointed out the disadvantage of enforcing our ultimatum, and then coming in with the fresh requirements, as well as the certainty that by this method we should have to pay more than was really necessary. Secretary Moore rather sided with Judge Day as to the disadvantage of going outside the protocol in an ultimatum.

On our side all insisted on the disadvantages of having it begin all over again with a statement of fresh demands, which the Spaniards could claim took them by surprise. Finally, Judge Day proposed a phrase to follow the ultimatum, to the effect that when these were agreed to, the Commissioners "would be ready to treat with reference to," etc.; and then proceed to enumerate the several points reserving the Islands' religious liberty, freedom of political prisoners, and so on. To this Senators Frye and Davis and myself agreed, and Mr. Moore accordingly proceeded to change the tentative draft in this sense. We also desired a pledge for the open door to the Philippines, and a specific agreement with Spain that her merchandise should be admitted on the same terms with that of the United States. After the discussion was over, it seemed as if all hands were about as well satisfied with the conclusion we had reached as if each had had his own way.

No session in the afternoon, and I continued to nurse the cold, not always with comfort. It threatens to be rather more serious than the last. . . .

Count Jean de Kergorlay made a long call, [which was] very interesting. Some question I had asked as to his not having tried for the [Chamber of] Deputies led to his expressing his views as to the present condition of rural France, particularly in the manufacturing regions. He deplored the Socialist tendencies and the increasing exactions of the working men and their unions. [They] were sure, he said, in the long run, to drive manufacturers largely out of France. The silk-weaving industry, for example, [might go] to Japan. He spoke of the wages as enormously increased. The hours of labor [were] greatly reduced, and the value of labor also reduced. [He noted] the lack of sympathy between the working men and their employers, the extraordinary advance in the mode of living, and in the expenditures of the working men. [He said] that in the manufacturing centres the liquor shops got the increase of wages. Thirty years ago he said the workingman rarely had meat more than twice a week, and then only salt pork. Now he had meat at least once a day and that almost always fresh meat, beef, veal, or mutton. He pictured the average day of a workingman as something like this: Before he started to work in the morning, a glass of brandy or of absinthe; work until nine o'clock, then a visit to the wine shop, [even if] he drank . . . the vilest cheap wine, which was not wine at all, but some sort of a chemical compound fortified with alcohol. Then a little more work and another visit to the wine shop about 11 o'clock; an hour for breakfast later on; and two more visits to the wine shop in the course of the afternoon. Formerly the workingman's wife received all his wages and kept a tight grip on the purse. The change in their mode of living, however, had changed her also. Now she made childish expenditures for hats, gowns, and gougaws [sic] unfitted for her station. These expenditures cost her her moral control over the husband. Since she was no longer a model of economy, he refused to let her control his earnings and thus came to retain a large part spent in the wine shops. Altogether, Count Kergorlay was extremely despondent as to the future, anticipating obviously some sort of a crisis and a revolution. . . .

Wednesday, November 16th, 1898.

The cold gave me a rather bad night of it, and work began in the morning almost before I was ready. . . .

[Lawrence] Townsend, our Minister to Portugal, came in sharp at 10 o'clock on the invitation of Senator Davis, got introduced to the various Commissioners as they arrived, and spent half an hour talking about the attitude of Portugal during the war, the feeling towards America and towards the Spaniards, etc. The French papers this morning have changed their tone again. [They] publish some official statements from Madrid to the effect that the Spanish Commissioners are not going to surrender the points at issue, and deny that there is any dissension among them or in the Cabinet. [I] translated several of these articles for the Commissioners. We all concluded that a long paper would be the only immediate result of today's meeting, and that we must soon be ready to put in our ultimatum, but that an elaborate reply to their last contentions would first be necessary. . . .

We were a little late in arriving at the Foreign Office, but were still ten or fifteen minutes in advance of the Spaniards. They came in with profuse apologies for the delay, which had been unavoidable, and with rather more than their usual cordiality of manner. A little private discussion sprang up among a few of us, as to whether Judge Day ought to imitate Montero Ríos's expressions of sympathy over the news of the explosion in our Capitol by referring to the news we had seen in the papers of an alleged attempt upon his life by a Spanish crank. The final conclusion, however, was that as this grew out of a private quarrel in which a scurrilous pamphlet had been published against Montero, it might not be in the best taste to stir it up in a quasi-public way. Senator Gray was a little inclined to press the point, but Secretary Moore and I finally agreed with Day in advising against it.

The moment the protocols had been read in English and Spanish and agreed to, Montero Ríos offered a paper which he said would serve two purposes, as a reply to the last paper filed by the American Commissioners, and as a counter proposition. He said that if the American Commissioners, after the arguments in the present paper had been fully considered, should still persist in their present views, he desired to call their especial attention to the suggestions made in the few last pages of the memorandum now presented.

Judge Day at once said that, in as much as the President of the Spanish Commission [Montero Ríos] had called attention to that particular part of their paper, he would like—without manifesting any lack of interest in what preceded it—to have the part specially brought to their attention read now. Montero Ríos assented at once to this, saying he knew, of course, the impossibility of taking time to translate the whole paper intelligently now.

Mr. Ferguson at once made a sight translation of the concluding pages in the Spanish memorandum. They proved [to be] a suggestion that if the question of the Philippines could not be agreed to by the two Commissions here, a settlement might be relegated directly to the two Governments. But . . . it would be more practicable and less objectionable if the meaning of the disputed passage in the protocol on that subject should be submitted to arbitration. Senator Davis, at the close of the translation, whispered to me that he considered it an extremely dignified and impressive [presentation] of their case. He could not free his mind from the feeling that it would greatly influence the considered judgment of men even in our own country. [He thought] they were adroitly placing us in a position where, in order to maintain our present ground, we would be compelled to throw over pretty much all we had ever said before in favor of arbitration. I did not concur in this view, but did not think it desirable to argue it then. Judge Day having suggested an adjournment till Saturday, with the usual reservations this was generally agreed to, and after a few moments chat and cordial leave takings, we all came out leaving the Spanish in possession of the field. . . .

Thursday, November 17th, 1898.

Was awakened in the night by an increasing oppression in breathing, and before morning found myself in an old fashioned asthmatic spasm, the first real one I have had for nearly two years. For two or three hours the distress was so great that I was extremely glad when Dr. Clarke turned up. He immediately added to his previous prescriptions, and promised me quite positively better rest the next night.

Kept shut up all day, but attended the usual meeting of the Commissioners in my room. The translation of the Spanish paper was read throughout. It proved extraordinarily prolix, and in various particulars rather offensive. They were especially stirred up by the passage which I had contributed to our last paper, and made many little efforts to display their temper. They were more offensive to Judge Day, since they succeeded in getting something tangible with reference to his part of the paper, producing some passages from Cambon's notes which did not fully sustain Judge Day's versions of the transactions preceding the protocol. They had also some vicious slaps at the portion of our paper contributed by Senator Davis. The reading was heard in comparative silence, and Senator Gray did not repeat upon it, at its close, the eulogium which he had expressed to me the day before. My own feeling was that the whole paper was unblushingly disingenuous and almost incredibly contentious and pettifogging. Judge Day asked me especially to prepare a memorandum for the next paper, setting forth in detail our reasons for taking the Philippines. I remarked that I should also reply to one or two passages in this one. We had already prepared a proposal presenting quite fully our demands as to Cuba, Puerto Rico, and the Philippines in the form of an ultimatum. When these were agreed upon, we should be ready to proceed to treat with reference to the acquisition of an island in the Carolines, religious liberty, "the open door," etc. This had been telegraphed to Washington and approved. It was now agreed that our reply to the present Spanish paper should precede it, and that the Spaniards should be distinctly advised that this was the end. . . .[17]

[17] The following pages show clearly that the Americans were at the end of their patience, and wished to end the conference quickly. "We are now disposed to force this matter to an issue, realizing that we have been here a long time, and that argument is exhausted on the subject," Day wrote McKinley (November 19, 1898, McKinley Papers, Library of Congress).

Friday, November 18th, 1898.

No trouble at all in breathing; ten hours' sleep; and an almost entire disappearance this morning of asthmatic symptoms. . . .

After we got settled down to business [this morning] there was some more discussion of the Spanish paper. Gray spoke of it as an able document. I dissented and said it struck me as pettifogging and dishonest. Day dwelt a good deal on the efforts to impugn his veracity in his account of the transactions preceding the protocol, and is evidently bent on giving it very serious attention. On renewed suggestions from several [Commissioners], I undertook to prepare our reasons for taking the Philippines and spent the afternoon in doing it. . . .

Saturday, November 19th, 1898.

. . . [I] spent the morning dictating some new points on the Spanish paper and revising some others. Senator Davis seemed particularly interested in this, and I read to him what I had written on the subject of the Philippines. He expressed great satisfaction with it. So did Senator Frye when he heard it. Judge Day was less enthusiastic, but equally positive in his approval, and he carried it off together with all my other memoranda to be incorporated in the paper. I said that, so far as I was concerned, there was no reason why our paper should not be ready for presentation this afternoon; but he [Frye?] insisted that on other grounds it was quite impossible, and said we would have to exercise the liberty we had reserved for postponing the meeting. From something someone else said, I suspect he has cabled the President for permission to use his name in some way in distinct confirmation of Day's own statements about what happened before the protocol. There is a subdued, but rather strong, feeling that Cambon was so anxious to achieve the signing of the [armistice] protocol that he concealed some things from the Spanish government.

Senator Gray strolled in an hour and a half after we had been [in] session, and just as Day was going off with all my memoranda. It struck me that [Day] was a little inclined not to let Senator Gray know of these contributions, the Senator on a previous occasion [having] expressed the opinion that it would be better if Moore prepared all the correspondence in the form of tentative drafts to be subsequently revised and patched in the meetings of the Commission. . . .

Addition to No. 19th, 1898 [*sic*].

[In the evening I had dinner at the Westminster Hotel with our Minister to St. Petersburg and Mrs. Ethan Allen Hitchcock.] Mrs. Don Cameron and the Ambassador [Horace Porter?] were also Mr. Hitchcock's guests. He [Hitchcock?] interested me with his curiously strong Russian views about their right to Chinese ports as an outlet to their railroad through Siberia, and to save their fleet from being ice-locked in the winter. A nation, he argued, has the same right as an individual to force an outlet to the highway. In this case he thought the Pacific Ocean was the highway, and a harbor free from ice the necessary outlet. He considered the English claim to being champions of the open door singularly unfair, and protested that they exacted [special privileges] as well as other nations [did]. After some talk, however, he was rather inclined to assent to my view that the imposition of duties in no way conflicted with the open door policy; that the only necessity was that these duties should be uniform to all comers of whatever nationality; and that it would be absurd for us to talk about an open door in the Philippines in the sense of abolishing custom houses, since that would compel us to support the expenses of Philippine administration ourselves, or else resort to very different internal taxation. . . .

Sunday, November 20th, [1898].

[I received some] good letters from home, and a supply of papers, with no particularly bad news. [But] they gave [me] a feeling of loneliness here, which not even a stroll in the garden of the Tuileries was sufficient to shake off.

I had an interesting call afterwards from Jules Siegfried. In answer to some amiable remark of mine about [Félix Jules] Méline, their former Premier, he spoke in sharp censure of Méline's conduct in permitting the Dreyfus case to attain its great magnitude.

[*Editorial note*. The typescript of the diary in the Library of Congress contains no entries for November 21–24, inclusive. This is unfortunate, since those days were critical in the negotiations. On November 21, the Americans presented an ultimatum demanding all of the Philippines in return for a cash settlement of $20,000,000. The Spanish delayed while awaiting final instructions from Madrid, but on November 22 Day informed McKinley that "If the Spanish Commissioners refuse our proposition to-morrow, we shall give notice that our offer was final and nothing remains except to close the negotiations."[18] McKinley approved this course on the same day. But on November 23 the Spanish asked for further time, which was granted. On Thursday, November 24, the Spanish handed their counterparts the comprehensive alternative propositions they had received from Madrid[19] on the Philippine problem. Reid resumed his diary entries on November 25.]

[18] *For. Rels. 1898*, p. 958.

[19] Moore summarized these proposals for President McKinley as follows:

First. Relinquishment by Spain of her sovereignty over Cuba and cession of Puerto Rico and other Antilles, the island of Guam in the Ladrones, and the Philippine Islands archipelago, including Mindanao and Sulu, to the United States, the latter paying to Spain the sum of $100,000,000 as compensation for her sovereignty over the archipelago and the works of public utility which she has executed during her rule in all the islands of the east and west [Indies], the sovereignty over which she relinquishes or cedes.

Second. Cession to the United States of the island of Kusaie, in the Carolines, of the right to land a cable on any of these or of the Marianas, while they remain under Spanish rule, and cession of the Philippine Islands archipelago proper—that is, beginning on the north, the islands of Batanes, Babuyanes, Luzon, Visayas, and all the others following to the south as far as the Sulu Sea, Spain reserving to the south of this sea the island of Mindanao and Sulu, which have never formed a part of the Philippine Islands archipelago proper. The United States as compensation for said islands, for the right to land cables, and for the public works executed by Spain in said islands during her rule will pay to Spain the sum of $50,000,000.

Third. Spain relinquishes her sovereignty over Cuba and gratuitously cedes to the United States the Philippine Islands archipelago proper, besides Puerto Rico, the other West Indies, and the island of Guam, which she cedes as compensation for the expenses of the war and as indemnity to American citizens for injuries suffered since the beginning of the last Cuban insurrection. The United States and Spain will submit to an arbitral tribunal what are the debts and obligations of a colonial character which should pass with the islands the sovereignty over which Spain relinquishes and cedes.

On these propositions the Commissioners hold the following views: Messrs. Day, Davis, and Reid think we are committed to our final proposition of last Monday; Commissioners Frye and Gray favor submitting a proposal to leave to Spain, Mindanao and Sulu group and take instead Ualan or Strong Island in the Carolines, paying only $20,000,000. Mr. Day would favor this if it were an original proposition. He believes that Mindanao and the Sulu group can be readily separated from the other islands and that with their population they are likely to be a source of trouble and expense, and are not desirable for us. He thinks Ualan or Strong Island would be very valuable to us, and he would prefer it. He also thinks that this concession would probably bring a treaty and that it may be that our present ultimatum will; but, as already stated, he thinks our only consistent course now is to stand by that ultimatum. Commissioner Gray prefers above all acceptance of third proposition . . . (See *For. Rels. 1898*, pp. 958–959.)

Friday, November 25th, 1898.

The first Commissioners [to arrive] this morning were full of pleasant talk about their enjoyment of the Thanksgiving festivities. One or two spoke of slight headaches left among the guests!

The written translation of the Spanish message received just as we were going to dinner last night and afterwards discussed in the smoking room was now presented. The secretary [Moore] and some others seemed to think that the closing sentences were now less obscure and were consistent with a mere effort to get us to consider alternative propositions. They impressed me as intended to be somewhat obscure. In fact, the Spanish pride had been stung by the receipt of an ultimatum, and [they] felt that it could only be vindicated by hurling back another. At the last moment [I thought] discretion got the better of their pugnacity, and their ultimatum was so veiled as to leave a possibility still of their crawling out and accepting our proposals.[20]

Senator Gray, however, was still very low in his mind, believing as he did last night that the Spaniards would refuse to sign, and we should get no treaty unless we yielded them something. Now, as all along, he was eager to yield them everything in the East. After a good deal of earnest discussion, he proposed the acceptance of their proposal which withdrew Mindanao and the Sulu group, left us the rest of the Philippines, and gave us Kusaie in the Carolines and asked $50,000,000.[21] Senator Frye

[20] In a dispatch accompanying Moore's summary of the Spanish proposals, Senator Davis said:

I desire to add to my views as stated in Mr. Moore's telegram that I think the propositions there stated are an afterthought contrived to protract and embarrass the negotiations after Spain had received our deliberate ultimatum, which has been given out as such to our people and to the world. The United States having so taken its position ought not to recede. I think that Spain will accept our ultimatum if we firmly insist upon it. (See *For. Rels. 1898*, pp. 959–960.)

[21] Gray's dispatch recommending arbitration read as follows:

Our having submitted an ultimatum does not in my opinion preclude us from adopting a course that will prove more advantageous to our country. My reasons for accepting [the] third proposition in the letter of the president of the Spanish Commission are, briefly, that in paying twenty millions we do not prevent the raising hereafter of the question of the liability of the sovereign of the relinquished and ceded territory for some part of the so-called colonial debts. When raised we must either flatly refuse to consider it and take the consequences, or must arbitrate. We have nothing to fear from arbitration, but have much to gain in moral prestige and maintenance of our preeminence in recognizing the obligations of international law. By adopting this course we pay

repeated his old declarations that he too would be glad to get rid of Mindanao and the Sulus, and that in fact he cared little for anything excepting the three islands, Luzon, Mindoro, and Palawan. The fifty millions suggestion was the only thing that prevented him from falling in with Senator Gray; and, in fact, the inclusion of Kusaie on that basis seemed to tempt him a little. Senator Gray, however, persisted in making a motion to the effect that the second proposition be accepted, subject to the approval of our Government, which got only one vote.

I found a good deal of difficulty during these proceedings in keeping quiet, since the whole affair seemed to me to indicate such a trivial and utterly inconsequential attitude on the part of the Commissioners, sending in an ultimatum one day and sending me to the Spanish Ambassador to tell him that we meant exactly what we said, and then turning around to undo it all.

Then the third proposal was read, which involved sacrificing the lower third of the archipelago, but getting rid of the money payment altogether and reserving the whole question of the Philippine and Cuban debts to arbitration. To my utter amazement some of the other Commissioners seemed inclined to side with Senator Gray in the belief that it might be wise now for us to ask our government for permission to accept this in place of the ultimatum we had given. Gray talked a good deal and maintained that this would be the most honorable way out of all difficulties as to the ratification of the treaty and everything else connected with the subject. Judge Day also expressed regret that this proposal had not come before the negotiations had advanced so far. Senator Frye was inclined to favor it.

I had continued to keep entirely out of the discussion, but, at last, felt compelled to say that the question of the Cuban debt was a thing which I should not consent to arbitrate under any circumstances, any more than I would consent to arbitrate a question whether we would or would not obey the moral law. To me the question of paying, or compelling the Cubans to pay the cost of the long, bloody, and finally unsuccessful efforts to enslave them, was primarily a question of morals. I would not consent to say that such a question was a fit subject to be arbitrated, or agree to be bound by an adverse decision on such a point if unfriendly arbitrators should find one.

Senator Frye said if we could get a fair arbitration he wouldn't mind.

---

nothing to Spain, and settle instead of postpone the question of liability and carry the principle of arbitration with us into the new century. (See *For. Rels. 1898*, p. 960.)

He would be willing to leave it to the sole arbitration of the Chief Justice of England. Davis interposed with some warmth that such an arbitration as that would be resented by the Spaniards as an insult, and that it would be impossible to get a court of three arbitrators on such a question without having one or two of them against us from the outset. Davis at last roused up and talked pretty vigorously against the proposals. I interposed at one stage of the talk to say that it seemed to me the whole suggestion of consulting our government as to whether or not we should accept these proposals, after having been instructed to present an ultimatum, having presented that ultimatum, and having then informally and in the most earnest way privately told them that it was an ultimatum, would be to make ourselves ridiculous. Thereupon Frye laughingly told me that I was using undiplomatic language. Day rather agreed with my view of the subject, but persisted in the statement that if the arbitration had come as an original proposal, he would have been glad of it. Moore also talked in this sense. I began to fear that there was even a possibility that a majority of the Commission would commit itself in favor of the proposition. [But] it sobered their sudden zeal a little to be reminded that since we were under positive orders to present our ultimatum, we should be compelled to ask permission from our government before departing from it. At last, Senator Gray asked for a vote on his motion to accept the third proposal subject to the approval of our government. Secretary Moore called on the members for their votes. Gray and Frye both voted for it. Day explained that as an original proposal, he would have supported it but felt constrained by our present situation, and voted no. Davis voted no. I had said scarcely anything beyond what is above reported during a discussion which had lasted now for some hours, and was walking up and down behind the table rather outside of the current, when I suddenly realized that the casting vote was in my hands. I voted no, of course.

Judge Day then prepared a dispatch to the President summarizing the situation, copying the three proposals of the Spaniards in full and stating the attitude of each of the Commissioners as disclosed in the discussions and the votes. [He] asked if we agreed to it. It struck me as somewhat favorable to the minority. But before I decided to make any criticisms, Senator Davis had said that he was not satisfied, and would insist on sending a separate dispatch which he began writing. Senator Frye said something about doing the same thing. Thereupon I remarked that if telegraphing became general, I thought I should send my views also. [I] repeated that I regretted to have the Commission putting itself in an attitude at Washington, which our own government could only construe as proving that we didn't know our own minds.

Davis' dispatch proved to be a terse and rather curt statement of his opposition to any modification of our ultimatum, both on the ground that things had gone too far for a change, and because the changes were not desirable any way. He considered the proposals merely a Spanish scheme to secure delay, and if possible introduce division. He came so nearly expressing my views that I was at first inclined to say that I should merely send a line concurring with him.

Others deprecated sending any dispatch excepting Day's, and Frye especially tried to prevent Davis from telegraphing. Davis at last spoke with a little more warmth than usual, though with perfect good feeling, saying: "Of course I take what you say at it is meant, but this is a question of public duty, which I must decide for myself, and on which my resolution is fixed." Gray and Frye then apparently abandoned the idea of telegraphing, and I made up my mind to do the same. The consideration which really controlled me was an unwillingness to put myself on record as refusing to consider a settlement by arbitration without writing a much longer dispatch than any of the rest of them were contemplating. [I would have shown] why we ought not at this stage of a negotiation to stultify ourselves by withdrawing an ultimatum in order to accept an insidious scheme for arbitrating a question which we had already placed on incontestable moral grounds.

There was considerable strain at different periods during the morning discussion, which was not ended until nearly half past one o'clock. There was, however, at no time any indication of anything but the best of feeling. For myself I was really amused to see how after two months of laborious work leading up to an ultimatum, our Commissioners had apparently been swept off their feet by these proposals. Of course the catching thing was the proposition to waive the question of money, providing they could get arbitration accepted. On this the really controlling consideration with the other members was apparently the conviction that they could not get a fair arbitration. . . .

Count Münster came in [this afternoon], remarking as he entered: "You are to dine with me in a little while, but I may not have a chance to talk with you there, and I want to speak again of your negotiations." He then produced a dispatch from his government, saying: "Our colonial department is very tiresome. They seem to think we want this [Ualan?] island, and can't believe that you need it on account of a cable, because it is too far south; they think you only want it because you have some missionaries there. They say it is an island with three fine harbors." I explained to him that the fact that the island was the headquarters of the American missionaries did have a certain interest for us, of course, but it was not a controlling reason. These missionaries were on other islands also. The real reason why we wanted this one was because it was the nearest to us, and therefore gave us the best landing point for a cable. I again took the map and showed him how an unbroken cable from Honolulu to Guam was thought by the cable experts probably impracticable. No cable of that length had up to this time ever been successfully laid in any part of the world. There was no satisfactory island nearer to us than the one we had chosen in the Carolines for an intermediate station.

He seemed interested about the nature of the island and I finally said that I would treat him with the utmost frankness in the matter and show him what we knew about it. I got a pamphlet therefore containing compilations from British Admiralty reports containing details concerning all the Caroline Islands. [I] pointed out that while Ualan was nearer us, and therefore most useful for our purpose, it had only about four hundred inhabitants, while Yap, which would be otherwise as useful to them had 8,000 to 10,000, and that Ponape was also a larger and more valuable island. He dwelt on the remarks in his dispatch about the three harbors of Ualan. I quoted to him what Commissioner Bradford and others had said about the whole Caroline archipelago being full of good harbors. I then pointed out that they merely enjoyed an option for an agreement between the United States and Spain to choose a point on some island in the group for a naval and coaling station and had now for over twelve years utterly failed to exercise this option.

I then explained to him the exact stage of our negotiation with Spain, bringing out the fact that provided our ultimatum was accepted we had then given notice that we should desire to treat for the acquisition of this island. He thought, under the circumstances, it was rather a good thing that we had thus stated our desire, since it seemed to relieve him. "I think," he said, "the natural course for me is to telegraph my government just what the state of your negotiation is and to advise them that if they wish to pursue the subject to take it up either in Madrid or in Washington." I concurred in this expression, whereupon he suggested that he might say that he got this suggestion in conversation with me. To this I objected, saying it would not be proper for me to be recommending any course to his government, and I preferred that he should not give them any indication of my opinion. I said, however: "I am quite willing to say to you personally that the course you propose seems to me the natural one." He seemed a little vague as to their exact rights in the Carolines. I therefore got the protocol following the Pope's decision in the arbitration between Germany and Spain, and showed him precisely what was accredited to Germany.

He then asked about the Sulus, and said he had not seen of late years the Sulu protocol, and did not recall it distinctly. Fortunately, I had this at hand in the French text, and, at his request, read it to him. After I had read a page or so, he said: "I begin to recall it now." He acquiesced in my statement that it merely gave them trading privileges without any right to a coaling or naval station. [He also acquiesced] in my previous statement that their right to the latter was limited to one island to be agreed upon between them and Spain, which might be either in the Caroline group or in the Pelews. He dropped the remark, in speaking of Ualan, that his people said it belonged more properly to the Marshall group than to the Carolines anyway. He was, as always, most amiable and cordial. But the impression left distinctly upon my mind by the sentence which he read from his dispatch, by the questions he asked, and by the whole scope of the conversation was that his government was jealous of our proposed acquisition. [It was] desirous of interposing obstacles and [was] probably anxious of using these as a means of getting itself introduced into the negotiations, and in some way laying claim to the Carolines. He said distinctly that his people ought to have the Carolines, to which I replied: "Yes, but you left it to arbitration and lost."

Before going out to dinner I had just time after the Count had taken his departure to visit Judge Day and give him the subject of the conversation. I think he was impressed with the idea that this situation furnished one reason more for having as little delay as possible in completing our negotiations. . . .

Saturday, November 26th, 1898.

Frye, Day, and Moore appeared about the usual hour. As the latter two came in, Frye and I were engaged in a little talk about the previous day's debate. I was expressing my regret that we had not within twenty-four hours sent a categorical rejection of all the propositions the Spaniards had made in order that they might realize that when we told them we had given them an ultimatum, we were not merely playing a Spanish game. Day said: "I don't regret it, because we have now the advantage of saying that we have submitted their proposals to the government, and are instructed by it to reject them." I at once called for the dispatch, which Moore read. It proved quite clear and satisfactory.[22] Moore then read a draft of a reply to Montero Ríos, with which I immediately expressed complete satisfaction. [I] urged that it be copied out and sent at once, or at least as soon as we could get the other members. We sent out for them, and in a moment Senator Davis appeared. He was entirely satisfied. . . . I now urged that the reply be copied at once pending Senator Gray's arrival. But just as the secretary was about to start off to do this, Senator Gray appeared—as usual, over three-quarters of an hour late. Everything had to be gone over again for his benefit, so that it was well towards noon before the secretary got off to copy the reply. It will still, however, give the Spaniards a chance to consult with their government fully between now and Monday afternoon.

With Senator Gray's appearance the discussion of yesterday revived a little. Senator Frye and Judge Day both repeated their desire to get rid of Mindanao and the Sulus in exchange for Kusaie. I replied laughingly that this outraged my yankee ideas of comparative acreage. Judge Day retorted that he didn't want so many acres of Mohammedans. My remark that England had seemed to be able to get on fairly well with Mohammedans produced no impression. I finally contented myself with laughing at their proposal to trade off a continent for a sand bank. Or as I put it at another time, to give up what the Spaniards valued at $50,-000,000 for a little island, which in our wildest moments we never thought worth more than a million. Judge Day and Secretary Moore were full of the idea all the morning that it was a great pity that the third Spanish proposal (that for an arbitration) had not been submitted at the beginning of the negotiations. That, they said, would have enabled us to mark diplomacy with a white stone, etc., etc.

I protested against this view. I said: "What you want to do is to arbi-

---

[22] The dispatch read as follows:

The President has considered the three proposals of the president of the Spanish Commission presented to you. He finds no reason for departing from his last instructions and your proposal thereunder. His instructions are that you adhere to your last proposal and decline those of the Spanish Commission. He repeats his instruction of November 13, by which you are authorized, in case of cession of an island in [the] Carolines, and other concessions mentioned by Messrs. Frye and Reid, to offer additional compensation. If negotiations in regard to [the] Philippines are successful, you will communicate to the President what amount is required for Strong Island, and he will instruct you. (Hay to Day, November 25, 1898; *For. Rels. 1898,* 960.)

trate the question whether an enslaved people, who have at last gained their independence shall immediately be taxed with every penny of the costs entailed in the long years of war for their enslavement. That seems to me distinctly a question of morals not to be submitted to arbitration, any more than the question whether you shall steal or shall commit murder is to be determined by the decision of three outsiders." Rather to my surprise Senator Gray seemed a little impressed by this aspect of the case. Senator Davis burst out with a declaration that he believed they were all wrong; at any rate, in the idea that under international law a partition of territory necessarily involved a partition of debts. He cited Belgium and was apparently proceeding to fortify his position with other arguments when Senator Frye interrupted him by saying: "You make such a speech as that in the Senate, as you say you are thinking of doing, and you will defeat your treaty without a question. Prove to the Senate that there is nothing in international law to lead to the payment of these debts, and the Senators would rather arbitrate than pay the $20,000,000." Davis rejected this idea, and the talk became again rather fervid though entirely good-natured.

Frye and Day next turned up with an idea that if the Spaniards should accept our ultimatum, we might still take advantage of their second proposal and say: "Since you seem in this to value Mindanao and the Sulus at $50,000,000, we will give them to you and only take Kusaie in return, besides retaining the $20,000,000 we should otherwise pay you." Frye insisted that the cash payment was the only difficulty the treaty would encounter. [He said] the American people didn't care a straw about Mindanao, and that we would be well rid of it, if we escaped the cash payment, especially, if besides, we got Kusaie. I insisted that on this point we should certainly not commit ourselves or cross any bridges till we reached them. We must first have an acceptance of our ultimatum, and that we would then have no authority to make such propositions as he suggested without the approval of our government.

Altogether we have had in the last two days the most erratic suggestions of changes in the policy that have marked any part of the two months' negotiations. But as we got an adjournment by half past eleven in the morning, there is probably not much danger now until the Spaniards have either accepted or rejected our ultimatum. I still incline to the belief that with all manner of protestations and outcries they will in the end accept.

Late in the afternoon Judge Day came down with a memorandum of a few remarks dropped by Count Münster to Gen. Porter in the talk after dinner the other evening at the German Embassy, in the same line with his talk to me earlier in the evening. The only additional significance of what he said seemed to lie in his use of the word "indemnity" in relation to Spain's inability or failure with reference to Germany's claims in the Carolines. The use of such a word on so shaky a foundation, even though unaccompanied by any details or explanations seemed to give further confirmation to the idea that Germany was hunting for a pretext either to interfere with the negotiations, or to seize territory from Spain as she recently did from China. Judge Day said he felt at any rate that my conversation with the Ambassador [Castillo] ought to be reported to the [State] Department, and that it would probably be wise to add [Ambassador] Porter's memorandum to it. He wished I would prepare a dispatch giving the essential facts, setting forth the policy of the Commission to go ahead on the line we had taken and acquire the island of Kusaie if we could. It was agreed that it would be better to have a meeting of the full Commission at nine o'clock to hear the dispatch. "Our colored Talleyrand," as Senator Davis has named the State Department messenger "Eddie," was sent around to give the notice. . . .

Monday, November 28th, 1898.

. . . Commissioners all a little late coming down. Finally started with Frye, Day, and Gray in carriage—Davis, who has uniformly gone with me, not having appeared. They sent up for him and he arrived a little later with Moore. His clock had been wrong. The Spaniards were in the inner room awaiting us; much more somber than usual and more distantly courteous.

We moved towards the table almost at once, and the protocols were read in English and in Spanish and approved in a moment. Judge Day was to have proposed at this point that the correspondence which had since taken place between Montero Ríos and himself should be attached to the last protocol. But the instant the approval of the proposals was announced Montero Ríos began presenting their reply. He merely said they had considered the paper presented at the last meeting and desired now to present the reply authorized by their Government. As it was handed to the translator, Abarzuza suggested that he would better read it over in Spanish before giving the English translation. This was done during a profound and rather painful silence. Ferguson then read it aloud in English. It proved to be exactly what had been foreseen; a maintenance of their conviction of the soundness of their proposals, an unwillingness to reopen the war and subject their country to greater calamities, and a submission therefore to the inevitable.

During the reading all the Spanish Commissioners sat in their places with a certain air of mournful dignity, Cerero with his head bowed on his hands. The American Commissioners were equally sober, and all were in their places excepting Frye, who at the beginning had been walking up and down the outer room. But as the reading of the reply began [he] entered the Salle de Conference and dropped into one of the window seats behind our side of the table.

Nearly all of the American Commissioners were smoking, and before the reading was finished nearly every Spanish Commissioner had also begun on a cigarette. This smoking habit, by the way, has continued from the first week. About the second or third meeting Montero Ríos remarked that he had observed in the ante-room that the Americans nearly all smoked. As it was the Spanish custom to smoke even in their legislative assemblies, and during the progress of business, he thought it might conduce to the general comfort if the same rule should prevail here, and there had been a prompt agreement.

As soon as the reading was finished, Judge Day suggested that it might be well now to have formal articles presented on the further subjects on which the American Commissioners had proposed to treat.

Montero Ríos remarked that he now wished to follow in the subsequent negotiations whatever course might seem to the American Commissioners most desirable, having in view the wish to expedite matters as well as to avoid long written discussions. Judge Day thought the plan of having tentative articles on other subjects for the proposed treaty submitted at the next meeting might have this effect. Montero Ríos repeated that he thought it desirable to get on without further written papers, unless, of course, in the case of something exceptional. Day assented to this, though, of course, reserving all rights under the rules with reference to the filing of papers, provided the American Commissioners should think it necessary.

Montero Ríos thought it might be advisable with this understanding to adjourn until the secretaries were ready to report. Day thought they would probably be able to report by Wednesday. Montero Ríos said he would be ready to return any day the American Commissioners desired. Day thereupon fixed Wednesday, reserving, as usual, the right of delay in case of unforeseen obstacles. Montero Ríos reported that all the Spanish Commissioners desired to urge in that particular was that all possible haste should now be exercised in order to complete the negotiations. To this there was general assent, and the Commission adjourned.

Just as the Americans were preparing to leave the room, the clouds cleared away for a moment, and a burst of sunlight illuminated the green table at which Ojeda was finishing his notes of the protocol. As I happened to be standing at his side at the moment I said to him I hoped that meant good fortune for both countries. He replied rather mournfully: "No, everything is gloom around us." Abarzuza approached at the instant and I repeated the wish to him. He seemed a shade less despondent, and at least received the expression with a smile.

In a moment or two we had all taken our leave of the Spaniards, who evidently desired to remain. In the ante-room were numbers of French reporters, who besieged me to know first whether the negotiations were now finished, and then when the next meeting was to be. Escaping, I got three of the Commissioners into the carriage with me and drove home. [I was] full of pity for the actors in the depressing scene we had witnessed, and at the same time convinced that they had brought it upon themselves. [They had] made it far worse by their pertinacious obstruction, acrimonious argument, and especially by Montero Ríos' hot-tempered outburst a week ago when the ultimatum was presented. . . .

CHAPTER VI

Finishing the Treaty

Tuesday, November 29th, 1898.

[There was] long discussion over preparing [the] draft for [a] complete treaty to be presented now at [the] next meeting. Moore furnished [a] synopsis of [the] contents of the various articles which he proposed. [The] chief points to be considered were what should be paid for Kusaie; how much time should be taken for payment of $20,000,000 [for the Philippines]; whether Spaniards should be required to take their own prisoners back from the Philippines, or whether we should be at once magnanimous and send them back ourselves; whether there was any possibility of extending the "open door" idea to Puerto Rico as well as to the Philippines; and points over which the lawyers on the Commission disputed a great deal as to the precise way in which the consideration for the payment of $20,000,000 should be expressed; and the way in which the danger of having to confer citizenship upon Asiatics might be avoided. . . .

A great deal of congratulations [at dinner this evening] over the results of the negotiations, and apparently a general feeling of exultation that the United States made good her claim to what she clearly had a right to. They all seemed to think the work practically done, although the Commission would be glad to think the remaining details easy. Immense desire on all hands, however, to get away early. Senator Frye declares we must sail by the 10th. Judge Day [is] extremely anxious to get in a little trip over the Riviera and sail from Genoa by the German boat. Senator Davis [is] unwilling to sail in any case before the 17th.

Wednesday, November 30th, 1898.

In spite of the fact that it was desired to submit the tentative text of the entire treaty to the Commission this morning and discuss it article by article, work was only begun a full hour late. Even then Senator Gray was absent as usual, but at last his presence was secured by sending for him.

A dispatch of thanks from the President was first read, and one reminding us of the need of reviving copyright stipulations from the State Department. Then came an interruption by Ojeda of the Spanish Commission, who brought in various suggested changes in the articles on which he and Moore had been in consultation. These mainly came, as we understood, from Montero Ríos.

As soon as the article was reached for the payment of $20,000,000 I proposed that the blank in the date be filled by the insertion of the words "three months." Senator Frye opposed it on the ground that so short a time would entail the danger of an extra session [of Congress] in order to secure the appropriation. Senator Davis at first was rather inclined to the same effect. I argued that the necessity for prompt action might be an additional reason to be urged for speedier action on the treaty, and that the actual appropriation need not take half an hour on the last day of the session. I pointed out privately besides to Frye that if we were to let it go past the 4th of March, [1899,] in order to avoid an extra session, we could not reasonably expect to pay before the first of January, [1900,] next. Such a delay in the case of a rich nation dealing with a prostrate and impoverished one would seem to be so long as to require explanation. He finally fell in with this view, and the Commissioners uniformly agreed to the three months.

In this discussion I had taken the ground that now that we had gained the essentials, it was desirable that over small matters, where we could afford it, we should not seem to stickle, but could afford to be magnanimous. For this reason I moved that the figure to be offered for Kusaie should be fixed at a million. Frye objected that the island was not worth so much, and thought that the expenditure of half a million at Midway Islands would probably make them as good a point for a cable landing. On the other hand, I urged that it was desirable at any rate to get Kusaie on account of our missionaries, and for the mere prestige besides of succeeding in what we had asked for. [I] thought the million dollars ought to be something of a temptation to Spain. The figure was finally unanimously agreed to.

On the same theory of being generous to a needy and fallen foe in unimportant matters, I proposed that the prisoners in Manila, concerning our right to hold which there was some doubt, at any rate, should be returned to Spain at our expense, and that the same policy should also be extended to the prisoners held by the Filipinos. . . . The probable cost was speculated over, and it was finally agreed that ships could probably be found to bring them at an average price of about $50 or $60 a head, and that the total outlay need not exceed, and possibly not approach, a million [dollars]. The Commissioners finally agreed that the article might be drawn with the provision that the prisoners held by either side should be returned to their homes at the expense of the country holding them.

When the clause for the "open door" in the Philippines came up, a blank had been left for the insertion of the number of years for which this privilege was guaranteed to Spain. It was proposed to make it ten years on the same general principle of being liberal, and of not making a term of years so short that commerce could not fairly and profitably adjust itself; and there was finally no objection. When Judge Day and Senator Gray talked rather cautiously about extending this to Puerto Rico, Senator Frye gave notice that he should protest most vigorously against such a course. . . .

Secretary Moore mentioned that Ojeda had communicated the feeling of the Spanish Commissioners that they had made the utmost possible concession and hoped that nothing more would be asked of them. He interpreted this [to mean] that they did not want to be asked for stipulations about religious liberty in the Carolines, the sale of Kusaie, or anything else outside the protocol. A feeling began to be expressed among the Commissioners that there was a possibility of our finding in the end that we could get nothing from the Spaniards except what we had already extorted by our ultimatum.

The articles as finally agreed upon, owing to the lateness of the hour at which we began, had to be sent down piece-meal, to be typewritten in a rush, and Secretary Moore only escaped with the last of them about half past one o'clock. The meeting with the Spaniards was to be at 2 o'clock, and a few minutes before that hour I rushed off with Judge Day "to hold the fort," as we expressed it, until the secretary [Moore] could come along with the articles. Senator Gray and the other Commissioners came a little more leisurely. We kept the Spanish Commissioners waiting over half an hour.

As soon as the daily protocols were read our articles were submitted, read in English and Spanish, and mutually agreed to up to that on the Philippines. At this point Montero Ríos objected to the provision that the United States "will, as far as possible, preserve order and protect property throughout the Philippines, until the ratification of this treaty." This, he said, presupposed an immediate exercise by the United States of the functions of sovereignty. He did not feel ready to stipulate for such an exercise before the sovereignty itself was ceded. Senator Gray remarked that the protocol itself as to the harbor and bay of Manila was not a cession of sovereignty. This provision merely extended the powers conferred by that protocol over the rest of the archipelago provisionally, and obviously for the common good. Montero Ríos repeated that the Spanish Commissioners were not now authorized to give such authority, but he saw no objection to laying it before [his] government. The Spanish Commissioners were not at present authorized to take any executive action such as this would be. Senator Davis said the only desire of the American Commissioners was to provide temporarily for the preservation of order. Montero Ríos replied that their objection was not to the thing desired, but as to the authority of the Spanish Commissioners to give it.

Senator Davis then offered in writing the clause, "provided nothing in this shall be construed as a cession of sovereignty before the ratification of this treaty."

Montero Ríos repeated that he recognized the weight of the suggestion offered by the American Commissioners, but the Spanish Commissioners were without power in the premises, and would at once apprise their government and ask for instructions. Judge Day replied: "We know that disorders are existing there now, and that there is destruction of property, if not also danger to life. All the proposed clause does is to charge the United States at once with the duty of protecting life and preserving order." Since there was objection, however, he thought it better to pass the subject provisionally till the Spanish Commissioners could get authority and then have it incorporated in the treaty. To this Montero Ríos agreed. Gray then repeated that it was only proposed because we have the power to do this [since it] was incidental to the general powers we already possessed. Montero Ríos replied rather tartly: "The American Commissioners are, no doubt, perfectly conversant with the powers *they* possess; but we do not consider our powers sufficient for this act, although we recognize its desirability." The secretaries then read the next article and Guarnica immediately said that the cession here did not include all the war material, artillery, etc., reserved to Spain in the agreement of the evacuation commissioners [in Cuba]. All heavy artillery that can be removed should be reserved to Spain [he said]. Their understanding was that this particular, if not already settled by the evacuation commissioners, should be settled here. He did not now refer to cases already agreed to in the West Indies, but thought the same principle should be adopted here.[1]

Judge Day said the purpose of this article was to do just that. If there were some suggestions concerning artillery on which the commissioners in Cuba and Puerto Rico have not been able to agree, then on those points we would undoubtedly have to reach some decision here. Meantime he thought it would be desirable to telegraph and ascertain exactly what had been agreed upon in Cuba and Puerto Rico.

Guarnica replied that there was no evacuation commission for the Philippines. He would like an agreement now that all war material and heavy artillery should be definitely reserved for Spain. Judge Day repeated his suggestion that the American Commissioners would prefer first telegraphing to ascertain exactly what the joint commissioners, charged with the decision of this very subject in Cuba and Puerto Rico, had determined. Abarzuza here interjected: "Certainly, we can't lose anything by that." A little debate here sprang up among the Spaniards themselves at the table, it seeming as if Abarzuza did not quite agree with the persistency of Guarnica. While it was going on, Montero Ríos asked if there was any objection to reserving all the war material in the Philippines, and all not already agreed upon in Cuba and Puerto Rico. Judge Day stuck to the position that he preferred to telegraph and ascertain what had been agreed to by the joint commissioners charged with this question in Cuba and Puerto Rico before undertaking to go farther here. [He] preferred, therefore, that for this purpose the articles should be passed. It was thereupon so agreed.

Montero Ríos next objected to the phrase "in consideration of the provisions in this treaty." The objection was obviously based upon the difficulty of a Spanish lawyer, trained only in the civil law, in understanding the exact meaning which American lawyers attach to this legal phrase.

---

[1] The American government argued in evacuating Cuba and Puerto Rico that the Spanish might remove small arms, artillery, and stores, but not fixed installations or fortifications. "The President thinks it undesirable to include in [the] treaty any preferential privileges to Spain in Cuba or Puerto Rico; and if such privileges tendered by you in [the] Philippines are accepted, care should be taken to avoid possible embarrassments to legislation by Congress or demands by other governments under [a] favored-nation clause" (Hay to Day, December 1, 1898, *For. Rels. 1898*, p. 963.)

The American Commissioners generally agreed that they might as well leave it out. [However,] Judge Day whispered to me that it might nevertheless be of some value as proving that the cession of the Philippines was not in the nature of a gratuity, and so might have a bearing on future claims as to responsibility for the debts. Montero Ríos finally agreed that this question might be left to the secretaries.

The article permitting free entry of Spanish ships and goods in the Philippines for ten years was next reached. Montero Ríos asked in a very quiet way if there was any objection to extending this privilege also to Cuba and Puerto Rico. Day replied that was not a question which had been considered, but the American Commissioners would be glad to take it into consideration, and take it up at the next meeting. Montero Ríos said he hoped that in considering it they would bear in mind that the customs of a people could not be changed between night and morning. The sovereignty might so be changed, but customs were harder to disturb. Any effort at an immediate change would also give a sudden wrench to industry in Spain. It was most desirable that Spanish commerce might have a little time to find new channels before it was abruptly turned out of the old ones. Gray had been listening to this sympathetically, and interjected in an audible "aside" addressed to me that this was a very weighty and just observation. Day replied that the American Commissioners fully appreciated the weight of the suggestions advanced and would take them into consideration.

The next question taken up was that of the release of prisoners and transport to the nearest port in their own country. Frye inquired if any idea could be given as to the number of prisoners in the hands of the Filipinos. Montero Ríos said he had no idea, and was not sure if his government knew. He thought, however, that the number was not great. Frye asked again if what the Spaniards desired on this article would include other prisoners than those now held by the Americans and by the Filipinos. Montero Ríos said that he understood there were no others.

Frye next asked how lately any artillery had been sent to the Philippines. Montero Ríos referred the question to Gen. Cerero, who said he thought none had been sent since 1885. With this the examination of the articles, the double text of which in English and Spanish had been agreed upon by the two secretaries, was completed. Montero Ríos then said that the Spanish Commissioners were quite at the disposition of the American Commissioners as to their proceedings. He thought, however, that time would be gained by having the secretaries get the rest of the articles also into a settled text in both languages, to be then taken up tomorrow afternoon. Day suggested that perhaps the secretaries themselves could agree on some of them. Montero Ríos said that his understanding was that by tomorrow we could take up everything the secretaries should have ready in both languages. Day proposed three o'clock as a better hour for meeting, and it was finally agreed upon.

As soon as the Joint Commission adjourned, Day proposed that the American Commissioners remain and prepare a dispatch at once on the points raised by the Spaniards with a view to getting news from home at the earliest moment.

Gray was eager to recommend the extension of the "open door" to Cuba and Puerto Rico, as requested by the Spanish Commissioners. Senator Frye was strong to the point of vehemence against it. Judge Day said he would be ready for it if it could be used as a means of securing Kusaie and religious freedom in the Carolines. Senator Davis did not express himself with quite his usual vigor, but did not favor the proposal. Finally, Frye and Gray wrote individual dispatches on the subject, and it was then agreed that all might as well do the same. The following was the text of mine:

Reid objects to Commission's taking initiative on subject no way covered by our instructions; especially as proposed action would injure the future extension of present long-standing policy of Government to Puerto Rico and Cuba. He thinks no step of such gravity should be proposed here without action of President, if not also of Congress.

[We were] surrounded by French reporters at the door, who insisted on knowing whether the treaty had been finally signed; how many articles had been considered and agreed upon, etc., etc. As I was the only American they could get at, they made a dead set for me. But, as usual, [I] escaped with as brief answers as possible. . . .

Thursday, December 1st, 1898.

The first thing that came up on the meeting of the Commissioners this morning was a dispatch from the State Department saying the Germans object strenuously to our getting Kusaie, and claim that they have an assurance from the American Commission that nothing will be done in contravention of German rights and interests. The President was not

aware of any such assurance, but if any had been given, it must be remembered and recorded in our negotiations.[2]

Day said in presenting it that he had no doubt that this illustrated
the danger of ever having anything to say to a Dutch diplomatist. I said
at once that there were no assurances beyond what were reported in my
two dispatches, and sent for them. Day [said] he thought it would be
well for me to prepare a dispatch, after examining those previously sent,
which would set the whole subject clearly before our government.

Gen. Merritt made his appearance before the Commission for the
first time since his marriage. He reported his wife nearly recovered from
typhoid fever, already sitting up, and very cheerful about future progress. The General was at once examined by Frye and others as to the
character of the heavy guns at Manila, which would be surrendered if
the Spanish amendments to our article were accepted. He referred for
details to Major Strother, the staff officer who accompanied him Strother reported these to be modern Krupp guns, and quite important. [He]

[2] Kusaie is an island in the East Caroline Islands group. The Germans had
been more of a nuisance than actual threat throughout the Spanish-American
crisis. When the war came, they were pro-Spanish, and Kaiser Wilhelm II had
unofficially attempted to rally European opinion against American interests. At
the Battle of Manila Bay the German fleet observing the conflict seemed to oppose the Americans, and public opinion in the United States was briefly inflamed
against supposed German desires in the Orient. Hay, then ambassador to England, reported that the Germans wanted assurances of a coaling station in the
Philippines if the United States acquired the Islands, and in general saw them as
our chief competitors in the Orient, with England as our chief ally. See Hay to
Day, July 14, 1898, cited in A. L. P. Dennis, *Adventures in American Diplomacy*
(New York, E. P. Dutton, 1928), p. 93. The Germans were not in fact willing to
challenge the Americans in the Philippines, and lacked etiquette rather than
sense. See Thomas A. Bailey, "Dewey and the Germans at Manila Bay," *American Historical Review*, 45 (October, 1939), 59–81.

But during the peace conference they continued to annoy the State Department. The dispatch mentioned here reads as follows: "German government
greatly dis-satisfied at our intention to acquire Kusaie. They say they have been
assured by Commission that nothing will be done in contravention of German
rights and interests. The President is not aware of such assurances, but wishes you
to be governed by them, if they have been given" (Hay to Day, November 30,
1898, Records). Day hastily denied the German statement on the same day
(*Ibid.*). Though Münster may have been sincere in his personal protestations
against acquiring the Carolines, Spain had secretly agreed provisionally to allow
Germany to buy the Carolines and the Marianas, minus Guam, on September 10,
1898. This tentative agreement became a formal treaty in 1899. The United
States did not acquire Kusaie. The League of Nations made the islands a mandate
to Japan after the World War in 1919, and they became a trust territory of the
United States in 1947.

said that to remove them would not only dismantle the fortifications of Manila and leave it for the time defenseless from the land, but would also compel the immediate shipment of other guns from the United States. He was strongly opposed to surrendering them. His report quite shook not only Frye but all of us about yielding to the Spanish request on this subject. Frye and Davis expressed apprehension that the Spanish Commissioners, if refused on this point, were not likely to take the ground that they could not do anything outside the protocol. Some of [our] other Commissioners intimated a similar fear. I suggested that in this case it would be wise to go slow about making such concessions as the surrender of artillery, returning their prisoners gratuitously, etc., until we could find out whether they were willing to concede anything.

Gen. Merritt thought the return of the Spanish soldiers from the Philippines might cost us two millions. After some consultation, however, he felt that it might be reduced considerably below that figure. He believed that it was costing about 30 cents [each a day] to feed them, although the army ration could not be furnished them in Manila at that figure. He believed the best way to deal with Aguinaldo would be to give him office not of a military nature. . . .

Friday, December 2nd, 1898.

Davis and Frye, as usual, [were] promptly in the room at 10, and for a wonder Gray [was] only a few minutes later. Day himself and the secretary [Moore] were this time nearly half an hour late, and Frye whose impatience over the tardy meetings has been gradually growing, broke out upon them. Day replied, with a face as grave as a grave-stone, that he had been at work since six o'clock in the morning over those articles, and wanted to know how much Frye had done in that time.

A dispatch was at once presented from the government giving the agreement of the joint commission as to the return of arms and munitions of war from Cuba and Puerto Rico. Applying the same principle to the Philippines, we should not let the Spaniards get any of their heavy guns, but they would get all of the field artillery. Major Strother, who was present again with his chief [General Merritt], for a few moments, expressed his regret at this. [He said that] field artillery would be especially necessary in the Philippines, and necessary at once, provided the insurgents became troublesome. Gen. Merritt and Major Strother took their leave to return to London in the morning. The General was given formal letters granting leave and arranging about his expenses.

A large number of Spanish proposals were then presented. The first one taken up stipulated for religious liberty, rights of property and position, etc., for the Apostolic Catholic Church in all the territories ceded. It was at once agreed on all hands among the Commissioners that no specific guarantee of this sort could be given to the Roman Catholic or to any other church by name. [We agreed] that religious liberty should be assured substantially in the language adopted by the United States in its treaty with Spain for the cession of Florida [in 1819]. I suggested that in view of the apprehension that the Spaniards were first going to get everything from us, and then grant nothing outside the protocol, we should try to tie our demand for religious freedom in the Carolines with this stipulation for religious freedom in the Philippines. But there was a rather hasty outcry against this by Gray, in which the others seemed to join. I thought, however, their opposition was rather to any idea we could refuse to grant this in the Philippines, unless we also secured it in the Carolines, and that it thus arose from a misapprehension of my purpose. Later on, I again insisted on the desirability of endeavoring to connect the question of religious liberty in the Carolines with the same question here taken up in its proper place as to the Philippines. [I] was not without hope of ultimately carrying the point.

The next important Spanish proposal was that the pensions now paid from the Cuban, Puerto Rican, and Philippine treasuries to the Duke of Veragua should be continued.[3] I at once expressed myself as ready to do this, although regretting that the beneficiary of what seemed to me a proper obligation, towards the descendent of the discoverer of America, for the United States to assume, was not personally better deserving of it. [I] referred to his effort to introduce bullfighting in Paris, and his undignified mendicancy in the United States. Judge Day was quite unwilling to give him anything, and Frye took the same view. Finally, a roll was called and Veragua got in on my casting vote.

All this business was done with difficulty and by snatches under the interruption of three or four calls in the hall from a dealer in rings to whom Senator Gray had given an order for a comparatively cheap Cornelian seal ring, and to whom he had also recommended Judge Day.

---

[3] Christopher Columbus and his lineal descendants were awarded titles in the New World. In 1537 Charles V granted the family heir the title Duke of Veragua, with an income to be paid from colonial revenues. The title is still in existence and the present Duke lives in Madrid.

When he came they couldn't communicate with him, and I was called out three times to bargain, give orders about measurements, engraving, etc. It was all to prepare for affixing their seals to the anticipated treaty. Judge Day, more than a month ago, had reminded such Commissioners as did not possess seals, that they should provide themselves for this contingency, but it seems that they put it off till today.

When at last we got to work again, a Spanish proposition came up for the appointment of a mixed Commission to investigate the cause of the explosion of the *Maine*. A certain number of Germans, French, and English [were] to be appointed on the nomination of each country. Everybody objected to this that it was doing what they could against us at once on a question already decided and fought out. All thought that the *Maine* chapter had been closed by the war, which grew out of it. [It] should not now be subjected to this scheme of quasi-national arbitration, however uneasy Spain might feel at the existing situation. Moore explained that Ojeda had told him the Spaniards only put this in because of our reference to the *Maine* in our last long paper.

Another Spanish proposal, which was taken up, was that for the free importation for twenty years of Spanish books, periodicals, etc. It was unanimously agreed, at any rate, that the term was too long, and it was changed to ten years. Frye, however, opposed it altogether, and Day did the same, on the ground that it was in the nature of tariff legislation. Gray and Davis were both in favor of it, and the casting vote thus came again to me. I expressed myself as cherishing a hearty contempt for the provision of our present tariff imposing a duty upon importation of books. [I] said I should be glad to wipe it out anywhere if I could. [I] was heartily in favor of the principle of getting rid of it in these Spanish territories, not merely because such a tax was wrong in itself, but because it would be particularly unjust in its application to a people who would thus be suddenly taxed upon the only sort of books they could read. My only hesitation would be lest our apparent effort to legislate here on tariff matters should endanger the treaty in the Senate. Since Senators Davis and Gray thought it would not have an appreciable effect there, I was in favor of it. . . . The remaining Spanish articles were understood to be of a still more serious nature, and it was decided to postpone them to another day. Before the Commissioners separated, however, I succeeded in gaining general assent to my proposal that we should not commit ourselves finally on questions of taking back their prisoners free of cost, returning artillery, etc., until we had ascertained whether they were going to refuse what we asked with reference to the Carolines.

After a hasty luncheon we all got off to the Foreign Office nearly on time, and immediately after the reading of the protocols, Judge Day announced that we were ready to proceed with the articles in the American draft not considered in the last meeting.

Montero Ríos at once announced that they had consulted their government on the doubtful points in these articles, but had not yet received a response. The Spanish play was instantly obvious. They intended to draw our fire, to get us committed on every point which we were ready to concede to them, and so maneuvre us into a position in which it would seem more ungracious for us to withdraw concessions already made, while they would still be at liberty on their side to refuse anything.

Judge Day asked how soon they could get a response from their government, and Montero Ríos replied today or tomorrow. Judge Day said: "Might we not take up some of the other questions? That of Guam, for instance?" Montero Ríos said he did not see anything to be gained, although he had no particular objection. He did not remember whether the need of instructions applied to all the remaining articles or not. As he remembered it, the points submitted to the government were those concerning an island in the Carolines, certain cable landings, religious liberty in the Carolines, and the revival of certain treaties. Judge Day said he thought that was about all.

[In the] meantime Senator Gray had been expressing himself rather audibly to me, as seeing no sense in the delay, saying we were going to have another day wasted, and wanted to know why we could not immediately go on without reference to the points on which the Spaniards still professed to be without instructions. The danger of this course seemed to me too serious. I passed along the table, first to Frye and then to Davis and Day, [a note?] insisting that we ought not to be tempted into playing our full hand until we got the Spaniards committed on some of the questions they were holding in reserve. Frye was impatient for progress. Davis and Day seemed impressed and Day finally asked for a few minutes delay for a conference among the American Commissioners. Contrary to our usual custom, however, Senators Frye and Gray merely took places in the window seat directly back of the table, so that our conversation went on almost, though not quite, within the hearing of the Spanish Commissioners. Senator Gray was eager to proceed at once. [He] saw absolutely nothing to be lost by showing our full hand, and nothing to be gained by delay. Senator Frye, though more moderately, took the same view. Davis and Day concurred in the view I had already expressed strongly deprecating committing ourselves on the last thing we had to concede, while leaving the Spaniards free on all the points on which we still desired concessions. The Commission thus stood three to two and resumed its place at the table. Senator Gray, however, seemed to be under some excitement, and took little pains to conceal his discontent and disapproval of our course. He continued to grumble against the arguments advanced by Day in the subsequent discussion. [His tone was] quite audible, and some of the things he said must have been intelligible to the Spaniards, if they gave the least attention.

Meantime Judge Day, resuming the discussion across the table, said it seemed to the American Commissioners that we could not make satisfactory progress till we were all on the same footing around the table with equal powers to treat on the articles presented. He hoped this might be the case by tomorrow. Montero Ríos said very plausibly that the desire to make as rapid progress as possible was entertained by the Spanish Commissioners, but with this difference from the attitude of the Americans: at the last session three points of detail in the articles already formulated and considered had been referred to the American government. He desired to know if the American Commissioners were not now prepared to treat on these articles. He would like to know also if the American Commissioners were not now prepared to express an opinion on the additional articles, which the Spanish Commissioners [had] submitted.

Judge Day replied that as to a number of these articles, including perhaps one or two of the most important of these, the translation of which had been received only late last night, the American Commissioners had not yet had adequate opportunity for discussion among themselves. Rather than attempt to take these up now, while the other sides were avowedly without full powers, he thought it would be better to take time for the discussion among themselves on these latest articles. [They could] come together tomorrow fully prepared to discuss everything that had been submitted on both sides. Montero Ríos again observed that the Spanish Commissioners were inspired by the same desire for speedy action. They had asked for final and definite instructions on all the questions in their hands. They hoped the American Commissioners, if not already prepared on all [points] would do the same. But he desired to call attention to the fact that it had already been determined that the treaty should be discussed in the order of the articles formulated, and submitted by the American Commissioners. This was the proper order: first the necessary and essential conditions of the peace; then the things that the Commissioners on both sides have desired to add. With respect to the points which the American Commissioners have subsequently raised, he had no doubt that the Spanish Commissioners would receive instructions authorizing them to reach some sort of agreement. Referring again to the order followed at the last session, he called attention to the fact that eight articles had been taken up and virtually approved, excepting as to three questions of detail on which the Americans had reserved their decision. He thought those questions ought now to be taken up first.

Senator Gray said: "That is right, what are those three articles?" Montero Ríos said they [were]: first, whether Cuba or Puerto Rico shall have extended to them the same privilege for the free entry of Spanish ships and Spanish goods, which it has already been agreed shall be given them in the Philippines; second, whether the prisoners mutually released by the two countries shall be transported at the expense of the releasing countries to the nearest port in the country to which the prisoners belong; and third, whether the arms, field batteries and heavy artillery in the Philippines shall be returned to the Spaniards.

Day at once interposed [that] there [was] still another question, which was reserved, and a more important one: whether the United States shall be permitted to arm, control, and protect persons and property throughout the Philippine archipelago in repression of existing disorders before the execution of this treaty.

Montero Ríos said: "That is correct, but on that point we were compelled to ask instructions, which we have not yet received. So great, however, is the anxiety of the Spanish Commissioners, that if the American Commissioners will give us their answer to the first three questions, we will, on our own responsibility, undertake to answer the last."

Day said: "Would that answer be subject to the subsequent approval of the Spanish Government?"

Montero Ríos said: "Yes, but we are willing to assume that our government will sustain us in any position we take on that subject, or, indeed on anything else we decide to do."

Judge Day replied: "Since the Spanish Commissioners are willing to assume such a responsibility as that, why not take it on all the points on which the delay is caused and proceed at once?"

Montero Ríos replied: "We cannot agree to go so far beyond our instructions. As to matters integrally connected with the treaty of peace we are ready to proceed at once. We are even ready not to leave the chairs in which we are now sitting at this table until those integral articles of the treaty of peace are signed and sealed. We have full authority for that. On one point mentioned before we have not received authority; a mere point of detail as to the protection of life and property in the Philippines pending the ratification of the treaty on that point. We are satisfied our government will support us in any decision we reach."

Judge Day then said: "If the learned President thinks that his government would support the Spanish Commissioners in any decision they might reach on this subject, which he refers to as one of the essential matters of the treaty, does he not think it would support them on the minor matters, which are causing the delay?"

Montero Ríos said he must again differ. "The other matters referred to are graver and more serious, and the Spanish Commissioners feel they ought not to proceed upon them without final instructions." They believed, however, there would be no trouble about coming to conclusions upon them that [would] be mutually satisfactory.

Judge Day said the adoption of the other articles submitted by the Americans would largely prompt and facilitate the establishment of better relations between the two countries. He had hoped that the Spanish Commissioners would have come today prepared to close upon the American proposals on these subjects. It was still the view of the American Commissioners that better progress could be made if we could only meet in this room with full authority on all matters with which we were about to deal.

Montero Ríos said he had already stated that it was only [upon] accessory matters that they were awaiting instructions. The order pursued at the last meeting for the discussion of the things particularly belonging [to] and essential to the treaty of peace might be pursued again. It was his private opinion that there would be no trouble at all on any of the matters that had been raised. Judge Day again asked whether we could not come fully prepared for the whole subject tomorrow.

Montero Ríos again said he thought we could, but we should have to begin at the same place then at which we might begin now.

Judge Day said: "Now we are fully prepared to treat on all matters now; we are ready to proceed on the basis that we are meeting Spanish Commissioners of equal authority. If not, we hope that they can come tomorrow armed with that authority."

Montero Ríos still regretted that he was unable to concur in these views. Both sides were fully authorized on the essential points. He did not see why the American Commissioners could not go into these now. He desired the fact of the Spanish Commissioners' readiness to be spread upon the minutes.

Judge Day repeated that at the last meeting both sides needed instructions, and agreed to get them. "The American Commissioners have done so, and are here ready. We hope the Spanish Commissioners may be able to do so now, and come here tomorrow ready."

Montero Ríos said at the last session there were three points on which the American Commissioners agreed that they would get instructions. These were the extension of the privileges for Spanish vessels and merchandise in the Philippines on the same terms to Cuba and Puerto Rico, the return of arms and artillery from the Philippines, and the repatriation of prisoners. There was another point on which the Spanish Commissioners were to get instructions. On that point he desired to say frankly that they had not yet received them, but they were willing now to assume the responsibility of acting upon that also. He understood that the American Commissioners were to come here ready today to give their answer on the former three points. The Spanish Commissioners were now ready to do the same as to the remaining point. They could thus finish up eight articles of the treaty. Beyond that there were four other points on which they expected instructions tomorrow. If it was the desire of the American Commissioners not to take up first these essential and necessary conditions of the peace, well and good.

Judge Day said it was the hope of the American Commissioners that this treaty was not going to depend [upon] or be limited merely to subjects which had been embraced in an ultimatum. With that view they had on last Wednesday submitted certain articles and hoped to be able to take these up. They have received a still larger number of additional articles from the Spanish Commissioners, only getting the translation of them late last night. These had been partly considered. The time would not be lost if an adjournment were made now in order that the American Commissioners might take up the remainder of these at once, so that we could be prepared tomorrow on both sides to consider all questions yet remaining undecided between us.

Montero Ríos said he did not desire to insist any further, but would only express the very lively wish of the Spanish Commissioners that the relations growing out of the peace might be mutually satisfactory and beneficial, as well as permanent. "According to the ease," he said, "with which the main points are now settled will be the ease with which the other points still remaining can be disposed of."

Judge Day responded that he had stated several times, and he believed, that both sides ought now to be here with full authority from their respective governments before undertaking the final disposition of the questions yet before the Joint Commission. He hoped the Spanish Commissioners might have such authority by tomorrow. Meantime, the American Commissioners would take up and consider the remainder of the Spanish articles, which had reached them last night.

At this point the Commission rose, and my American colleagues left the room in such haste that they all seemed to forget to take leave of the Spaniards. Overtaking them in the coat room, I reminded them of this, and one or two went back for the purpose. There [were] signs of more discontent with the attitude taken by the majority than we have had at any time during our sessions. Senator Davis and I rode home together, the rest walking. On the way Davis spoke of Senator Gray's expressions of discontent, as quite differing from anything he had ever witnessed in him before, and good-naturedly said: "It is not like him at all. His luncheon must have disagreed with him."

Saturday, December 3rd, 1898.

Senator Frye and Day appeared by half past nine this morning, and for a wonder by a few minutes after ten all were gathered. Walter Neef [a newspaper reporter] had been around before with a story of dispatches from Berlin to the effect that Germany was negotiating for the purchase of the whole Caroline group. Dispatches from Washington furnishing something of the same sort had also appeared in the Paris edition of the [New York] *Herald*, and the Commissioners were generally inclined to believe the story. I found them all more or less imbued with the idea that we should get little outside the protocol unless we made additional concessions. Frye, Davis, and myself were agreed on an unwillingness to make any further concessions unless provisional, and with the understanding that they were conditioned upon our getting Kusaie, religious liberty, and the release of political prisoners. Judge Day and Senator Gray, on the other hand, thought nothing but the open door in Puerto Rico would bring these, and if it were not offered nothing could be given. . . .

[The] subject of contracts was first taken up. The Spanish proposal was read with a memorandum of such outstanding government contracts as they could remember, and a copy of the contract with the British Ocean Cable Company having the monopoly in the Philippines. This last when read proved to be extremely binding and comprehensive, and it was generally concluded that most of its provisions would bind us.

Senator Gray was ready at once for an article in the treaty corresponding in scope with the article between the Germans and French in the Treaty of Frankfurt [in 1871]. The others all thought this too sweeping. After a great deal of discussion pro and con, Senator Gray continued to talk in favor of magnanimity, and the obligations of cordiality and civilization, but offering nothing practicable. Judge Day challenged him to prepare such an article as he would be willing to incorporate in the treaty and defend in the Senate. He spent the next fifteen or twenty minutes in trying to elaborate such an article. When finally read, it proved to be a plan for a joint commission of which three members should be appointed by the President of the United States and two by the Spanish Government, which was to examine and report to the United States Government on such contracts as should be taken over. By the time this had been read and discussed a few moments, he did not seem to be very well satisfied with it himself, or to think that the Spaniards would be; nor did he see anything he could prepare in its stead.

From the beginning of the discussion I had constantly expressed myself as greatly attracted towards the idea of assuming, man-fashion, every obligation that rightly belonged to us, provided they could suggest an article, properly safeguarded, which would accomplish this purpose. None of the rest suggested anything. I finally moved, as the sense of the Commission, that we should reject the Spanish article. But in doing so [we] should enter upon the protocol a statement of the desire of our government to accept every contract obligation of a civil and public character by which it would be bound in the forum of international law or morals. [We would also] unite in procuring legislation which would admit foreigners holding such contracts to the privilege of our Court of Claims or other judicature to enforce their rights. After some discussion, and with the general understanding that this was intended merely to draw out the general feeling of the Commission, it was finally adopted unanimously. Even Senator Gray [voted] for it, with a quasi-admission that his own article was not satisfactory, and that the Spanish article was unacceptable.

The next question that came up was that of the return of artillery. At this stage Senator Frye interposed a strong objection to making any concessions excepting provisionally. [Everything would] depend on our getting corresponding concessions with regard to Kusaie, political pris-

oners, religious freedom, etc. Senator Davis spoke in the same sense. I
had previously shown to these Senators a memorandum which I had
hastily penciled myself, to the following effect:

The American Commissioners
  Believing that the terms required by their Government in its ultimatum
were just, though the indemnity exacted was inadequate to the cost of the war;
and
  Believing that the subsequent offers to return prisoners at their own cost,
to give up artillery and make specially prompt payments, are unusually liberal—
  Agree that these offers shall be made only provisionally, dependent upon
the Spanish response as to our requests concerning Kusaie and religious freedom in the Carolines, and release [of] political prisoners.

Senator Gray repeated with a good deal of vigor his objection to
"dickering" of this sort. [He] insisted that we were already committed
to the free return of prisoners. He, for one, would never consent to withdraw or modify that committal.

The fact of the committal was questioned by some of the others, to
most of whom, like myself, it was new. We had not realized that this
provision had been embodied in one of the last articles rushed through
at the previous joint session. But Judge Day announced that it had been
agreed upon, and that the fact of the agreement had been telegraphed to
our State Department. [At this,] there was on the part of Frye, Davis,
and myself, an expression of regret that we were committed to an unusual expenditure which could only be justified on the ground of magnanimity to a fallen foe, which was also exhibiting a disposition to be
conciliatory to us. Senator Frye insisted, however, that we were not yet
committed to the free return of the prisoners held by the Philippine
insurgents, and I proposed that we should make our agreement to that
return provisional. Judge Day then showed that this would imperil the
return of political prisoners, since the Spanish had submitted an article
in lieu of ours. In [it] their liberation of the political prisoners they held
was coupled with our undertaking to procure the liberation of prisoners
held by the insurgents. In each case the liberating government was to
return the prisoners at its own expense. This expense would, of course, be
trivial to the Spanish and very heavy to us. But unless we were ready to
imperil the liberation of the Cuban and Philippine political prisoners
held by the Spaniards, on which our instructions had been early and spe-

cific, there seemed no safe way of escaping the further concession into which we had been hurried.

At this point, Judge Day and Senator Gray revived the question of the "open door" for Puerto Rico and Cuba . . . Judge Day expressed the belief that unless we practically granted the "open door" in Puerto Rico, we should get no further concession of any kind from the Spaniards, and that our treaty would be limited practically to what we had extorted in the ultimatum. He added, however, that he and Senator Gray had asked for authority to do this from the government, while the majority of the Commission had been against him. The answer of the government to the dispatches had been so peremptory that he was unwilling to raise the question anew. Senator Gray still thought it might be raised, and repeated his expressions of dislike to being tied up by such rigid instructions.

As they referred frequently to the attitude of the rest of us against their proposal of an unlimited extension of the "open door" to Cuba and Puerto Rico for five years, I threw out the suggestion that the change would not be so revolutionary or offensive to supporters of the historic national policy of the United States on this subject if we got permission to offer this for a single year. Senator Gray vehemently opposed this as beneath the dignity of the nation, and wholly worthless to the Spaniards. I resisted this contention with some vigor; [I] said it was idle to maintain that while an industry like the Compañía Transatlántico would be practically destroyed by being cut off immediately, it would not be given a fair chance for its life if given a year in which to arrange its affairs and seek new channels of business. He continued, however, to denounce such a proposal with more heat than he has heretofore shown. Both Senators Davis and Frye agreed with him that a year would be too short a time, although they thought two or three years might form a very valuable concession.

It was at last suggested by Judge Day that he might greatly restrict and narrow the original offer he had asked the government for leave to make by limiting it to the precise words employed in the treaty with Spain concerning the cession of Florida, granting access to Spanish ships sailing from Spanish ports, and laden exclusively with goods of Spanish growth or manufacture on [the] same terms with vessels of the United States. It was generally agreed that in following this early precedent we should be giving a substantial privilege to Spain without embarrassing our friends in Congress, endangering the treaty, or materially injuring American business interests. On this theory a dispatch was sent expressing the uniform desire of the Commission for authority to make this offer for a term of years not to exceed five, in return for the concessions from Spain, which we still sought to secure.

By this time, the commissioners were pretty tired, with as near an approach to sharp controversy and long argumentation as they have had at any time during the negotiations. It was therefore agreed that we should postpone the meeting with the Spanish Commissioners till Monday, by which time it was hoped we might have the desired authority. The commissioners accordingly adjourned about half past one o'clock.

While the discussion was going on, Secretary Moore was called out by a message that Ojeda was waiting for him in the office. When he returned he said he could tell us exactly what the Spaniards were going to do. Ojeda had said to him substantially this: You give us the "open door" concession for Puerto Rico and Cuba, as you did in the Philippines, also our proposals as to the legal status of Spaniards in the ceded territory, and as to contracts now in full vigor. If you do this we will then consider the renewal of all the treaties excepting the protocol of '77 and landing rights for cables, as well as the cession of the whole group of the Carolines and the Ladrones too, if you want them. . . .[4]

Sunday, Dec. 4th, 1898.

Just as I was settling down to read the paper while the family were starting to Church, two or three of the Commissioners appeared at the door. It seemed that a dispatch from Hay had been received refusing the unanimous request of the Commissioners for leave to exercise their discretion in granting in return for concessions to us a limited privilege of trade to Puerto Rico and Cuba for five years modelled on the lines of the similar concession in the treaty with Spain about Florida.[5] Judge

[4] The reference to "the protocol of '77" is apparently to the agreements of 1877 between the United States and Spain which defined legal rights for the respective citizens and extradition privileges. Their texts are too long and complicated to be cited or summarized here, but can be found conveniently in *U.S. Statutes at Large*, Vol. 19, pp. 650–657.

[5] Day had telegraphed Hay on December 3:

We are unanimously of the opinion that unless we are invested with discretion to allow for a limited period, not exceeding five years, Spanish vessels coming laden only with productions of Spanish growth and manufacture directly from

Day and Senator Gray both expressed a lively disappointment and Gray was especially inclined to resent the refusal to entrust to the Commissioners the slightest discretion in such a matter even when unanimously asked for. I concurred in the expression of some surprise that in view of the unanimous request it had not been granted. Gray thought they might almost as well send clerks over here to do their work. When Frye and Davis came in their expressions were rather more restrained but tended in the same direction; and some one commented on a headline in the newspapers this morning that "Col. Hay remains firm."

Judge Day next presented a circular from the London Committee of the Filipinos protesting vehemently against what they called the brutality of the language used by Gen. Merritt as to the aid rendered by the Filipinos in the operations at Manila, as to their capacity for self-government, general character, etc. [It] referred to Merritt with great scorn as "this decrepit old man."

The possibility of a concession as to Puerto Rican trade being abandoned, a discussion sprang up as to whether we should adhere to our previous purpose of allowing the prisoners held by the Tagalogs to be returned to Spain at our expense. Gray again declared that we had been utterly wrong in taking the sovereignty of the Philippines, and that our position was indefensible by the law of nations and the judgment of the civilized world. Davis contented himself in saying: "Oh, Gray," in a sort of appealing tone, and Frye with something of the same sort. Then I

---

ports of Spain or of her colonies to enter ports of Cuba and Puerto Rico without paying other or higher duties on cargoes or tonnage than are paid by the United States vessels, it may be impracticable to obtain anything not contained in our ultimatum and therefore necessarily forming [the] subject of mutual concession—such as Kusaie, and religious freedom in Carolines, the release of political prisoners, cable-landing rights, and revival of treaties in force between the two countries before the war. The privilege above mentioned is different from and much more restricted than that referred to in our telegrams of 30th ultimo, and is in conformity with precedents cited in that telegram from [the] Florida and Louisiana treaties. (*For. Rels. 1898*, p. 964.)

Hay replied for the President:

The President is still of the opinion that preferential privileges to Spain in Puerto Rico and Cuba are not desirable. He would even prefer that [a] treaty should be made on [the] basis of ultimatum rather than risk the embarrassments which might result from such concessions. (Hay to Day, December 3, 1898, *ibid.*)

"The embarrassments" the President had in mind were probably the protest in Congress from tariff protectionists and jingoes alike should such concessions be granted.

made a rather earnest appeal to Gray to recognize as to this question the maxim *stare decicis*; and, leaving all that behind us, see if we couldn't use this question of the return of the prisoners held by the Tagalogs at our expense as a concession, which might serve the purpose of a lever to pry out of them the sale of Kusaie and the renewal of their old agreement as to religious liberty in the Carolines. He at last admitted his willingness to make this effort. Then to my surprise Day broke out against it, saying that if we tied strings to any of our propositions, they would do the same, and we would soon be hopelessly tangled up. At last a vote was taken on the matter, and Davis voted with Day, Frye did the same, with obvious reluctance, and then Gray. I renewed the expression of my opinion that we were throwing away another, and almost our last, chance to get anything out of them, but yielded to the majority.

We then worked for a time over the Spanish proposal as to existing contracts. Moore read an article he had prepared. Although there had been a little talk about it, I said it struck me as a Bunsbyism pure and simple. Moore then laughingly admitted that he thought it was himself. Others took the same view, and it was passed to see if something better might not be devised in the afternoon. . . .

Monday, December 5th, 1898.

At the meeting this morning, which began within half an hour of the time, we took up at once two or three proposed forms for an article on contracts. All seemed, however, to involve a possible obligation to the priests, whom the Spanish government had been supporting, and some an obligation for the Cuban debts. I objected to these because if we adopted them, we were at once in trouble at home. If we amended them so as to specifically exclude the priests, we should not only have trouble in getting the Spaniards to adopt them, but we should also kindle a fire in our rear at home among Catholic sympathizers before we were ready for it. It seemed to me much wiser to leave contracts out altogether than to put them in only at the risk of having a religious antagonism to the treaty from the outset. If left out they could subsequently be dealt with in other negotiations, or by Congress. The same view was entertained by the others.

. . . Senator Davis made a motion that the Chairman [Day] reply to the Spanish request for such an article substantially in the language I had just used, which was: "It has never been our practice to make such stipulations in treaties; there were none in our previous treaties for the cession of territory either from Spain or France; and it seems best now to follow our precedent in the matter for the reason that under our form of Government such questions belong primarily to the legislative department." This motion was carried unanimously, Senator Gray assenting to it at the last. [He said] that he still hoped to devise something further from the objections named, which we could put into the treaty. The rest of us all cordially agreed that if he did we should be glad to adopt it.

The next troublesome article was that relating to existing litigation. It was believed that this, like most of the other articles which the Spanish have offered, was primarily inspired by a desire to help the Marquis de Comillas, in his effort to save something from the wreck to which he was exposed by his relations to the Spanish government, and his enormous advances. This article would certainly cover his contracts for the Compañía Transatlántico, and it was believed that it would also cover many other dangerous contracts. In this apprehension, the words "suits by or against the Government" were taken out. It was concluded that we could explain this action by the same reason given in the previous paragraph; that under our system, suits against the government were not permitted, although claimants were given access to the Court of Claims. . . .

Moore was again instructed to re-draft the article relating to litigation in the light of the amendments and suggestions made. Senator Gray said in presenting it: "You can explain our good will but say that Col. Hay is firm." This was only another of several recent instances of dislike on the part of the Senators [toward] the tone of recent dispatches from the State Department, as well as the tone of the Associated Press dispatches concerning the State Department's control of the negotiations here. . . .

It was announced that the Spanish Commissioners had requested the postponement of today's session until 3 o'clock.

When we got off, we found the Spaniards in the outer room, where they seemed inclined to linger, drawing Judge Day alone into their circle. The rest of us passed into the Salle de Conference, and presently began to think, from the unusual stay of the others outside, and the appearance of earnest talk, that they must be making some effort at direct negotiation. At last they joined us. But even after we were all seated at the table there followed long consultations between the two secretaries and afterwards between each secretary and the president of his Commission. Montero Ríos seemed very discontented with anything in the protocol which Moore was willing to agree to. Abarzuza once attempted to persuade Moore that their view was correct. These whispered consultations continued until 3:40, when the reading of the protocol at last began. It proved to be very long, and to be practically a report of the entire debate of the previous session, obviously from the Spanish point of view. Montero Ríos had plainly revised the original notes of his part of the debate and had placed his entire afternoon's argument in much more symmetrical and consistent shape. Under this practice the American side appeared at a disadvantage.

Even [so], Montero Ríos was not satisfied. As soon as the reading was finished, he said that he wished the protocol to show that his declaration that he understood all the war material of every description in the Philippines belonged to Spain had not been contradicted or objected to by the Americans. If they assented to this his statement could stand as it appeared in the protocol. If not, he wished it now to appear on the protocol of today's proceedings, that the American dissent had not been expressed until today.

Judge Day remarked that the American Commissioners had understood that the rule concerning war material as now maintained by the American Commissioners in Puerto Rico and Cuba should prevail, and that for the sake of absolute accuracy and certainty, they had undertaken to telegraph their government to find out what this rule was. Montero Ríos said that if there was a difference of opinion between the Commissions on this point, the best way out of it would be to spread upon the minutes the exact facts as to the understanding of each, together with his undisputed fact that his claim on behalf of Spain for all the war material in the Philippines passed without objection at the time it was made. He wanted now to add specifically that, in the judgment of the Spanish Commissioners, all the war material in the Philippines legally and properly belonged to Spain.

Thereupon, Judge Day remarked that the President of the Spanish Commission [was] now passing from the question before us, namely what the protocol of the last meeting should be, to another question, namely, what the president [Montero Ríos] thought he should have said more explicitly and wished now to say. The fact remained, and he [Day] understood that nobody questioned it, that the whole matter had been left open until the American Commissioners could telegraph to their government to ascertain the decision taken in this matter in the Puerto Rico case. They had done so. They now had that decision, and were prepared at the proper time to offer what might be satisfactory to the

Spanish Commissioners. Whether it was or not, the American Commissioners were now fully prepared to take up that matter at the point where it had been left off at the previous session.

Montero Ríos again responded that the only point he desired to insist upon was that the protocol of the last session and of today's should make absolutely clear the opinions advanced by him and by the president of the American Commission [Day]. Senator Gray interposed that that seemed to be the only solution and Judge Day (thus foreclosed) said: "Very well."

The Judge [Day] then referred to the questions which had been called up at the last session, on which the Spanish Commissioners had expressed their inability to act through lack of instructions from their government, and had promised to get instructions. He desired to ask if they had heard from their government on these points.

Montero Ríos responded with some asperity and with visible heat that they had in fact heard from their government on the subject, but that he refused to take it up for the reason already given. He wished it distinctly understood that the Spanish Commissioners [would] not take up the questions thus referred to in the American proposals till all the articles which they (the Spanish Commissioners) considered essential or naturally belonging to a treaty of peace have been considered and completed. Judge Day responded very quietly that he made the inquiry now, not for the purpose of immediately taking up these articles, but for the purpose of ascertaining if the American Commissioners were now meeting and dealing with Spanish Commissioners having like themselves full power over all the questions now before them.

Montero Ríos proceeded again to develop his idea that the first thing for the Joint Commission now to do was to take up the four points he had already referred to in the last session, as matters properly and necessarily connected with a treaty of peace. After that would come subsidiary points proposed by the American Commissioners, and then similar points proposed by the Spaniards. Following this order he desired now to inquire from the American Commissioners what action they proposed on the first point, to which he called attention, and which he considered necessarily and essentially connected with a treaty of peace. [It concerned] the extension to Puerto Rico and Cuba of the same trade privileges in behalf of Spain already extended to the Philippines.

Judge Day said quietly [that he could] not now make such an extension. At the proper time and place [he would] be ready to take up and consider what special facilities, if any, can be given to Spanish trade.

But [he would] not now answer any provision on that subject in a treaty of peace.

This remark seemed to produce a decided sensation among the Spaniards. Up to this time their air had been curiously dogmatic and triumphant. They evidently felt that they had been thwarting the Americans, and had them at a disadvantage, since they believed the Americans extremely anxious about the remaining points on which they were delaying a decision. Apparently they had hardly doubted that they were going to get some concession in Puerto Rico. [They] had persuaded themselves that at this stage, at least, the American Commissioners would not have the nerve to give them a plump denial.

Montero Ríos rallied in a moment, and said that the second point on which they desired to have action was the question whether the prisoners on both sides should be liberated at the expense, in each case, of the liberating.

To this Judge Day replied that the American Commissioners had already agreed to return at the expense of their government all the prisoners of war we held in the Philippines. There had been some talk about the further question involved in the Spanish proposal, since this called also for the repatriation of the prisoners held by the [Filipinos]. We had thereupon naturally inquired how extensive an undertaking this might be, which was thus proposed to us. [We had] therefore asked how many of these prisoners there were, [and] the President of the Spanish Commission had promised to ascertain. Had he done so? (Frye, who had been afraid of the magnitude of this undertaking, as well as like myself averse to giving so much to the Spaniards, and getting so little, here whispered with Day about the desirability of covering the case a little more thoroughly.)

Meantime, Montero Ríos replied rather indifferently, that they still had no knowledge on the subject. Judge Day then remarked that it was a long and expensive trip from Manila to the nearest port of Spain, and that we would like to know something definite about the extent of the undertaking which was asked of us. Montero Ríos still said that the Spanish Commissioners were unable to give even an approximation towards the definite number. The Spanish army in the Philippines had been largely composed of natives. His government did not want those on any terms. . . . They certainly did not want the natives transported to Spain. It might be possible, if the American Commissioners insisted upon it, to reach a common agreement as to a maximum or minimum number that should be covered by the article.

Judge Day at once said: "We agree to that." Whereupon Frye inter-jected: "Have that distinctly understood." Montero Ríos said as an ad-dition to the article: "Let it be made clear that we don't want the natives."

He then continued immediately: "Now as to the material of war of whatsoever kind in the Philippines?" This question, however, was not translated for a moment or two, owing to some further talk by Frye and Davis with Judge Day about the previous subject. When it was finally translated, Judge Day responded: "As to that the matter is settled in Puerto Rico by another commission, with which we have no authority to interfere. We are willing to do in the Philippines what has been agreed to in Puerto Rico." He thereupon handed to the translator the summary of the information telegraphed from the State Department as to the terms proposed by the American commissioners in Puerto Rico. [It was] practically that everything above nine centimetres calibre should re-main. Montero Ríos, as soon as this was translated, said: "This state-ment differs from the information we have received from our govern-ment with respect to the armament of forts and fixed batteries. We understand that the question has not been decided at all by the com-mission, but has been left to the decision of the two governments."

Judge Day replied: "That is possible. We are without information on that point. What we do know is what our government has done or held with regard to Puerto Rico, and we are willing to do the same with re-gard to the Philippines."

Montero Ríos said that the instructions received from their govern-ment, and the instructions likewise given to their commissioners in Puer-to Rico, were to claim all material of war. He understood, however, that as to fixed batteries, etc., the Puerto Rico commission had unani-mously agreed to refer the question to the two governments for decision. [He suggested that] we could do the same here if the [Peace] Commis-sion preferred. He wished it understood, however, that as to the Philip-pines, the Spanish Commission here claimed all war material, everything that could be transported. None of this material had been included in the cession of the territory.

Judge Day replied: "As to Puerto Rico and Cuba, the question has not been committed to us. As to the Philippines, we have power [to de-cide], and we understand that heavy guns in fortifications are fixtures in law, belong to and stay with the territory."

Montero Ríos responded again testily, and with some vigor and rhe-torical effort: "The article here cannot be accepted by Spain. As it is not essential, a treaty can be made without it." But he wanted to make the statement and would insist on having it spread upon the minutes that in such a position the United States was treating Spain with more harshness than Russia showed to Turkey in the treaty of San Stefano. Gen. Cerero followed this up by exclaiming: "These are not fixtures at all. They are guns with carriages, all movable."

Judge Day said: "We understand that many of the guns are mounted in the fortifications for the defense of Manila and other important points. It is perfectly known that it would be embarrassing in the present situation for the United States to dismantle those fortifications, even if there were a just claim regarding it." Gen. Cerero repeated that they were all portable in the Philippines, as well as in Cuba and Puerto Rico. Even those of the largest calibre were in no respect fixtures in the fortifications, but were arranged to be moved from point to point, and could be so removed. Senator Davis asked if that statement was not true in a sense of all modern artillery, and Gen. Cerero replied: "Yes, all over the world now."

By this time Judge Day, who seemed impressed with the necessity of avoiding a flat breach on this point, and had apparently been considerably affected by the charge of a harshness greater than that of Russia to Turkey, consulted privately with some of the Commissioners as to whether we might not strike out the limitation as to field artillery above nine centimetres. The several Commissioners in a rather weary mood assented.

Gen. Cerero continued: "We don't want to make a gift to you of all our war material, having already given up the archipelago." Judge Day asked if they had field artillery there of more than nine centimetres, and Gen. Cerero said he couldn't say.

Senator Frye here interposed with the remark: "We have some disquieting late subjects largely belonging to Spain called Tagalogs. Would the Spanish Commissioners consent that these guns should remain in their present position for six months?"

Montero Ríos' reply was characteristic; he did not think this remark was in place here. We were engaged in making a treaty not in conducting a campaign; and the business of the treaty makers was to tell to whom this war material belonged.

Frye said to the translator: "He does not understand my question. Tell him that assuming that we put in the treaty what he asks, we inquire whether he would insist on the immediate disarmament of these fortifications, or whether he would be willing to delay it six months."

Montero Ríos again replied: "The question to be treated now is one of ownership. If that is settled there would probably be no trouble about an arrangement for time of delivery."

A rapid consultation now followed on the American side. Judge Day was evidently desirous of allowing the claim to all the war material on this condition, and Davis and Gray led off in seconding his proposal. Frye finally yielded to it. I remained quiet, but in the end concluded to make no objection. It would have been useless any way, and I was about half persuaded that we had gone so far already in the matter that it was hardly worth while to make two bites of the cherry.

Day then agreed to make the concession asked by the Spaniards as to all war material in the Philippines, to take effect as to field artillery only six months after the ratification of the treaty. Montero Ríos then said there was no need of delaying here for the details. The recognition of the right of Spain to this material and the agreement not to remove a part of it for six months were the essential features. The latter requirement was to apply only to heavy siege guns. All war material belonged to them, and all to be removed at pleasure, save the heavy siege guns, and these after six months.

Frye here interposed that it should be distinctly understood that all artillery exceeding the nine-centimetre calibre was to remain for six months. A little discussion here sprang up in Spanish between Cerero and Montero Ríos, during or at the close of which, Judge Day remarked that he had no doubt the two secretaries could now draw an article embodying the terms here understood, and we could pass at once to something else.

Montero Ríos replied that in order to avoid any mistake he wished to repeat his understanding that Spain's right was recognized to all war material of every description in the Philippines, and that only heavy artillery was to remain for six months. To this I replied that my understanding was that everything of over nine-centimetre calibre was to remain six months. Several Spanish Commissioners cried "No, No," and Montero Ríos said he did not have that understanding. Thereupon Judge Day remarked that [since] the secretaries were in accord, and would bring in an article on which we could agree, we might better pass to something else.

Montero Ríos at once said: "There is a fourth point, the preservation of order throughout the archipelago, and the proposition of the United States to undertake it, as well as the protection of life and property." On this point it seemed to him that whichever power was in possession in

any region should keep order there. There should be agreement between
the two powers now existing in the archipelago until the final cession of
sovereignty.

An immediate informal consultation was held at the table among the
American members. I declared myself at the outset strongly opposed to
any such partnership with Spain, and said it would involve the possibility
of innumerable troubles and complications. Judge Day and Senator
Davis expressed themselves with equal strength against it. In a moment
Judge Day, speaking again across the table, said: "The United States are
now holding the harbor, bay, and city of Manila under the protocol pending this cession of sovereignty. It was the purpose of the American proposal that the responsibility attaching to these provisions of the protocol
should be so extended as to include the entire archipelago. We understood that this was the assumption of a greater responsibility; and in the
common interest of all we were willing to undertake it. If the Spanish
Commissioners object, we prefer to make no agreement as to any change
from the existing status." Montero Ríos replied instantly and indifferently: "Very well."

Judge Day then asked as to the remaining articles. Montero Ríos replied that he first wanted to know if the first eight were now definitely
settled and agreed upon, saving the modifications which had been here
settled and were left to the secretaries to be put in shape. Judge Day suggested that the articles were not numbered alike, and it would be better
to read them over as we have them to be sure of avoiding any misunderstanding. This was done, and when the article was reached leaving the
time of evacuation to the two governments, the Americans held a short
consultation. I objected to this as again leaving a chance for dangerous
delays in case of a failure by the Spaniards to agree to time desired by
the Americans. Gray was quite willing to accept it. Judge Day finally
found another clause which, taken in connection with this one, seemed
to him to guard against the dangers I apprehended and the article was
finally agreed to; though I must confess with some reluctance on my
part.

We came next to the article, which contained the words "in consideration of." They were left out. Judge Day said he understood that the
President of the Spanish Commission [Montero Ríos], after their legal
significance under English and American law had been explained to
him, had agreed that they should go in. Montero Ríos replied tartly:
"The gentleman is in error." What he had agreed to was to think [about]
it. Reflection had convinced him in the conclusion that these words

should not be in. Judge Day then said that he understood the article as
read to express the fact that the cession of the territory was made "without consideration." That language, of course, could not be admitted for a
moment. Ojeda explained that these words did not appear in the article,
but that he had used them merely to indicate that the article had been
recast so as to appear without any words whatever in it relating to the
subject of consideration.

Recurring to the question of the transport of prisoners, Montero Ríos
explained that it would be preferable to the Spanish Commissioners to
let any prisoners stay in the countries they are now in, where they wish
to do so, since that would save the expense of transportation.

Judge Day said he presumed the next subject to be considered would
be the articles proposed by the American Commissioners. But it was almost immediately agreed, to avoid confusion, [that] the eight articles already discussed should also be read in Spanish. When this was done Montero Ríos again persistently recurred to his old inquiry: "Is it understood that these are all agreed to excepting as to the changes in article
eight, which have been decided upon and left today to the secretaries
to be put in shape?" There being no negative response, he next proceeded to say that in his judgment what now ought to be taken up would
be other articles either necessary or natural to a treaty of peace; such as
one relating to citizenship in the ceded territories.

Judge Day responded: "It was the understanding of the American
Commissioners that we were now to receive the answers of the Spanish
Commissioners on what have been styled the subsidiary articles proposed sometime ago by the Americans. We understood this was agreed
to at the last session, and again at the beginning of this session." Montero
Ríos at once responded tartly that this was a mistaken idea, as would be
seen from the minutes in the protocol itself. Judge Day said: "No,
the protocol should show that the Spanish Commissioners only asked to
delay their answer on these questions because they were without instructions. We said then they should get instructions, and it was the understanding that when instructions were procured these articles were to be
taken up. We yielded the point readily this morning to allow the first
eight articles to be revised, and supposed that then, as a matter of course,
ours filed long since would be taken up."

A long silence followed, during which Montero Ríos busied himself
in hunting through the text of the Spanish protocol. This, as already
noted, had obviously been framed to fill up the gaps in what he had actually said, in such a way as to sustain him in his present position. He

read with emphasis various sentences dwelling on the necessity of first disposing of articles, which as he claimed were either necessary to a treaty of peace or naturally belonged in it. The Spaniards had delivered to the American Commissioners drafts of still other articles, which, in their view, came within these divisions as forming natural or necessary parts of a treaty of peace. He then said, somewhat bluntly, [that] the Spanish Commissioners would not discuss the American articles till the answer of the Americans had been received on these articles which the Spaniards had submitted. He had said the same thing, as the protocol showed, on yesterday; he repeated it today.

Judge Day said: "This is insistence on an opinion expressed by the President of the Spanish Commission as to what would be proper or desirable. Is it anything more than such insistence? Has there been any agreement between the Commissioners to that effect?" Montero Ríos replied that he did not claim that the Americans had agreed to this view. He only read these extracts from the protocol to show that the Americans had misunderstood him, if they supposed he had agreed to anything else. He had made no agreement to take up the articles which the Americans proposed, and he repeated that the Spaniards would not take them up.

Judge Day said: "We supposed it was a common understanding; now we are told that there has been no agreement on the subject. Very well. We still ask to take up article No.—[sic], being the article which we proposed on the subject of the revival of treaties."

Montero Ríos replied that a strict procedure would prevent the Spanish Commissioners from discussing anything not properly belonging to a treaty of peace. It might be possible, perhaps, to bring about a greater agreement by discussion of outside questions. But this could only be done informally, and must not appear in the protocol.

Judge Day asked what that meant; whether they desired to keep such matters entirely out of the record? Montero Ríos said it was true the American Commissioners had presented a draft including articles necessary to a treaty. They had also presented some having nothing properly to do with a treaty of peace, or no way provided for in the protocol. The Spanish Commissioners, for example, had never agreed to sell any islands or grant any facilities for landing cables or treat on any such subjects. Yet here these were brought forward in American articles. On receipt of such articles, the Spaniards had themselves prepared others, which they thought essentially connected with a treaty of peace. In the natural order there must be taken up first. If the others to which the Americans refer are to be discussed now it can be only informally.

Guarnica followed this up by repeating that the articles presented by the Spanish Commissioners were intimately connected with the eight which had been approved today. For example, they related to the status of inhabitants in ceded territories and to kindred subjects, which were in a sense vital to the treaty, and certainly must be disposed of before we began to discuss buying islands.

Montero Ríos continued that these articles are really needed. "We have no power to enforce them on the attention of the American Commissioners; but what is to be done? We regard them as articles necessary for a treaty of peace, which we wish to perfect and conclude. We do not say we will not treat on other questions; but we do say they do not belong here. In a word, every article we have presented relates distinctly to Cuba, Puerto Rico, and the Philippines. Not one of the articles now insisted on by the Americans relates to any of these subjects."

Judge Day said: "No one is authorized to declare what a treaty of peace must include. No doubt it should include what the Joint Commissioners may choose to put into it. Certainly, however, there can be no dispute that a revival of treaties belongs in it, and that is the first article to which we have invited attention. We have considered the remaining articles of the Spanish Commissioners. Some of them no doubt properly belong to a treaty of peace. Others, like the article relating to the explosion of the *Maine*, or that relating to pensions to the Duke of Veragua, certainly do not belong to a treaty of peace. As to some of ours, long since filed, there can be no question on that point. If the Spanish Commissioners mean to refuse to take them up, we would like to understand it."

Montero Ríos replied: "As to the pension to the Duke of Veragua, Spain will continue to pay it if the United States doesn't." To this Judge Day responded: "The President of the Spanish Commission will please note that we have not as yet refused to consider it. We have said that it was not a necessary article of the treaty of peace." Montero Ríos replied: "The article relating to the Duke of Veragua may perhaps not belong strictly to a treaty of peace, but the article relating to the explosion of the *Maine* does. It has been brought into this situation by a paper filed here by the American Commissioners with the implication that the explosion was due to what might at least be described as the carelessness of the Spaniards. We want to show to the world that the ports of Spain are safe to its marine. This explosion was one of the causes of the war, and necessarily it must be settled by this Commission."

At this stage the American Commissioners began to confer privately while the Spaniards settled back with sardonic smiles of triumph and presently began chatting and laughing among themselves. It seemed evident that they thought they had played with the Americans to their hearts' content all the afternoon, and, in the slang of our newspapers, "had put them in a hole." Frye had wandered out towards the close of the discussion, apparently too impatient to listen to it longer. The rest of us expressed decided dissatisfaction with continuing this kind of discussion. Davis was ready to close on the eight articles already agreed without another line to the treaty rather than submit further to what he considered to be an unnational [sic] dictatorial tone and persistent bullying. Judge Day thought it would be better to refer the question of the order of procedure to the secretaries. I expressed my sympathy with Senator Davis's view of the Spanish conduct, but thought the best thing for the moment was to adjourn the present session without any action, and take it up afresh at the next meeting. Day continued to urge the suggestion that the secretaries could probably adjust it. I resented the idea that we should formally abandon our functions, after a scene like this, to the secretaries of the two Commissions. Davis vehemently approved this view. Gray also favored my suggestion for an adjournment till tomorrow and Davis finally came over to it.

All this time the appearance of the Spaniards was that of great enjoyment and hilarity. They clustered together at the table with lively conversational sallies, repeated laughter, and every evidence of great enjoyment of the situation. At Judge Day's request I went to the outer room to see if Frye could be found, but he had evidently gone. Judge Day seemed to think that Senator Gray would probably still side with his proposal to leave it to the secretaries and apparently fancied he could get Frye to favor this view also. As it was, he considered the Commission was practically tied. At last he turned to the Commissioners on the other side of the table (we had all been gathered about the table during this whole scene) and said: "Are we right in understanding the Spanish Commissioners to refuse now to consider any of the American articles?" Montero Ríos replied: "We are ready to consider them now informally." Judge Day said: "Does that mean you are ready to give your answer?" Montero Ríos at once said: "Officially we will not give any answer, but we shall be quite willing to discuss them informally, and unofficially." Judge Day then said: "I think we understand." [He] was evidently going on to make some further statement when Ojeda interrupted with a proposition on their behalf that the matter be left to the two secretaries, saying he thought they could agree. Day and Gray were now willing to accept this proposal. Davis and I both felt that to abnegate our functions in this way on the invitation of the Spanish secretary, and at the end of such a discussion would be unseemly, and still persisted in our proposal to adjourn until tomorrow. Day thereupon said that owing to the lateness of the hour there seemed nothing better to do than to adjourn the session until two o'clock tomorrow afternoon, and the session was closed. . . .

Tuesday, December 6th, 1898.

Before the Commissioners were all gathered this morning, the conversation which sprang up led me to suggest that a line of procedure might be adopted at the next joint meeting, which would have quite as much justification as that of the Spaniards. This would be to hold that we should take up the articles which the Spaniards spoke of as being naturally or in some case necessarily connected with the treaty of peace in the order in which such articles had been filed. There could be no question that our article reviving treaties which the war had suspended would come under this classification. It had been filed a week or more before any of the Spaniards', while notice of it had been given even a week or two earlier than that. The revival of the agreement as to religious freedom could then come up in the same way, and we might try to get a Spanish assent or rejection to these. By way of providing for a possible refusal, which would be the signal for a failure on everything else before us, I suggested that if that refusal came it would be of great advantage to us to have religious freedom distinctly connected with it. This could easily be accomplished by avoiding having a separate article on religious freedom and adding the agreement on this subject, which we proposed to revive, to the list of other treaties and diplomatic agreements to be revised. Frye and Davis favored such a consolidation in the revival of all treaties and diplomatic agreements. Day feared first that it would complicate the question, though why none of us could see. [He] next considered that it would be better for us to have it rejected clearly and by itself, if it were to be rejected at all. On this, as on everything else, Gray was opposed to anything except allowing the Spaniards to have their own way.

Frye interrupted the talk with an outburst against the Veragua pensions. He said he had consented with a good deal of reluctance to this payment, but after yesterday's performance he was quite convinced that our vote ought to be reconsidered. He was confirmed in this by talk with Americans, who expressed amazement that such a proposition should be made or entertained for a moment, and he predicted that it would arouse a storm of opposition in the United States. I said at once and frankly that my motive for it had been simply the desire to yield to the Spaniards on a point like this, to which they seemed to attach a sentimental importance, and to show a conciliatory disposition. But after yesterday's performance I was satisfied there was no use wasting conciliatory measures of this kind upon them. Even Gray agreed to this and the previous action in favor of the United States' assuming the payments to Veragua was reconsidered.

Gray then took up the parable again as to the general necessity of yielding to the Spanish contentions and finally began lecturing us for expressing our dissatisfaction with their conduct yesterday. His remarks, for a time, were general, but at last he seemed to single out Davis and myself, although neither of us had said one word at the joint session which was not absolutely quite courteous and cordial to the Spaniards and to everybody.

Davis finally turned on him and met him pretty squarely, remarking that while he had said and done nothing in the joint session to show it, he had been mad at their insolence and evident desire to provoke us, and he had a right to be. I repelled [Gray's] attempt to reproach us with loss of temper good-naturedly but with some vigor.

Finally, he went on criticizing the general course of the American Commissioners in not yielding yesterday to the Spanish demands about procedure until he fairly aroused Judge Day. For a little time the Judge evidently resolved to say nothing, but at last he resented Senator Gray's remarks rather sharply with one or two pointed and rather stern questions as to what he (Gray) would have done if called upon personally to make the answer for the Commission to the remarks of Montero Ríos. At last with obvious temper he broke out: "Well suppose you take charge of the discussion then."

Gray seemed suddenly startled at this effect of his persistent inclination to the Spanish side. [He] immediately disavowed any desire of that sort, and said quite earnestly that he thought he had done or said nothing to expose himself to such a remark. He repeated this idea in two or three more sentences within a few minutes. Desultory talk went on about the table for a little while on the question of reviving the treaties, and against the idea of tying up the religious freedom in one article with such a revival. While this was in progress Gray quietly went out, and did not return until the session was ended.

Frye rather urged the union of the articles as I had originally proposed, and Davis did the same. Day seemed, however, so much impressed with his point of view, that I finally said: "I [don't] care, my only motive for the suggestion being to try to provide for making the Spanish action in rejecting our articles as striking and effective at home as possible."

We all finally agreed that we would call up simply the treaty articles this afternoon. If they refused to consider this, we would repeat our opinion that it was properly the first in the order of procedure. But [we] would say that we were so anxious to finish the work in hand that we would be willing to waive that point and proceed as rapidly as possible with the Spanish articles in the order in which the Spaniards themselves desired to present them. With a view to this, we went over the Spanish articles carefully to make sure that we had conceded nothing more than we had intended. When this work was finished, Day referred to Gray's continued absence and remarked quietly that he hoped he had not abandoned the Commission. He then made a few remarks about the frequent provocations Gray had given to which he had made no replies, and of which he had taken no notice. For the first time within my hearing [he] referred to one or two remarkable scenes which I have mentioned heretofore, when Gray persisted in vehement expressions of his discontent at the course Judge Day was taking in a tone quite audible to the Spanish Commissioners sitting opposite. After the others went out Day continued talking with me about it. [He] expressed regret at his own impatient expressions, saying that while he thought the provocation had been ample, he was afraid one or two of his own remarks had been needlessly pointed, if not petulant. I assured him that they seemed to me to have been warranted by the circumstances and that he need have no particular uneasiness about them. We agreed fully in our general estimate of Gray's generous and manly character. [It was necessary to make] all possible allowance for his position here as an ultra-conservative Democrat, opposed to the war, opposed to any annexation of territory, and opposed vehemently to taking a foot of land in the Philippine archipelago.

It was comical, as well as thoroughly characteristic, when we were ready to start at a quarter to two for the Foreign Office, to find Davis standing at the door and saying [that] we must wait a minute for Gray, who had just rushed off to get some luncheon. In a few moments Gray appeared with his mouth apparently still half full of a sandwich, and as amiable as if he had not left the conference in the morning.

As soon as we were seated at the table with the Spaniards, it was evident that the secretaries had their minds burdened. After conferences back and forth, Judge Day finally announced that the secretaries had not been able to agree on the protocol of yesterday. To expedite business he suggested that the reading and consideration of it be passed therefore until tomorrow. Montero Ríos interposed that he believed the difference only on one paragraph, and, as the point there involved would come up again in the article about the descendants of Columbus, he had no particular desire to insist on it now. Judge Day responded that there were a number of questions still open between the secretaries on which they could probably agree when they had time to get together. Montero Ríos and Ojeda then held a private conversation, after which Montero Ríos remarked that he now understood there was a difference also about the nature of the ordnance which was to be left in the Philippines for six months, and also about the *Maine* disaster, as well as about the descendants of Columbus.

Judge Day then inquired if he desired to have these questions taken up and decided, or to let the secretaries see if they could agree. Montero Ríos replied that he thought the regular order required that there should be no session without the approval or disapproval of the protocol of the previous session. He suggested, therefore, that points on which disagreement existed should either be submitted now to the full Commission, or that they should adjourn for a few minutes to see if the secretaries could adjust them. After a few minutes consultation on the American side, Judge Day said he thought it best to let the secretaries see if they could harmonize the difference. If not they might report.

A long delay followed. Montero Ríos and one or two of his colleagues arm in arm walked up and down the outer room. The Americans lounged about the table or gathered at the fireplaces. Gen. Cerero elaborately wrote over the agreement about artillery to suit himself, claiming this time for Spain everything belonging to the army even down to live stock. The secretaries struggled over the documents on the other matters and ended by expunging a whole typewritten page or more of Montero Ríos' remarks about the *Maine,* etc. At last the Commissioners gathered again at the table and at four o'clock the secretaries again began reading the protocols.

When these were finally finished, Judge Day at once said: "The matter, which at present seems to divide the Commission is merely a question on the form of procedure. It has been the contention of the Spanish Commissioners that their articles, although filed later than ours, are essential to the treaty of peace, while in their judgment the American articles are outside the natural or proper provisions of such a treaty. It is the desire of the American Commissioners to expedite business, and they do not therefore wish to dwell so much on a mere question of order. There is one American article about which it is difficult to see how there can be any division of opinion. The treaties between the two countries having been suspended as a significance of the war, it seems a necessary accompaniment of a restoration of peace, and therefore of a peace treaty, that such of these previously existing international agreements as are applicable to the present condition of affairs should be ratified." The Americans had offered an article on this subject, and he proposed now to take that up. They would then be quite ready to consider the articles which the Spanish Commissioners thought naturally or necessarily connected with the treaty of peace, and then the remaining articles of the American Commissioners. He believed this was a substantial compliance for which the Spanish Commissioners had contended, and would tend to expedite business.

Montero Ríos instantly replied that he was compelled to insist on their original claim as to the mode of procedure. He begged to differ from the American Commissioners as to their article about treaties. He did not consider it a necessary element in the present negotiation. He would be willing to take it up in its proper order. In all treaties of peace, however, where such an article was inserted, it was naturally and necessarily the last and must be taken in that order now.

Judge Day responded that the American Commissioners felt very decidedly that the order of procedure, which they had proposed today, was inherently right. They were more anxious, however, to expedite business than to prolong discussion on such a point. He desired therefore to ask if it were now the wish of the Spanish Commissioners that all their articles be immediately taken up.

Montero Ríos said that was his idea; not because these were questions presented by themselves, but because these subjects properly belonged to a treaty of peace. One of them was an article relating to citizenship. It had been proposed by the Americans themselves, and a modification of it had been offered by the Spanish Commissioners, and it was now the first which they wished to consider.

Judge Day asked if it was the understanding that all the articles proposed on either side were to be taken, and Montero Ríos said yes, that all were to be discussed. Judge Day thereupon said that the article now in question had originated with article six of the first American draft. The Spanish Commissioners had proposed two articles on this subject. These and the original American article have now been considered by the American Commissioners. From these they have drafted the following substitute (the American substitute for the Spanish article was then read in English and Spanish, and Judge Day continued) : "This article involves some obligations as to Cuba. The American Commissioners have prepared a general article limiting such obligation wherever it may appear in the period of United States occupancy of Cuba." He then presented this article, and it was read in Spanish. He then explained that the answer of the American Commissioners to the Spanish article which the President of the Spanish Commission had called up was the offer of the substitute just made, together with the general article limiting responsibility in Cuba to the time of United States occupancy of Cuba.

Montero Ríos said the mere reading of this substitute showed that it was almost on the same lines as the original American proposal. There were four or five points of marked difference between this and the Spanish proposals, which come out at once, on this hasty reading: (1) The Spaniards who may reside in these islands hereafter should be entitled to the same treatment and privilege as to citizenship, the same right of option, with those residing there now. (2) Spaniards should not only be entitled to hold property, but should be entitled to acquire property. (3) Spaniards should be specifically guaranteed to engage in the mechanical or liberal arts. (4) The American reference to the law of Congress is a limitation of the privileges agreed in the Spanish article. Spaniards who should arrive in any one of these islands towards the end of the first year after the ratification of these treaties, ought not only to be allowed to choose their citizenship, but ought to be given a full year in which to exercise their option. He then went on to say as to the general clause limiting United States' responsibility as to Cuba, any obligation assumed in this treaty by the United States must run current with the treaty.

When Montero Ríos closed these remarks, Day briefly consulted as to whether reply was desirable. I instantly gave advice strongly against it, and one or two others joined in this view. Judge Day then said he did not wish to provoke discussion as to this article. It seemed to the American Commissioners that it fully protected Spanish subjects. It gave them a year to choose which citizenship they preferred. As to guaranteeing the privileges of practicing handicrafts or engaging in liberal pursuits, the practice of the United States on this subject had been invariable. The field was open to all. The right of Congress to determine the status of natives in the islands was clear. In a word, there was nothing whatever in the article in any way undertaking to approach the rights of Spain. As to limiting the United States' responsibility for Cuba to the period of its occupancy, it was sufficient to say that the United States [would] not consent to take these obligations unlimited. If the general article on this subject [could not] be answered, the American Commissioners [were] constrained to reject the article, and leave the treaty silent on the subject.

Montero Ríos asked if the article referred not only to Spaniards now in the islands, but to those who may go there. Judge Day replied that the article very clearly applied to those now there. Those who chose to remove there later naturally come under the general laws of the country to which they removed. Montero Ríos said he could not agree to the conclusion that Spaniards who came later should be covered by laws applicable to laws in general. The article extended no special privileges to Spain. If there were no such article in the treaty, Spaniards would have all that this article gave. It has therefore no *raison d'être*. In treaties of peace it had been the custom to embody provisions as to the status either of inhabitants belonging to the country, which made a cession of territory, or of those who may come in from that country.

Judge Day replied: "This article intends to fix the status of people now there—to protect and preserve all their just rights. Beyond that, the United States must reserve its control." Gray here interjected: "Providing that they shall not be discriminated against. This part of the article is in fact taken exactly from the draft of the Spanish Commissioners."

Montero Ríos did not see any privilege whatever granted to Spanish subjects in allowing them at the end of a year to elect to retain their Spanish nationality. It was just the opposite of a privilege; in fact, it was a right. No statute could take from a man his right to belong to any government he pleased. This draft was silent on rules that have heretofore been made to all treaties.

Judge Day replied that all clauses here as to Spaniards were intended to give them special security. The clauses as to the United States dealing with the status through Congress were limited to *new* inhabitants. It would be an extraordinary anomaly to have all these inhabitants Spanish. The privilege is given to Spaniards to choose their allegiance. Passing to another phase of the subject, he thought it as well to say that if the Spanish Commissioners intended to object to the general clause limiting responsibility as to Cuba further discussion was unnecessary, since the United States must insist on that limitation.

Montero Ríos seemed surprised a little by this last remark. He said the first intimation they had had of this article was gathered today in listening to the hurried translation of it at the table. As to the remark just made concerning the limitation of responsibility with reference to Cuba, he would like to give it more careful consideration. He would like copies of the article, and would like to give a categorical answer on behalf of the Spanish Commission during the first hour tomorrow. Judge Day said he would be entirely contented with the understanding that the answer on this article and on the general limitation should be given tomorrow. This particular subject was not treated of in any other article. Montero Ríos said time would be gained if the American Commissioners could give copies of all the other articles tonight, so that they could be prepared for discussion. Judge Day suggested perhaps preparation for discussion would not be so desirable as preparation for an answer.

Montero Ríos inquired if this was the only Spanish article modified, and Judge Day said: "No, there are others." Montero Ríos again said it would be wise and a gain of time, if the Spaniards could have them all. Judge Day, addressing the translator, said: "Give them another now." [He] handed up the one as to pending suits, while Senator Davis remarked: "The reading of this paper is its formal presentation on behalf of the American Commissioners, and becomes a part of the protocol." Montero Ríos at once said, "And the same rule holds as to ours." To which Judge Day responded: "Certainly."

Montero Ríos wanted to know what differences there were in the article, and whether the articles not modified were to be accepted. Judge Day replied: "That will appear as we develop the articles." Montero Ríos wanted to know if the draft covered them, or if [we only had] to consider them. Day responded: "Excepting as to some which we reject, and on which we are willing to have the treaty silent." At this point Day and others called for the translation of the article thus submitted. Montero Ríos waived a translation, and said it could be entered on the minutes as presented.

It seemed to me at this moment that it might be a mistake to file all the other articles at once, and thus play our whole hand before the Spaniards had given any answer whatever. Without in the least insisting on it, I whispered an inquiry on this point to Judge Day; but he was clear in the belief that it was better to "play the whole hand at once" and get the Spanish answer once for all tomorrow.

The article on patents and submission to the jurisdiction of courts was then accepted as proposed by Spain. Their article on consuls was

accepted. Their article on deposits and bonds rejected. Their article on
public contracts read and rejected and another on grants and contracts
also rejected. Day remarked, at this point, that these were not rejected
because the government of the United States proposed to repudiate any
contract properly binding on the United States by international law. It
was a fact, however, that the treaties of the United States had been uniformly silent on this subject, whether with Russia, with Mexico, or
with France, and the American Commissioners proposed here to follow
the same rule.

Judge Day next called for the article on the practice of retention. The
Spanish article was read and the American one formally submitted. The
article on the *Maine* was then rejected. Judge Day remarked that it was
not the purpose of the United States or of the Commissioners to reopen
that subject; they regarded it as closed.

Montero Ríos, with obviously suppressed passion and flashing eyes,
here burst out that if the subject had been closed by the government, the
President of the United States would not have revived it in his [annual]
message just delivered to Congress. To this Judge Day responded: "We
have not had an opportunity to read that message, and at any rate we
have no observations to make." Montero Ríos retorted with heat: "We
have read it and copied it. I have a copy of this passage in my pocket,
and would be glad to offer it now." Judge Day replied: "We do not care
to open a discussion on that subject."

The Spanish article for pensions to the Duke of Veragua was then
read and rejected.

Judge Day then remarked: "We have now indicated the action of the
American Commissioners on all the articles proposed by the Spanish
Commissioners. We have either accepted, modified or rejected every
one." Montero Ríos said: "We will take them under consideration."

Judge Day said this left still the American articles, and Montero Ríos
retorted, still evidently in a temper: "We will pursue the same course as
to these, you have taken as to ours." Judge Day said: "Shall we adjourn till tomorrow?" Montero Ríos replied: "There is no objection; we
may need more time. The American Commissioners have had these for
some time." Judge Day said: "We have no desire to dictate as to time,"
and Montero Ríos replied: "We will come tomorrow if possible," Abarzuza adding, "With the usual reservation."

The American Commissioners left the room rather hastily as the
Spaniards gathered together in an apparently excited group on their
side of the table. Almost for the first [time], I think, some of our people

forgot to take leave of them at all. When I returned for that purpose, after a moment's talk in the outer room, they seemed to be engaged in such an earnest conversation that I preferred simply to make a general bow to them and take my leave. They were ceremoniously polite in returning it, as usual, but certainly not cordial.

As soon as we began to compare notes, we found we all had the same impression, that after the bullying to which they had subjected us on the previous day, they were stunned and almost dazed at finally realizing how composedly we had taken their conduct, and how calmly we had modified or rejected their articles. They had apparently convinced themselves that they were making headway with us, and that we were likely to accept their dictation and then proceed to accept their articles in the hope that afterwards they might accept some of ours. I was myself absolutely convinced that for days they had had no such intention. [I thought] that in fact we lost every opportunity of getting anything from them in the way of revival of treaties, cable facilities, the purchase of Kusaie or otherwise, when we freely gave them the concessions about the return of their prisoners, artillery, etc., without making these concessions provisional. Nonetheless, they had certainly expected to lure us on into assenting to some, at least, of their more objectionable articles, and particularly those about contracts, deposits, and the Church.

Day and others commented on the fairly savage look, which had come into Montero Ríos' face as he realized how all these hopes were being shattered. Even Ferguson, the translator, thought "the old man was madder this time than ever before, and wickeder."

Wednesday, Dec. 7th, 1898.

Senator Frye had thought the morning after our last blow at the Spaniards would be a good time to hear Gen. [Charles A.] Whittier, and so caused him to be called for this morning. All the Commissioners excepting Senator Gray were on hand promptly, and the examination was begun. Senator Davis, however, soon excused himself, and retired, on the ground of business, to his room, and Senator Gray presently came in.

Whittier began with a brief statement of his services in the army, assignment to Manila, and action there, and then proceeded to read a paper, which he had prepared with some care, and which he interspersed with numerous explanations and additions. It proved to be, on the whole, as interesting a piece of testimony as any we have had from the Philippines, and perhaps more favorable both to the character of the people and [to] the commercial and industrial possibilities of the Islands. He gave some account of talks with Aguinaldo, and was pretty confident that with tact there would be no great difficulty in managing him. He was extremely reassuring as to the ease with which good soldiers could be made out of the natives, provided they were led by white officers. [But he was sure] that it would be a mistake to have any of the natives hold any rank higher than that of a non-commissioned officer for the present.

He produced a large number of photographs of people and places in and about Manila (including an admirable photograph, with autograph attached, of Aguinaldo) and concluded his statement with the introduction of four wooden carvings made by a native of Manila, who had been imprisoned for a year or two by the Spaniards. These purported to give faithful representations of the nature of the torture inflicted in four different typical cases. The name of each of the victims tortured was given, with the particulars of the crime with which he was charged, the nature of his preliminary punishments and final execution. Nothing more horrible has been seen outside the records of the Inquisition, and the worst atrocities of our own North American Indians. One of these cases was that of a reputable and industrious native of Manila, who was suspected of being a freemason, and tortured in order to make him confess. His punishment, after severe flogging on the naked back, consisted in having the nose pierced, a cord run through the central cartilage and tied to a spike on a post above his head. Unless he stood on tip-toe, the body was partly supported by the string in the nose. Another torture was applied to a man, placed half-naked in the stocks, where after the soles of his feet had been beaten, he was kept with a rough, wooden instrument rubbed up and down the naked spine. A number of other tortures, which the General declared were equally well authenticated, were of too revolting a character to bear description. All of these had been [carried on] during the year 1897.

The effect of the testimony upon the Commission was marked, though different in some cases. Senator Gray seemed much more reconciled to our not having given the Philippines back to Spain. Senator Frye was greatly encouraged as to their commercial value and the ease with which they could be defended. Judge Day was almost convinced that with good management, they might be made valuable, and that after all it was not so bad that he had failed in the effort to get them divided.

About the time the examination was over, we received word from the secretary of the Spanish Commission, which had not been altogether unexpected. They found it would be impossible for them to be ready to meet us today, and asked to have the meeting postponed till tomorrow. . . .

Thursday, December 8th, 1898.

. . . The Spaniards were rather more stately than usual at the afternoon meeting.

As soon as the reading of the protocols began, and the first article came up, Judge Day proposed to save time by skipping the reading of the articles. Montero Ríos after a moment's hesitation said he should be contented, provided the secretaries had verified the text. Moore explained that he had the originals there, but had not compared the copies here transcribed in the protocol. It was finally agreed that the protocol should be approved subject to a careful comparison, to be subsequently made by the secretaries. Thereupon the further reading was abandoned.

Abarzuza then suggested the desirability of something in the article about Cuba to the effect that the United States would endeavor to secure from the government that succeeded it an assumption of the same obligations it was now itself assuming. Day suggested an entire willingness that if the secretaries could agree on a phrase to that effect it should be added.

Gen. Cerero next came forward with a suggestion. He thought that the treatment of the *Maine* had been entirely *ex parte*, and that under the circumstances Spain ought to be heard on that subject. Judge Day's only response was to call for the reading of the passage relating to the *Maine* in the last protocol. He then asked if an agreement might not be had at once on the general clause relating to Cuba. The Spaniards seemed disposed to accept it, but it then appeared that our clause as proposed was in rather clumsy shape. Moore has been overworked. Some suggestion of mine seeming to meet the approval of the other Commissioners and of Moore himself, I finally wrote it out. Moore carried it over to the Spaniards, who at once accepted it, erasing, however, the words "so far as they remain unexecuted." They considered these words as surplusage, and I thought so too.

Gen. Cerero again asked if it were possible that the question of the *Maine* could be left as it is. If the American Commissioners would not accept the Spanish proposal on that subject would they not recommend something else instead. Judge Day replied very quietly that on that subject the American Commissioners had nothing to recommend.

Montero Ríos then for the first time today came forward with the remark that they must then use their privilege to file a memorandum. Judge Day immediately added this under the rule about filing articles giving the reasons in favor of rejected proposals. Montero Ríos then presented a paper of several pages and the translator read it over slowly in Spanish. This was obviously the critical moment when Judge Day's fears were to be confirmed or dissipated. While their translator was studying the paper, the American Commissioners preserved countenances almost as immobile as those of North American Indians. The Spaniards were equally grave and somewhat subdued. The paper when translated proved to be an earnest protest, as vigorous as the forms of diplomacy would permit, against the rejection of various articles, particularly those relating to the *Maine*, contracts, etc.

At the close of the reading, Judge Day said he would like to understand more precisely just what the Spanish Commissioners had done with reference to the American modifications of all substitutes for the articles they had presented. The translator read the passage over again and Montero Ríos then explained that the Spanish Commissioners agreed to conform more closely to the facts they submitted to the American action. They accepted therefore the substitutes, modifications, etc., made by the American Commissioners at the last session. Judge Day responded that after this paper had been carefully translated it would be attentively considered, and the American Commissioners would reserve the right to file a reply to which Montero [Ríos] assented.

Judge Day then said, addressing the translator: "Will you now call attention to the American articles long since filed, which have not yet been disposed of."

Montero Ríos at once said he had no objection to stating the Spanish decision on them. Judge Day thereupon asked that they be taken up in their order, and called for article 10 relating to Kusaie and to telegraph landings in the Canaries and on the peninsula.

When it had been read, Montero Ríos at once said that the Spaniards still insisted on the fact that an article of this nature was entirely extraneous to a treaty of peace. Even if they had been willing to entertain such a proposal, it was prohibited by the constitution of Spain, since they could not alienate property without the consent of the Cortes. As to cable landings, even if they were willing to assent to what was here asked they would still be prohibited under the law since it would be the equivalent to a conveyance of land without authority. Furthermore, even if they were allowed, they were not disposed to grant such privileges. The Spanish Commissioners were therefore unable to accept the article.

The next article read was that relating to the revival of the agreement in diplomatic correspondence in 1886 as to religious liberty in the Carolines. Montero Ríos immediately followed the reading with the remark that the Spanish Government had heard no claim that there were any troubles or inconveniences for the Missionaries in the Carolines. All matters of this sort were already regulated by the broad, liberal views of Spanish law, and while these lasted there was no need for such an article. It was declined.

The next article was the one on which Senator Frye's heart had been centered, that equalizing port charges in the two countries. To our amazement Montero Ríos asked for what term this was asked. Frye said he had proposed no limit, but if they preferred to make one, he thought the same term agreed upon as to the "open door" in the Philippines, ten years, would be proper. To everybody's amazement Montero Ríos said: "Very well, our only objection would be as to the form. We should prefer that Spain and the United States should make a reciprocal agreement, and we would accept it for ten years, with the proviso that either side could withdraw from the agreement on six months' notice. We could not, however, accept an agreement as to a commercial convention. We do not [control] the obligations of our government in that regard; but if free to enter upon such a convention, it could do so at any time without the need of any article here."

We were all so delighted and surprised at this acceptance that we were only too glad to delay while the article was immediately reconstructed in the sense to which Montero [Ríos] had agreed, and then accepted [it].

Next, the article proposing the revival of treaties was read, and Montero Ríos said they would be unable to accept that. There were many provisions in several of the treaties, some, in fact, in nearly all of them, which were either entirely obsolete, or which depended upon conditions no longer existing. The treaties therefore required a more thorough examination than this Commission could now give. Some of them undoubtedly ought to be revived, and the two governments [could], at their convenience, come together on this subject. For the purpose of this treaty, however, the article must be declined. Senator Gray inquired if this remark applied even to the extradition treaty, which had been recently revised. Montero Ríos said: "It applies to that also, for the reasons which I had not intended to express. Since you raise the question, however, I may say that the treaty is defective on some points of law. For instance, it calls any violent entry into a house a robbery, which is a legal definition Spanish law would not sustain." With this remark the subject was dropped for the moment, and the next article relating to the period within which ratification should be had was agreed to. There then sprang up a little discussion as to the time required for engrossing the treaty, and as to when it should be signed.

Senator Frye made us a little uneasy by suggesting that he would like to recur again to the article that had been accepted concerning port charges, with a view of having it use the exact language of the United States statutes, when it referred to the United States coast-wise trade. Montero Ríos objected, though he was willing to have the two secretaries consider it.

I then asked the attention of the Spanish Commissioners to the unfortunate situation in which the two countries were left by their refusal to revive the extradition treaty. I was perfectly sure they could not intend or desire that either country should become a secret and favorable resort for criminals from the other. It would certainly be in the common interest not to permit such provisions for the return of criminals to lapse, merely because a treaty with which the two governments had appeared to be entirely contented, up to the outbreak of the last war, was now thought to be less accurate than could be wished in one or two of its legal definitions. I therefore asked if, in view of this public necessity for an international police arrangement, they could not agree in the interest of both countries, to the revival of the extradition treaty, to serve until it could be replaced by something better.

Montero Ríos replied that he did not think the difficulty would be great. The two countries were so remote from each other that the chances of criminals from one reaching the other would be limited. To this I replied that the distance of the countries from each other and the infrequency of communication, would be the precise reasons which would recommend each country to the criminals of the other, and added that it was sure to result in their becoming the favorite haunts for such criminals. Montero Ríos insisted, however, that the difficulty would not be great, that extraditions had not been frequent in the past, and that if there were clear cases of criminals being wanted, Spain would be willing to give them up without a treaty.

I continued to urge the point, insisting that it was a step backward to go without an extradition treaty which was really in the interest of both nations, and offered no special advantages to either. Bad as the present treaty might be, in their opinion, it must be better than none. I therefore asked whether in view of their unwillingness to have it revived, they would not consent to accept it merely as a *modus vivendi* for a year, or even for six months, so that time might be given for the negotiation of another without offering safe resorts in the meanwhile to criminals.

At the same time I called attention to the copyright and trademark arrangements, and asked if they might not be revived in the same manner, merely as a *modus vivendi* proposition, for a year or six months. Montero Ríos was evidently staggered by the *modus vivendi* proposition, and it seemed as if his colleagues wanted to assent to it. He asked some questions about the existing copyright arrangements, but finally fell back on the suggestion that anybody could take out a copyright in Spain by simply registering, and that no international agreement was necessary. He therefore adhered to his rejection of the article.

With this the Joint Commission adjourned to give time for the engrossing of the treaty. The majority of the Spanish Commissioners seemed well pleased to have the thing over, and were quite cordial. Old Montero [Ríos], however, was obviously dissatisfied with the position into which he had got himself by rejecting even a *modus vivendi* on such things as extradition and copyright, and was rather more stately than usual when I took leave of him.[6]

Emerging from the Salle de Conference, we found an unusual number of French, English and American reporters. The Frenchmen, as usual, made a descent on me, and I thought it best to say frankly that we had finally agreed on all the articles that were to go into a definite treaty of peace, and that nothing remained [except] to engross them and sign the document. They seemed much surprised, and were full of questions as to whether there had been much discussion, how many articles there were, whether anything had been done with the Carolines, whether there were any expressions of gratification or the reverse, etc., etc. I escaped as soon as possible, having said as little as possible beyond the pure facts above mentioned. . . .[7]

[6] Montero Ríos had a characteristic view of the final treaty:

The treaty is the pure expression of the immoderate demands of a conquerer, who, in order to appear great in history, ought to have made moderate use of its victory. The Spanish Commission succeeded in saving the name of its country and its dignity, although it was impossible to save its interests, irremissibly compromised. (Montero Ríos to the Duke de Almodovar del Rio, December 11, 1898, *Spanish Diplomatic Correspondence*, p. 364.)

[7] Judge Day spoke best for the American Commissioners when he surveyed the

Friday, December 9th, 1898.

The first man to arrive in my room this morning was Senator Davis, who said he came down early that he and I might express congratulations alone. We were the two in whom there had been no variableness or shade of turning, and we at least had a right to regard the triumph as entirely unmixed. When the others had gathered, the work of revising the protocol for yesterday was at once undertaken, so that the secretary might get at the task of having it engrossed and added to the rest, all of which had to be signed in duplicate so as to supply the Spaniards as well as ourselves. Various members had slight amendments to suggest on different parts of the procedure, and when the little encounter on the extradition and copyright treaties was reached, I caused it to be sufficiently enlarged to record exact facts. The secretary had been otherwise occupied at the moment and had overlooked the final attempt to induce the Spaniards to assent to the old treaties as a *modus vivendi* for a period of a year or even six months.

When this was finished, Moore was excused, that he might get the copyists at work. I undertook his duty, and read the careful translation of the Spanish paper, which had been filed yesterday. Day and others made notes as we went along, and the reading was frequently interrupted for the purpose of general discussion. Day undertook to reply on some of the more important points and I was assigned to the task of "jollying" the Spaniards a little at the close, as Day expressed it, the idea being to end our final paper with a few conciliatory and complimentary expressions. . . .

As soon as I could get a little leisure after the Commissioners had separated, I concocted, with Blanchard's revision, a note to Castillo asking him and his wife to *un dîner intime.* In the afternoon Day came in

---

finished treaty, and probably reflected the feeling of most Americans at home:

We obtain, when we shall have perfected our title, the Philippines, Puerto Rico and adjacent islands, Guam in the Ladrones, and Cuba in trust—a goodly estate indeed! Like other large properties, it will no doubt bring its responsibilities and burdens, but our country has proven itself equal to everything it has undertaken, and will no doubt be able to cope with this situation. . . . Few events compare in importance with this compact in its effect on our country and its institutions. That it may redound to the glory and credit of our nation, and promote the general approval with which I believe your administration is regarded at home and abroad, is the most sincere wish of all who have represented the United States in the negotiations here. (Day to McKinley, December 12, 1898, McKinley Papers, Library of Congress.)

with his proposed reply. I went through it at his request, with some care, and in one or two places suggested trifling verbal changes, which he promptly accepted. He asked me immediately to append the complimentary expressions I had been asked to arrange. I had done nothing; but, agreeing with him that only a few lines were necessary, wrote them out in pencil at once. I simply said that we could not close this final memorandum without expressing our appreciation of the learning, thoroughness, and devoted ability with which the Spaniards had endeavored to protect what they thought the interest of their country in these negotiations. Day was satisfied with it, and carried it off to be incorporated exactly as written. A fair copy was to be made out immediately and delivered to Villa-Urrutia within half an hour. He was then in our office below working over the arrangement of the Spanish and English text of the protocols with Moore.

Sometime afterwards, however, a hitch appeared. Judge Day came in with an anxious face to say that Senator Gray had intercepted his paper in the office, and had felt the need of modifying the reply we had agreed upon to the Spanish remarks about the *Maine*. Senator Gray's modification seemed to Judge Day to put us in the attitude of apologizing for our reference, or that of the President, [to the *Maine*], and in either view he thought this undesirable. I fully agreed with him, and on examining the passage Senator Gray had proposed, at once said I would not consent to it. It explained rather elaborately that the "Reference to the *Maine* in our former paper had not been made for any purpose of irritation, far from it, but with a view," etc. [It then went] into a rather thin explanation, which seemed to me rather disingenuous as well as apologetic. We therefore decided to call at once a meeting of the Commissioners, and Eddie [the doorkeeper] was sent off to summon them.

Before Senator Gray arrived Davis and Frye had been found and both of them agreed fully with us. When Senator Gray came in, he accepted quite graciously our view of the situation. His purpose had merely been to avoid irritation. He recognized that as he had phrased it we seemed to do a good deal more. Senator Davis had written the reference to the Spanish comment on the President's message. It was merely a dignified statement of the fact that under the well recognized prudence and practice of the United States . . . we could not discuss what the President had said. Judge Day finally proposed that we leave this as the only reference to the *Maine,* and strike out his paragraph altogether, including the insertion in it which Senator Gray had proposed. After some hesitation this was finally accepted. But I then pointed out that Senator Davis's paragraph about the President's message required a distinct reference to the *Maine* and proceeded to put this in. Davis and the rest assented, and the paper was again sent to the copyist.

Fortunately, Villa-Urrutia was again in the office, so that on his return to the Spanish Commission in the afternoon he took the paper back with him. We soon had occasion to learn that the few hastily penciled lines of compliment at the end had proved singularly successful, hitting the mark we had aimed at precisely.

An hour or so before dinner Count Münster called to congratulate us on the close of the negotiations, and to inquire precisely how things had been arranged. There seemed no reason to make a mystery of it with him, and so, making it confidential as between colleagues, I gave him a pretty good idea of the final arrangements. He was very generous in his congratulations. [He] told me frankly in the same confidence that he knew directly from the German Ambassador in Madrid that the Queen Regent and Sagasta had sent instructions today to Montero Ríos to sign the treaty as quickly as possible and get the matter ended. He was very confident that they would sign the moment the treaty was engrossed. [He] repeated to me two or three times that we need have no apprehensions on this score, no matter what tone they took or what people said.

He learned from me during this conversation (for the first time apparently) just what our offer for Kusaie had been. He apparently shared my belief that Spain had not been wise in its failure to embrace the opportunity. I told him that I did not believe they would ever get an offer of a million from us for the island. He was very frank in saying that he hoped his country would never give either that or any other sum even for the whole archipelago. He talked more strongly than ever against German acquisitions in that quarter, saying that with the Marshall Islands they already had all they could possibly have any need for and that such possessions were useless in time of peace, and an increased responsibility and anxiety in time of war. . . .

Saturday, December 10th, 1898.

More or less gossip this morning among the Commission over the possibilities of the day and still a little nervousness. I had not communicated Count Münster's assurance to any one excepting Judge Day, and even to him had not been at liberty to tell how direct it seemed. The secretaries had a mass of the daily protocols engrossed and ready for signature. The Spaniards seemed to think it indispensable that each daily protocol should bear the signatures not only of the secretaries, as is the American custom, but also of each one of the Commissioners on both sides. Accordingly, with some little good-natured grumbling, our Commissioners sat down and signed away vigorously for an hour, each of us putting our signatures on each of the protocols in the order in which our names had been arranged on the letter heads of the Commission.

When we arrived at the Foreign Office in the afternoon it was evident that the treaty could not be signed till late in the afternoon, if then. There had been a panic about parchment at the Spanish Commission, and efforts had been made by the secretaries on both sides to exchange material in some way, so as to facilitate the engrossment. The Spaniards were confessedly behind, not having been able to begin the work, as Villa-Urrutia explained to me, till twelve o'clock, instead of at nine as they had expected. It was at first said that we might possibly be able to sign by half past three or four.

Meantime Grubayedoff, the Russian photographer and artist, who had been reminding me of his having begun his service on the [New York] *Tribune* twenty years ago, had established a powerful camera in the corner of the room, and was desirous of getting a photograph of the Joint Commission seated at the table. A little talk about it showed that the Spaniards were quite willing, and so we all took our seats. There was little light, and the calcium light on which he had expected to depend proved useless. He continued the exposure, however, as long as the members seemed willing to sit still, fully a minute I should think, and announced that the lenses were so powerful, that he was sure he had secured material for a good picture.

Then came the turn of poor Pirou, the photographer apparently recognized by the French Foreign Office. He had been unlucky in pursuing Senators Frye and Davis with too much pertinacity, and they had shown a genuine, American discontent at the prices he had charged for photographs they had previously got [from] him. In fact, Senator Frye, having tried to get rid of him otherwise one evening at his room, resorted to the only French word he could think of, and pointing to the door shouted at him "Sortie!" Frye had related to us with great glee how mad he had made the Frenchman, and how successful he had been in making him understand his meaning.

Poor Pirou now appealed to the Commission to go out into the garden of the Foreign Office (or, as Frye described it afterwards, into

the back yard) and stand for a moment in a group on the steps. He insisted that there was not adequate light in the room, but that he could
make a good picture of the group. Evidently Montero Ríos did not relish
this idea, but professed his willingness to go if the American Commissioners desired it. Senator Davis then objected suddenly, saying that he
did not care to expose himself to the cold for such a purpose. Thus re-
enforced, Montero Ríos absolutely refused, evidently having a feeling
that it was not a very dignified close to negotiations which he had conducted with such acerbity. Pirou couldn't comprehend no for an answer
and hung on arguing against hope. But both sides were firm, and at last
he retired disconsolate.

During this wrangle most of the Commissioners had remained seated
at the table. When at last the disconsolate photographer retired, the protocols were read and approved. I was standing over at the fireplace when
I observed that Montero Ríos, leaning over almost as if what he wanted
to say were confidential, had begun addressing our interpreter in a very
low but earnest tone. In a moment I got the idea that he was making a
little further expression to the Americans. The other Commissioners soon
had their attention attracted and became alert. Day [was] quite apprehensive (as he told me afterwards) that after all the old man might be
springing some trick upon us at the very crisis of the business. In an instant, however, it was evident that his intentions were far more amiable
than usual. He and his associates had been much touched, as Ferguson
[the interpreter] proceeded to translate it, by the concluding words of
the last American memorandum. They appreciated very highly the expressions therein made concerning the Spanish conduct of the negotiations. [They] desired to express to the American Commissioners their
gratitude for this appreciation, their own agreeable recollections of the
personal intercourse during the negotiations, and the value they should
attach throughout their lives to the souvenir of the words with which
the Americans had closed their last paper. Judge Day responded immediately with dignity and sufficient cordiality, reciprocating the expressions of personal good will which the Spaniards had used. [He said
that] the American Commissioners desired to preserve only the most
agreeable personal recollections of each of their associates during all
these long negotiations. A few words in a similar sense followed from
Montero Ríos as he bowed right and left to all of us, and we returned
the bows and smiles. It came nearer genuine cordiality than anything
we had had for months. . . .

Montero Ríos presently announced that recent advices from their

Commission led them to hope that the engrossed copies of the treaty would now be ready for us before five o'clock, so we all left the table and began general conversation.

Abarzuza and I fell into a talk about educational matters in America and Spain. He thought the tendency in Spain as strong as ever to depend on a thorough knowledge of the classics, as the basis of any liberal education, and had noted a revival of this tendency in the United States. He referred to his own experience at an English university, and talked with great good sense about the importance of laying a thorough foundation in the old-fashioned way in the classics and mathematics. Not so much for the sake of the information actually acquired as for the training of the memory, and for the acquisition of what he called educational tools. From this his talk diverged to English and American books, with which he showed considerable familiarity.

He spoke with enthusiasm of [William H.] Prescott, but with a still higher appreciation of [John Lothrop] Motley. [George] Bancroft he supposed to be a great authority, but he did not find him interesting. Of the later American historical writers, he did not seem to have much knowledge. Some talk about the French theatre led him to speak of the play we had lately seen at the Théâtre Français, "Struensee." He pronounced the play dull and the acting exquisite, and then went on to speak with little respect for even the best French dramatic art. Racine, Corneille, and Molière he thought admirable as works of art but never rising above that plane; and never for a moment to be compared with Shakespeare.

This discursive talk with Abarzuza lasted half an hour or more, and Gray, who had observed it, presently drew me aside and suggested that I ought now to tell Abarzuza that the American Commissioners would be glad to have the Spanish Commissioners dine with them, if they should find it convenient or consistent with their other arrangements.

Some idea of this sort had been in my own mind for weeks, but after learning that the Spaniards had discouraged Delcassé's proposal to have a breakfast or dinner for the Joint Commission, I felt sure that they would not accept and was not inclined therefore to give them the opportunity of declining. Gray agreed with me that they would probably not accept, but still thought I ought to get the credit of giving them the invitation. He seemed in fact rather troubled that I hesitated about it. Later in the afternoon he told me that he himself made some such hint to Ojeda, who replied frankly that they had themselves been thinking of something of the same sort, and would have been glad if it had been possible. But he considered it quite impossible on account of the criticisms already leveled at them in Madrid. [In some quarters there] they were accused of professing to defend the interests of their country against its enemies during the day, and spending the night feasting and drinking champagne with these same enemies, "with arms around each other's necks," as some of the Spanish journals had put it. Under these circumstances Ojeda said that it would not do at all, although they appreciated the Senator's courteous intention. Curiously enough, he still persisted in wanting me to make the same invitation to Abarzuza in the name of the Commission. I felt more than ever disinclined after hearing the account of his conversation with Ojeda. To say nothing of the fact that I had received in the morning a warm and cordial letter from Castillo, which nevertheless explained that he and Madame Castillo were "desolés" that they found themselves engaged for both the evenings I had named. It was clear to me that after two such intimations good sense would not dictate inviting a third. Gray was curiously persistent about it, asking me again later in the afternoon, but I made an effort to persuade him that it was better not.

Finally towards six o'clock word came, Montero Ríos announced, that he had received word again from the Spanish Commission that they could not be ready with the treaties before seven. Montero Ríos said he would go over and try to hurry them a little. By this time we were all somewhat wearied, and so it was finally arranged that the American Commissioners having a dinner engagement should go to their hotels, arrange for the delay of the dinner a little, if necessary, and return shortly after seven prepared to sign the treaty and go afterwards directly to their dinner....

... By half past seven [I was] in my carriage again on [my] way to the Foreign Office. Some of the Spaniards were already there, and the others came in a moment or two afterwards, and there was a greater crowd than usual of newspaper men and others haunting the vestibule. As we gathered about the table there was quite a contrast between the American Commissioners, all in correct evening dress, and the Spaniards who remained in their afternoon costumes. It was not till about eight o'clock that the treaties arrived.[8] Around the sides and corners of the room spectators were present for the first time during the long negotiation. The employes of our Commission [had] been given leave, on their request, to witness the signature. Two or three of the people from the Spanish Commission [were] also present.

[8] The treaty's text can be found conveniently in *For. Rels. 1898*, pp. 831–840.

APPENDIXES

I. *The Armistice Protocol of August 12, 1898*

On August 12, 1898, Jules Cambon, French ambassador to the United States, acting for the Spanish government, signed the armistice protocol in Washington that suspended the conflict. Its terms are listed below (From *For. Rels. 1898*, 828–830).

William R. Day, Secretary of State of the United States, and His Excellency Jules Cambon, Ambassador Extraordinary and Plenipotentiary of the Republic of France at Washington, respectively possessing for this purpose full authority from the Government of the United States and the Government of Spain, have concluded and signed the following articles, embodying the terms on which the two Governments have agreed in respect to the matters hereinafter set forth, having in view the establishment of peace between the two countries, that is to say:

Article I

Spain will relinquish all claim of sovereignty over and title to Cuba.

Article II

Spain will cede to the United States the island of Porto Rico and other islands now under Spanish sovereignty in the West Indies, and also an island in the Ladrones to be selected by the United States.

Article III

The United States will occupy and hold the city, bay, and harbor of Manila, pending the conclusion of a treaty of peace which shall determine the control, disposition, and government of the Philippines.

Article IV

Spain will immediately evacuate Cuba, Porto Rico, and other islands now under Spanish sovereignty in the West Indies; and to this end each Government will, within ten days after the signing of this protocol, appoint Commissioners, and the Commissioners so appointed shall, within thirty days after the signing of this protocol, meet at Havana for the purpose of arranging and carrying out the details of the aforesaid evacuation of Cuba and the adjacent Spanish islands; and each Government will, within ten days after the signing of this protocol, also appoint other Commissioners, who shall, within thirty days after the signing of this protocol, meet at San Juan, in Porto Rico, for the purpose of arranging and carrying out the details of the aforesaid evacuation of Porto Rico and other islands now under Spanish sovereignty in the West Indies.

Article V

The United States and Spain will each appoint not more than five Commissioners to treat of peace, and the Commissioners so appointed shall meet at Paris not later than October 1, 1898, and proceed to the negotiation and conclusion of a treaty of peace, which treaty shall be subject to ratification according to the respective constitutional forms of the two countries.

Article VI

Upon the conclusion and signing of this protocol, hostilities between the two countries shall be suspended, and notice to that effect shall be given as soon as possible by each Government to the commanders of its military and naval forces.

Done at Washington in duplicate, in English and in French, by the Undersigned, who have hereunto set their hands and seals, the 12th day of August 1898.

[SEAL]   WILLIAM R. DAY
[SEAL]   JULES CAMBON

II. *President McKinley's Instructions to the Peace Commission, September 16, 1898*

Shortly before the Peace Commission left Washington for Paris, President McKinley gave them formal instructions that outlined the general policies they were to pursue. They forecast most of the major problems that arose at the conference, and anticipated much of the argument that surrounded the question of overseas territorial expansion. The text of the instructions is given below (From *For. Rels. 1898,* pp. 904–908).

EXECUTIVE MANSION,
Washington, September 16, 1898.

By a protocol signed at Washington August 12, 1898, a copy of which is herewith inclosed, it was agreed that the United States and Spain would each appoint not more than five Commissioners to treat of peace, and that the Commissioners so appointed should meet at Paris not later than October 1, 1898, and proceed to the negotiation and conclusion of a treaty of peace, which treaty should be subject to ratification according to the respective constitutional forms of the two countries.

For the purpose of carrying into effect this stipulation, I have appointed you as Commissioners on the part of the United States to meet and confer with Commissioners on the part of Spain.

As an essential preliminary to the agreement to appoint Commissioners to treat of peace, this Government required of that of Spain the unqualified concession of the following precise demands:

(1) The relinquishment of all claim of sovereignty over and title to Cuba.

(2) The cession to the United States of Porto Rico and other islands under Spanish sovereignty in the West Indies.

(3) The cession of an island in the Ladrones, to be selected by the United States.

(4) The immediate evacuation by Spain of Cuba, Porto Rico, and other Spanish islands in the West Indies.

(5) The occupation by the United States of the city, bay, and harbor of Manila pending the conclusion of a treaty of peace which should determine the control, disposition, and government of the Philippines.

These demands were conceded by Spain, and their concession was, as you will perceive, solemnly recorded in the protocol of the 12th of August.

By article 1 of that instrument Spain agreed to "relinquish all claim of sovereignty over and title to Cuba."

By article 2 she agreed to "cede to the United States the island of Porto

Rico and other islands now under Spanish sovereignty in the West Indies, and also an island in the Ladrones, to be selected by the United States."

By article 3 it was declared that the United States would "occupy and hold the city, bay, and harbor of Manila pending the conclusion of a treaty of peace which shall determine the control, disposition, and government of the Philippines."

By article 4 provision was made for the immediate evacuation of Cuba, Porto Rico, and other Spanish islands in the West Indies, as follows:

Spain will immediately evacuate Cuba, Porto Rico, and other islands now under Spanish sovereignty in the West Indies; and to this end each Government will, within ten days after the signing of this protocol, appoint Commissioners, and the Commissioners so appointed shall, within thirty days after the signing of this protocol, meet at Habana for the purpose of arranging and carrying out the details of the aforesaid evacuation of Cuba and the adjacent Spanish islands; and each Government will, within ten days after the signing of this protocol, also appoint other Commissioners, who shall, within thirty days after the signing of this protocol, meet at San Juan, in Porto Rico, for the purpose of arranging and carrying out the details of the aforesaid evacuation of Porto Rico and other islands now under Spanish sovereignty in the West Indies.

The commissioners referred to in the foregoing article have been appointed, and they are now in session at Habana and San Juan, respectively. A copy of their instructions is herewith inclosed.

By these instructions you will observe that the evacuation of Cuba, Porto Rico, and other Spanish Islands in the West Indies is treated as a military operation, and will, when carried into effect, leave the evacuated places in the military occupation of the United States. The purposes of the United States during such occupation are set forth in General Order No. 101 of the War Department of July 18, 1898, which was issued by direction of the President on the capitulation of the Spanish forces at Santiago de Cuba and in the eastern part of the Province of Santiago and the occupation of the territory by the forces of the United States. A copy of this order is hereto annexed for your information.

As the evacuation of Cuba and the other Spanish islands in the West Indies by the Spanish military forces devolves upon the United States the duty of taking possession of and holding and preserving all the immovable property therein previously belonging to the Government of Spain, the evacuation commissioners of the United States are instructed to arrange for the taking into possession and to take into possession for the United States, all public buildings and grounds, forts, fortifications, arsenals, depots, docks, wharves, piers, and other fixed property previously belonging to Spain, and to arrange for the care and safe-keeping of such property under the authority and control of the United States. Small arms and accouterments, batteries of field artillery, supply and baggage wagons, ambulances, and other impedimenta of the Spanish army in Cuba and other Spanish islands in the West Indies are to be removed, if desired, by the representatives of Spain, provided such removal shall be effected within a reasonable time; but the armament of forts, fortifications, and fixed batteries, being in the nature of immovable fixtures, are not to be allowed to be taken, but are, in connection with such forts, fortifications, and batteries, to be taken over into the possession of the United States. The instructions of the evacuation commissioners also contain appropriate clauses in regard to the custody and preservation by the United States of state papers, public records, and other papers and documents necessary or convenient for the government of the islands, as well as all judicial and legal documents and other public records necessary or convenient for securing to individuals the titles to property.

It will be proper to confirm these transactions by appropriate clauses in the treaty of peace.

Similar clauses will be inserted in respect to the island ceded to the United States in the Ladrones. This Government has selected the island of Guam, and you are instructed to embody in the treaty of peace a proper stipulation of cession.

A rumor has reached us from various quarters to the effect that the Spanish Peace Commissioners will be instructed to claim compensation for the public property of the Spanish Government in Cuba, as well as in territories agreed to be ceded to the United States. This rumor is not credited, but it is proper to make a few observations upon it. No such claim on the part of the Spanish Government is to be entertained in respect to any territory which Spain either cedes to the United States or as to which she relinquishes her sovereignty and title. The cession of territory or the relinquishment of sovereignty over and title to it is universally understood to carry with it the public property of the Government by which the cession or relinquishment is made. Any claim, therefore, on the part of Spain, such as that above suggested, would be inconsistent with the express agreements embodied in the protocol.

In the correspondence leading up to the signature of that instrument you will observe that this Government waived, for the time being, the requirement of a pecuniary indemnity from Spain. This concession was made in the hope that Spain would thereby be enabled promptly to accept our terms. But if the Spanish Commissioners should, contrary to our just expectations, put forward and insist upon a claim for compensation for public property, you are instructed to put forward as a counterclaim a demand for an indemnity for the cost of the war.

By article 6 of the protocol it was agreed that hostilities between the two countries should be suspended, and that notice to that effect should be given as soon as possible by each Government to the commanders of its military and naval forces. Such notice was given by the Government of the United States immediately after the signature of the protocol, the forms of the necessary orders having previously been prepared. But before notice could reach the commanders of the military and naval forces of the United States in the Philippines they captured and took possession by conquest of the city of Manila and its suburbs, which are therefore held by the United States by conquest as well as by virtue of the protocol.

In view of what has taken place it is necessary now to determine what shall be our future relations to the Philippines. Before giving you specific instructions on this subject it is my desire to present certain general considerations.

It is my wish that throughout the negotiations intrusted to the Commission the purpose and spirit with which the United States accepted the unwelcome necessity of war should be kept constantly in view. We took up arms only in obedience to the dictates of humanity and in the fulfillment of high public and moral obligations. We had no design of aggrandizement and no ambition of conquest. Through the long course of repeated representations which preceded and aimed to avert the struggle, and in the final arbitrament of force, this country was impelled solely by the purpose of relieving grievous wrongs and removing long-existing conditions which disturbed its tranquillity, which shocked the moral sense of mankind, and which could no longer be endured.

It is my earnest wish that the United States in making peace should follow the same high rule of conduct which guided it in facing war. It should be as scrupulous and magnanimous in the concluding settlement as it was just and humane in its original action. The luster and the moral strength attaching to a cause which can be confidently rested upon the considerate judgment of the world should not under any illusion of the hour be dimmed by ulterior designs which might tempt us into excessive demands or into an adventurous departure on untried paths. It is believed that the true glory and the enduring interests of the country will most surely be served if an unselfish duty conscientiously accepted and a signal triumph honorably achieved shall be crowned by such an example of moderation, restraint, and reason in victory as best comports with the traditions and character of our enlightened Republic.

Our aim in the adjustment of peace should be directed to lasting results and to the achievement of the common good under the demands of civilization, rather than to ambitious designs. The terms of the protocol were framed upon this consideration. The abandonment of the Western Hemisphere by Spain was an imperative necessity. In presenting that requirement, we only fulfilled a duty universally acknowledged. It involves no ungenerous reference to our recent foe, but simply a recognition of the plain teachings of history, to say that it was not compatible with the assurance of permanent peace on and near our own territory that the Spanish flag should remain on this side of the sea. This lesson of events and of reason left no alternative as to Cuba, Porto Rico, and the other islands belonging to Spain in this hemisphere.

The Philippines stand upon a different basis. It is none the less true, however, that, without any original thought of complete or even partial acquisition, the presence and success of our arms at Manila imposes upon us obligations which we can not disregard. The march of events rules and overrules human action. Avowing unreservedly the purpose which has animated all our effort, and still solicitous to adhere to it, we can not be unmindful that, without any desire or design on our part, the war has brought us new duties and responsibilities which we must meet and discharge as becomes a great nation on whose growth and career from the beginning the Ruler of Nations has plainly written the high command and pledge of civilizations.

Incidental to our tenure in the Philippines is the commercial opportunity to which American statesmanship can not be indifferent. It is just to use every legitimate means for the enlargement of American trade; but we seek no advantages in the Orient which are not common to all. Asking only the open door for ourselves, we are ready to accord the open door to others. The commercial opportunity which is naturally and inevitably associated with this new opening depends less on large territorial possession than upon an adequate commercial basis and upon broad and equal privileges.

It is believed that in the practical application of these guiding principles the present interests of our country and the proper measure of its duty, its welfare in the future, and the consideration of its exemption from unknown perils will be found in full accord with the just, moral, and humane purpose which was invoked as our justification in accepting the war.

In view of what has been stated, the United States can not accept less than the cession in full right and sovereignty of the island of Luzon. It is desirable, however, that the United States shall acquire the right of entry for vessels and merchandise belonging to citizens of the United States into such ports of the Philippines as are not ceded to the United States upon terms of equal favor with Spanish ships and merchandise, both in relation to port and customs charges and rates of trade and commerce, together with other rights of protection and trade accorded to citizens of one country within the territory of another. You are therefore instructed to demand such concession, agreeing on your part that Spain shall have similar rights as to her subjects and vessels in the ports of any territory in the Philippines ceded to the United States.

We are informed that numerous persons are now held as prisoners by the Spanish Government for political acts performed in Cuba, Porto Rico, or other Spanish islands in the West Indies, as well as in the Philippines. You are instructed to demand the release of these prisoners, so far as their acts have connection with matters involved in the settlement between the United States and Spain.

It will be desirable to insert in any treaty of peace which you may conclude a stipulation for the revival of the provisions of our former treaties with Spain, so far as they may be applicable to present conditions.

I have directed Gen. Wesley Merritt, the late commander at Manila, to report to the Commission at Paris, where he will arrive October 2, with such information as he may possess; and it is understood he will carry with him, for the use of the Commission, the views of Admiral Dewey. To the views of these distinguished officers I invite the most careful consideration of the Commission.

It is desired that your negotiations shall be conducted with all possible expedition, in order that the treaty of peace, if you should succeed in making one, may be submitted to the Senate early in the ensuing session. Should you at any time in the course of your negotiations desire further instructions, you will ask for them without delay.

William McKinley.

III. *Opinions of the Peace Commissioners on the Retention of the Philippines, October 25, 1898*

The divergence of opinion within the Peace Commission on acquiring the Philippines and initiating a policy of overseas expansion symbolized the various views on the subject in the American government and among the people as a whole. The commissioners forwarded their views to Washington three days before the President's final formal instructions demanded cession of all the Philippine Islands. The Commissioners' opinions are given below (From *For. Rels. 1898*, pp. 932–935).

PARIS, October 25, 1898.

Differences of opinion among Commissioners concerning Philippines are set forth in statements transmitted herewith. On these we request early consideration and explicit instructions. Liable now to be confronted with this question in joint commission almost immediately.

Day

(1)

Information gained by Commission in Paris leads to conviction that it would be naval, political, and commercial mistake to divide the archipelago. Nearly all expert testimony taken tends to this effect. As instructions provide for retention at least of Luzon, we do not consider question of remaining in Philippine Islands at all as now properly before use. We therefore ask for extension of instructions.

Spain governed and defended these islands from Manila; and with destruction of her fleet and surrender of her army we became as complete masters of the whole group as she had been, with nothing needed to complete the conquest save to proceed with the ample forces we had at hand to take unopposed possession. The Ladrones and Carolines were also governed from the same capital by the same governor-general.

National boundaries ought to follow natural divisions, but there is no natural place for dividing the Philippines.

There is hardly a single island in the group from which you cannot shoot across to one or more of the others. Scarcely another archipelago in the world in which the islands are crowded so closely together and so interdependent. Military and naval witnesses agree that it would be practically as easy to hold and defend the whole as a part. Some say easier; all say safer. Agree, too, that ample and trustworthy military force could be raised among natives, needing only United States officers and a small nucleus of United States troops; also that islands could be relieved from oppressive Spanish taxation and yet furnish sufficient revenue for the whole cost of administration and defense.

Great danger must result from division. Other islands, seeing benefits from our government of Luzon, are sure to revolt, and to be aided and encouraged by natives of Luzon, thus repeating, in more aggravated form, our troubles with Spain about Cuba. Visayas already in revolt. Division would thus insure lawlessness and turbulence within gunshot of our shores, with no prospect of relief unless in Spanish sale of islands to unfriendly commercial rivals, which would probably happen if we hold the most important—Luzon—and release the others.

Generally expected now that this would be attempted the moment we released them. If such sale or transfer is to be made at all, would be less dangerous to our interests if done by us rather than by Spain. If we do not want the islands ourselves, better to control their disposition—i.e., to hold the option on them rather than to abandon it. Could then at least try to protect ourselves by ample treaty stipulations with the acquiring powers.

Commercially, division of archipelago would not only needlessly establish dangerous rivals at our door, but would impair value of part we kept. Present prosperity of Manila depends on its being natural center of import and export trade for the whole group. Large part of its business derived from Iloilo, Cebu, and other points in south. To yield these to unfriendly rivals would be to provide beforehand for diversion of business from our own possessions.

Moral obligations not to return Manila and Luzon to the oppressive power from which we have relieved them applies also to the rest of the archipelago, since Spanish power there is now broken and can not be restored without our consent. We believe public opinion in Europe, including that of Rome, expects us to retain whole of the Philippines, and would prefer that to any other solution save the impossible one of restoration of Spanish power over all the islands.

If a division should be insisted on, the only one that seems to us admissible would be by a line from the Straits of San Bernardino, south of Masbate and north of Panay, to the northeast corner of Borneo, leaving to the United States all to the westward, including Luzon, Mindoro, and Palawan. This would control the China Sea, and give excellent ports of call along the whole line from Borneo to Hongkong. But it would throw away the Visayas, including the best sugar, hemp, and tobacco islands. These contribute a large part of Manila's trade, and are inhabited generally by a people nearly as easy to manage as those of Luzon.

We are convinced that much injustice has been done inhabitants in published accounts of their character. Even the Mohammedans of Mindanao and the Sulu Archipelago, if left enjoyment of religious liberty and given freedom from oppressive taxation, would be found less intractable, in opinion of the experts, than under the rule of Spain; while the others would be comparatively easy to control, and glad to welcome strong and just rule of United States.

(Signed)   Cushman K. Davis
William P. Frye
Whitelaw Reid

(2)

I am unable to agree that we should peremptorily demand the entire Philippine group. In the spirit of our instructions, and bearing in mind the often declared disinterestedness of purpose and freedom from designs of conquest with which the war was undertaken, we should be consistent in our demands in making peace. Territory permanently held must be taken as war indemnity, and with due regard to our responsibility because of the conduct of our military and naval authorities in dealing with the insurgents. Whether this conduct was wise or unwise is not now important. We can not leave the insurgents to mere treaty stipulations or to their unaided resources, either to form a government or to battle against a foe which, unequal to us, might readily overcome them. On all hands it is agreed that the inhabitants of the islands are unfit for self-government. This is particularly true of Mindanao and the Sulu group.

Only experience can determine the success of colonial expansion upon which the United States is entering. It may prove expensive in proportion to the scale upon which it is tried with ignorant and semi-barbarous people at the other side of the world. It should, therefore, be kept within bounds. Accepting Luzon, strategic advantage, as shown by high naval authority, may require cession of that part of the group lying north and west of a line drawn through San Bernardino Strait, south of Luzon to San Bernardino Islet, and thence by the Naranjos Islands and certain courses and distances to Tambisan Island, to the northeast coast of Borneo, conveying to the United States Luzon, Mindoro, Palawan, and various other islands, thus controlling the entrance to China Sea, with additional harbors and ports of call.

The objection that other islands will be acquired by European powers without regard to our interests can be obviated by treaty stipulation for nonalienation without the consent of the United States. There should also be stipulations for absolute freedom of trade and intercourse among all the islands of the group. This gives us practical control of the situation, with a base for the navy and commerce in the East, and responsibility for the people to whom we owe obligation and those most likely to become fit for self-government. It affords an opportunity for lessening the burden of colonial government, with room for further expansion if desired. It does not leave us open to the imputation of following agreement to negotiate with demand for whole subject-matter of discussion ourselves.

(Signed)   William R. Day

(3)

The undersigned cannot agree that it is wise to take Philippines in whole or in part. To do so would be to reverse accepted continental policy of country declared and acted upon throughout our history. Propinquity governs case of Cuba and Puerto Rico. Policy proposed introduces us into European politics and the entangling alliances against which Washington and all American statesmen have protested. It will make necessary a navy equal to largest of powers, a greatly increased military establishment, [and] immense sums for fortifications and harbors, multiply occasions for dangerous complications with foreign nations, and increase burdens of taxation. Will receive in compensation no outlet for American labor in labor market already overcrowded and cheap, no area for homes for American citizens—climate and social conditions demoralizing to character of American youth. New and disturbing questions introduced into our politics, church question menacing. On whole, instead of indemnity—injury. Undersigned can not agree that any obligation incurred to insurgents is paramount to our manifest interests. Attacked Manila as part of legitimate war against Spain. If we had captured Cadiz and Carlists had helped us, would not owe duty to stay by them at conclusion of war. On contrary, interest and duty would require us to abandon both Manila and Cadiz. No place for colonial administration or government of subject people in American system.

So much from standpoint of interest. But even conceding all benefits claimed for annexation, we thereby abandon the infinitely greater benefit to accrue from acting the part of a great, powerful, and Christian nation; we exchange the moral grandeur and strength to be gained by keeping our word to nations of the world and by exhibiting a magnanimity and moderation in hour of victory that becomes the advanced civilization we claim, for doubtful material advantages and shameful stepping down from high moral position boastfully assumed. We should set example in these respects, not follow in the selfish and vulgar greed for territory which Europe has inherited from mediaeval times. Our declaration of war upon Spain was accompanied by a solemn and deliberate definition of our purpose. Now that we have achieved all and more than our object, let us simply keep our word. Third article of protocol leaves everything concerning control of Philippines to negotiation between the parties. Absurd now to say that we will not negotiate, but will appropriate whole subject-matter of negotiation. At the very least, let us adhere to President's instructions, and if conditions require the keeping of Luzon forego the material advantages claimed in annexing other islands—above all, let us not make a mockery of the injunction contained in those instructions, where, after stating that "we took up arms only in obedience to the dictates of humanity and in the fulfillment of high public and moral obligations," and that "we had no design of aggrandizement and no ambition of conquest," the President, among other things, eloquently says: "It is my earnest wish that the United States in making peace should follow the same high rule of conduct which guided it in facing war. It should be as scrupulous and magnanimous in the concluding settlement as it was just and humane in its original action." This and more, of which I earnestly ask a reperusal, binds my conscience and governs my action.

(Signed)   George Gray

IV. *Biographical Glossary*

The following glossary identifies the various characters mentioned in the text. In most cases identification has been established, but in some cases it has been impossible, and the names of unidentifiable persons are not listed here. Such individuals are almost always casual acquaintances, dinner guests, and minor correspondents, whose omission does not affect the main story. In many cases minor characters have been sufficiently identified in the text, and these names are not included here either.

Abarzuza y Ferrer, Don Buenaventura de: Member of the Spanish Peace Commission; a former crown minister, noted Spanish politician, and in 1898 a senator of Spain.

Adee, Alvey A (1842–1924): Holder of a legendary career in Washington in the diplomatic bureau of the State Department and as Assistant Secretary. He held his post for nearly fifty years, and was famous for his knowledge of protocol, procedure, and phraseology in state papers.

Agoncilio, Felipé: Filipino statesman. In 1898 he was a delegate representing Aguinaldo, and attempted unsuccessfully both in the United States and in Paris to achieve American recognition of the Filipino rebels.

Aguinaldo, Emilio (1869–1964): Filipino statesman and leader of the insurrection against Spain in the Islands after 1896, and against the United States between 1899 and his capture in 1901.

Alger, Russell (1836–1907): Secretary of War, 1897–1899; the center of a controversy during and after the Spanish-American War relative to the competence of his department; later a senator from Michigan, 1902–1907.

Bates, General John Colter (1842–1919): A prominent military figure in the Cuban campaigns, especially at the battle of El Caney. He later fought in the Philippines after giving testimony to the Peace Commission. For a time he was chief of staff, and he retired in 1906 after promotion to lieutenant general.

Bennett, James Gordon (1841–1918): American newsman and publisher. He was for many years chief of the New York *Herald*, which he ran from Paris, where he lived in self-imposed and happy exile.

Bigelow, John (1817–1911): Prominent as a minor diplomat, newsman, and essayist; an old friend of Reid's in 1898.

Blaine, James G. (1830–1893): American politician and diplomat; Secretary of State, 1881, 1889–1892; defeated Republican candidate for President, 1884. He tried to foster closer relations within the Western Hemisphere, and was chiefly responsible for the first so-called Pan-American Congress of 1889–1890.

Blowitz, Henri Georges Stephane Adolph Opper de: At the time of the Paris Peace Conference he was the Paris correspondent for the London *Times*.

Bradford, Commander Royal B.: Chief of the Bureau of Equipment, U.S.N.

Brisson, Eugéne (1835–1912): French politician of the *fin de siècle* period; premier of France, June–October, 1898.

Cambon, Jules (1845–1935): French diplomat and civil administrator; ambassador to the United States in 1898, when he acted for the Spanish in ending the war; later a ranking official in the Foreign Office, a signer of the Treaty of Versailles in 1919, and a member of the Academy.

Cameron, J. Donald (1833–1918): The son of Simon Cameron, Lincoln's first Secretary of War and long a dominant Republican in Pennsylvania politics; an international traveller; the younger Cameron was also a senator from Pennsylvania; he married the niece of John Sherman in 1878.

Carlisle, John G. (1835–1910): Prominent Kentucky Democrat; Speaker of the House of Representatives, 1883–1889; senator from Kentucky, 1890–1893; Secretary of the Treasury, 1893–1897; a strong supporter of the gold standard and of Grover Cleveland.

Carnot, Sadi: (1837–1894): Prominent French politician; President of the Republic, 1887–1894; assassinated by an anarchist in 1894.

Cerero y Sáenz, Don Rafael (1834–1906): Member of the Spanish Peace Commission; a regular-army general who had seen service in the Philippines.

Chandler, William E. (1835–1917): Prominent first in national politics as a Radical Republican from New Hampshire after the Civil War; Secretary of the Navy, 1882–1885; an ardent expansionist and free silverite; a senator from New Hampshire, 1887–1901; subsequently appointed by McKinley as president of the Spanish Treaty Claims Commission.

Chapelle, Archbishop Placide Louis (1842–1905): American Roman Catholic administrator, first prominent in the diocese of Santa Fe, then as archbishop of New Orleans; appointed apostolic delegate to Cuba, Puerto Rico, and the Philippines in 1898; spokesman for the Church before the Peace Commission.

Clarke, Lieutenant-General, Sir Andrew: British colonial administrator at the time of the peace conference; his views on rule of dependencies were used by the American Commission.

Clarke, Sir Campbell: The correspondent for the *Daily Telegraph* in Paris after 1872; widely travelled in the Near East and Orient.

Clunet, Edouard (1845–1922): A contemporary French authority on international law, whose books and opinions the American commission used.

Colwell, Lieutenant Commander John C.: United States naval attaché in London in 1898, who furnished information to the Commission.

Coquelin, Benoît-Constant (1841–1909): French actor, who performed with his brother Ernest in Paris during the season of 1898.

Corbin, Henry C. (1842–1909): Widely known and respected professional soldier in the U.S. Army; at this time he filled the post of Adjutant General, which he held for many years.

Creelman, James (1859–1915): A war correspondent for the New York *Journal*; his antics in Cuba prior to the war had caused a sensation.

Davis, Cushman Kellogg (1838–1900): Minnesota Republican politician; governor of Minnesota, 1873–1875, while active with the Granger movement; a senator from Minnesota, 1887–1900. An early expansionist and nationalist, he supported the war with Spain and the annexation of foreign territory; while a member of the Peace Commission in 1898 he was also chairman of the Senate Committee on Foreign Relations, and was very influential in securing the acceptance of the treaty in 1899.

Day, William Rufus (1849–1923): A close friend of William McKinley's, though not active in Ohio politics as an officeholder; assistant Secretary of State, 1897–1898; Secretary of State, 1898; president of the Paris Peace Commission, 1898; U.S. circuit judge, 1899–1903; associate justice of the U.S. Supreme Court, 1903–1922.

Delcassé, Théophile (1852–1923): French diplomat, foreign minister in 1898.

Denby, Charles (1830–1904): Scion of a prominent Indiana family; minister to China, 1885–1898; a member of the Dodge Commission, which investigated the War Department in 1898; a member of the Philippine Commission, 1898–1901.

Dewey, Admiral George (1837–1917): The chief hero of the Spanish-American War; victor of the Battle of Manila Bay, for whom the rank of admiral was revived for his lifetime only; a possible contender for the Presidency in 1900.

Draper, William F. (1842–1910): United States ambassador to Italy, 1897–1898.

Faure, Félix (1841–1899): President of France, 1895–1899.

Field, David Dudley (1805–1894): Famous authority on international law, whose works were consulted by the American commission.

Foreman, John: Author of a book on the Philippines, whose testimony was also taken by the American Commission.

Frye, William P. (1831–1911): Pursued a long and distinguished career in Maine politics as a Republican; member of the House of Representatives, 1871–1881; United States senator, 1881–1911; an expansionist and strict Republican, whose long tenure gave him considerable power within and without his party.

Fuller, Miss Loie (1862–1928): An interpreter of the dance, who was in Paris during 1898. She was later famous during World War I for her charity and Red Cross work.

Gage, Lyman (1836–1927): Secretary of the Treasury, 1897–1902.

Garfield, James Abram (1831–1881): President of the United States, 1881; assassinated the same year; and early and close friend of Reid's.

Gilman, Daniel Coit (1831–1908): American educator who also pursued a minor diplomatic career as a young man; famous chiefly as president and developer of Johns Hopkins University and as president of the Carnegie Institution.

Gray, George (1840–1925): Member of a prominent Delaware family active in Democratic politics; a United States senator, 1885–1899; a strong supporter of Grover Cleveland, and hardy opponent of both the Spanish-American War and, as a member of the Paris Peace Commission, of territorial expansion. McKinley appointed him a U.S. circuit judge, 1899–1914; he was in later life a member of the Permanent Court of Arbitration at the Hague, 1900–1914, and held other international legal posts.

Greene, General Francis V. (1850–1921): A professional soldier and expert in engineering, who resigned from the army in 1886 to enter private business; a volunteer army officer in 1898; governor of Havana, 1898–1899; police commissioner of New York City, 1903–1904.

Griggs, John W. (1849–1927): Attorney-General in McKinley's Cabinet, 1898–1901.

Guarnica, José de: Member of the Spanish Commission; also a member of the Cortes and of the Spanish Supreme Court.

Harrison, Benjamin (1833–1901): President of the United States, 1889–1893; Reid's running mate in 1892.

Hay, John (1838–1905): American statesman, diplomat, and author; private secretary of Abraham Lincoln; followed a diplomatic career in subsidiary posts until appointed Assistant Secretary of State, 1878–1881; ambassador to England, 1897–1898; Secretary of State, 1898–1905; a strong believer in an Anglo-American understanding; noted also for his novels and poetry.

Hayes, Rutherford Birchard (1822–1893): President of the United States, 1877–1881; Reid was instrumental in assuring Hayes' election after the disputed election of 1876.

Herschell, Lord Farrar (1837–1899): English jurist and diplomat; president of the Joint High Commission for the United States and Canada that in 1898 negotiated Canadian-American differences.

Hitchcock, Ethan Allen (1835–1909): American businessman, politician, diplomat; active in Republican Party politics, especially in relation to the tariff; minister to Russia, 1897–1898; Secretary of the Interior, 1898–1907.

Huntington, Collis P. (1821–1900): Railroad builder in the western part of the United States, especially California.

Huntington, Henry E. (1850–1927): Successor to Collis P. Huntington in California railroad interests; founder and benefactor of the famous library and art gallery that bears his name in San Marino, California.

Kergorlay, Comte Jean de: Large property owner in the department of Haute-Seine, in the vicinity of Lyon.

León y Castillo, Fernando de: Spanish diplomat and politician; ambassador to France in 1898.

McKinley, Ida Saxton (1847–1907): Wife of President William McKinley.

McKinley, William (1843–1901): President of the United States, 1897–1901; representative from Ohio, 1877–1891; author of the McKinley Tariff of 1890; governor of Ohio, 1892–1896; elected President in 1896 and again in 1900. He was assassinated on September 6, 1901, and died on September 14, in Buffalo, New York.

McMillan, James (1838–1902): Republican United States senator from Michigan in 1898.

Maria Christina, Queen Regent of Spain (1858–1929): An Austrian princess, who was the consort of Alfonso XII, and mother and regent for Alfonso XIII in his minority; prominent and respected for her talents in Spanish politics in the 1890's.

Méline, Félix Jules (1838–1925): French politician; a leading tariff protectionist in the 1880's; especially active in the so-called Méline Program based on protection and internal improvements between 1890 and 1902; Minister of Agriculture, 1883–1885, 1896–1898, 1915–1916; Premier of France, 1896–1898

Merritt, General Wesley (1834–1910); A professional soldier with a distinguished Civil War record; superintendent of West Point, 1882–1887; commander of the first Philippine expedition in 1898; gave testimony favorable to annexation before the Peace Commission in 1898.

Mills, Darius Ogden (1825–1910): American merchant, businessman, and philanthropist; prominent in the California gold rush of 1849 and later lived in New York, where he engaged in banking, mercantile and hotel interests; artistic philanthropist; the father of Mrs. Whitelaw Reid.

Montero Ríos, Eugenio (1832–1914): President of the Spanish Peace Commission in 1898; president of the Spanish Senate; prominent political leader in his country for many years.

Montsaulnin, Comte Charles de: A royalist member of the French Chamber of Deputies while Reid was in Paris in 1898. He held extensive properties in the department of Cher, in central France.

Moore, John Bassett (1860–1947): American international lawyer; he had a long and distinguished career as a legal counsellor to the State Department; professor of international law at Columbia University; secretary of the American Peace Commission in 1898; later a member of the Permanent Court of International Justice at the Hague, 1921–1928; the author of many widely used textbooks and monographs.

Münster, Count George Herbert (1820–1902): German ambassador to England, 1873–1885; and to France in 1898.

Ojeda, Emilio de: Secretary of the Spanish Peace Commission in 1898.

Otis, Harrison Gray (1837–1917): Newsman and publisher in California, where he owned the Los Angeles *Times*; a volunteer general-grade officer who saw action in the Philippines in 1898 and 1899.

Patti, Adelina (1843–1919): One of the most famous coloratura sopranos of modern times, noted for her interpretations of the operas of Bellini, Rossini, and Donizetti. She was in Paris for the season of 1898.

Peck, Ferdinand W.: United States Commissioner General to the Paris Exposition of 1900.

Platt, Thomas Collier (1833–1910): Republican politician, and party boss of New York during the latter part of the nineteenth century. A cohort of Roscoe Conkling's, he succeeded to control of the state party machine after 1885, where he perfected the techniques of political manipulation in which he delighted, winning the sobriquet "Easy Boss"; an early opponent of McKinley's, he nonetheless followed party dictates as a senator from New York; he was an avowed and bitter opponent of Reid and the *Tribune*, both of whom he considered agents of reform, which he detested.

Porter, Horace (1837–1921): Noted first as aide de camp to General U. S. Grant during the Civil War, prominent after the War in New York financial and political circles; chief motivating force behind the construction of the Grant Tomb in New York City; ambassador to France, 1897–1905, where he was noted chiefly for his gracious manners and his search for the bones of John Paul Jones, which he discovered and transported at his own expense (later reimbursed by Congress) to Annapolis.

Proctor, Redfield (1831–1908): A Republican senator from Vermont.

Puvis de Chavannes, Pierre Cecil (1824–1908): French painter, master of the fresco, and decorator; a transitional figure between Academicism and the early Impressionists.

Ribot, Alexander Félix Joseph (1842–1923): Prime Minister and Foreign Minister of France, 1892–1893; Prime Minister, 1895; in opposition to the governments until 1914; Prime Minister and Foreign Minister, 1917.

Roberts, Marshall O. (1814–1880): An old friend of Reid's, prominent in New York financial and social circles.

Rodríguez, José Ignacio: Expert on international law, particularly relating to Cuba and Spain. He was very useful to the American Commissioners, who employed his services.

Sackville-West, Sir Lionel (1827–1908): British diplomat; minister to the United States, 1881–1888; dismissed in 1888 for inadvertently becoming involved in the presidential election.

Sagasta, Práxedes Mateo (1827–1903): Prime Minister of Spain, 1887–1890, 1892–1895, 1897–1899.

Seckendorff, M. G.: Washington, D.C. correspondent of the New York *Tribune* in 1898 and a friend of Reid's.

Siegfried, Jules (1837–1922): French politician; Minister of Commerce, 1892–1893; senator from Seine-Inférieur in 1898; also interested in the arts and literature.

Sims, William S. (1858–1936): Naval attaché at the American Embassy in Paris in 1898; headed the intelligence system that gathered secret information for the Peace Commission; later commanded American naval forces in Europe during the First World War.

Sousa-Rosa, Conde Thomás de: Portuguese diplomat; former ambassador to Japan; minister to the United States in 1894; minister to France in 1898.

Speyer, James: Prominent New York banker and socialite; a friend of Reid; visitor to Paris during the peace conference.

Storer, Bellamy (1847–1927): American diplomat; minister to Belgium, 1897–1899; minister to Spain, 1899–1902; minister to Austria-Hungary, 1902–1906; prominent for his work as Roman Catholic layman, which resulted in his abrupt retirement in 1906.

Townsend, Lawrence: United States minister to Portugal, 1897–1899; minister to Belgium, 1899.

Vignaud, Henry: Secretary of the American Embassy in Paris, 1898.

Villa-Urrutia, Don Wenceslao Ramírez de: Spanish minister to Belgium and member of the Peace Commission, 1898.

Weyler y Nicolau, Valeriano (1838–1930): Spanish soldier and colonial administrator; fought Cuban rebels between 1868 and 1872; engaged in suppressing colonial rebellion in the Philippines in the 1880's; famous as the "Butcher" Weyler who tried to suppress the Cuban insurrection between 1896 and 1897, to cries of outraged horror from the press and public opinion of the United States.

White, Andrew D. (1832–1918): American diplomat and educator; noted chiefly as president and developer of Cornell University; held minor diplomatic posts under Grant and Harrison; minister to Germany, 1879–1881, and 1897–1902; minister to Russia, 1892–1894.

Whittier, General Charles A.: Member of the Volunteer Army, who reported to the Commission on his services in the Philippines, and who was later prominent in the campaign to suppress the insurrection.

Woodford, Stewart (1835–1913): Prominent New York banker and lawyer; the controversial but competent American minister to Spain during the crisis years, 1897–1898.

Young, John Russell (1840–1899): Newsman and correspondent for the New York *Tribune*; librarian at Library of Congress, 1897–1899.

INDEX

INDEX

Abarzuza y Ferrer, Don Buenaventura de: on minutes of joint sessions, 45, 194; on Protocol, 76, 85; at Castillo's dinner, 94; on purpose of negotiations, 111; and translation, 119, 167; and reading of U.S. Philippine proposals, 130; on Spanish Commission, 169; and war materials, 174; on Cuba, 216; and Reid, 226; on French drama, 226; U.S. invitation to, 227; mentioned, 84, 87, 104, 213
Abolitionists: in Ohio, 5
Adams, Charles Francis: 7–8
Adee, Alvee: mentioned, 3
adjournment (of joint sessions): possibility of, to Nice, 122; debated, 126; temporary, of last meeting, 227. SEE ALSO Commission, Joint: meetings of
Administration, McKinley: Hay on views of, 118 n; and elections of 1898, 134, 141. SEE ALSO McKinley, William.
Agoncillo, Felipé: in U.S., 82 and n.; Senator Chandler on, 86
Agricultural Department, U.S.: 25
Aguinaldo, Emilio: as rebel leader, 58, 82 n.; U.S. dealings with, 58, 178; Gen. Whittier on, 215; mentioned, 82, 86
All Saints Day: 126
Alsace-Lorraine: 107
ambassadors, French: mentioned, 132. SEE ALSO Cambon, Jules
ambassador, German: to France, 148; to U.S., 149; to Madrid, 223
—, Spanish: mentioned, 39. SEE ALSO Castillo, Fernando de León y
—, United States. SEE Porter, Horace
America. SEE government, United States; United States
American colony (in Paris): 70, 94
anarchists: and Montsaulnin, 92
antiexpansionism: and U.S. as world power, 14; Gray and, 14, 15, 59, 147, 149–50; bitterness caused by, 16–17
anti-imperialist. SEE antiexpansionism
Antilles Islands: 158 n.

anti-Semitism: and Dreyfus Affair, 90 n.
arbitration: Spanish hope for, 80, 88; Reid on possibility of, 145 n; and dispute on Protocol, 154; Gray on, 159–160; proposal of, 160–161, 165–166; possible court for, 161; Reid against, 162; and *Maine* explosion, 180
Arizona: and debt precedent, 108
Armistice Protocol: SEE Protocol, Armistice
arms: of Spanish soldiers in Manila, 47; small, disposition of, 174 n. SEE ALSO war material
army, Spanish: prisoners from, in Philippines, 30, 196; prisoners from, in Manila, 46–47, 50; evacuation of, 63 n; Reid on capture of, 121; as U.S. prisoners, 139; mentioned, 208. SEE ALSO prisoners
—, U.S.: influence of, on Philippine issue, 28; and evacuation of troops from Cuba, 62 n.
articles, treaty: SEE proposals, Spanish; proposals, U.S.
articles necessary to treaty: dispute over, 204, 205, 209
artists, French: mentioned, 87
artillery. SEE war material
Asiatics: citizenship for, 170
Asiatic territory: Gray on taking of, 147. SEE ALSO China; Orient
Associated Press: 126; and Republican victories, 142; on negotiations, 193
Atlantic Ocean: and trade, 29
Austria: and debt precedent, 107, 110
Avenue des Accacias (Paris): 146
Avenue Hoche: as Reid's address, 94
Avenue Rapp: 86

Babuyanes Island: 158 n.
Bancroft, George: Abarzuza on, 226
Barcelona: Comillas in, 97
Barnard, Mr.: 41
Bartlett, Mr. with N.Y. *Sun*): 23
Batanes Island: 158
Bates, General John C.: 38

—, U.S.: on Cuba, 51, 53, 63, 81, 112,
120, 133 n, 149, 155, 158 n., 210;
reaction of Spanish Commission to,
53–54, 66, 74, 84, 98, 106, 112, 122–
123, 130 and n., 149, 161,
217, 218, 220; on Guam, 81; and
debt issue, 118 n.; formal presentation of, 122, 168, 173, 181, 217; on
Puerto Rico, 123; Montero Ríos on,
123, 125; on preservation of records,
125; as subject to agreement on
treaty, 126 n.; on Philippines, 128,
130, 136, 137, 144, 151; and threat
of rupture, 151; as ultimatum, 155,
157–158, 158 n.; on war material,
173–174; on religious freedom, 179,
218; on *Maine,* 180, 216–217; Day
on acceptance of, 184; on litigations,
193; on revival of treaties, 202, 205,
218–219; as improper to treaty, 209;
on practice of retention, 213; on Kusaie, 217–218; on trade agreements,
218; on ratification of treaty, 219;
final paper of, 221–222, 225; mentioned, 82, 120, 137, 201, 217. SEE
ALSO issues
—, Spanish: on Cuba, 63, 64, 67–68,
69, 72–73, 99, 200, 203; American
Commission and, 63, 64, 67–68, 101,
103, 153, 156, 180, 182, 185, 204,
213, 221; on Puerto Rico, 64, 67–68,
72, 107, 119, 123, 203; on property,
99; on debt, 99, 112; on Philippines,
136–137, 138, 139, 141, 154, 158,
199–200; as counter-ultimatum, 159
and n.; worth of, 168; on Catholic
Church, 179, 214; on Veragua pension, 179, 213; on printed matter,
180; on contracts, 186–187, 192, 213,
214; on war material, 187; on
Maine, 188, 203, 213; on litigations,
193, 212; on patents and courts, 212;
on consuls, 212–213; on deposits and
bonds, 213, 214; on practice of retention, 213; mentioned, 104, 108,
155. SEE ALSO issues
protocol of '77: renewal of, 190 and n.
Prussia: and debt prededent, 107
Pullman strike: 10
Protocol, Armistice: Spanish complaints on, 35–36; and Spanish questions on Cuba and Puerto Rico, 40;
and order of negotiations, 40, 43, 51;
and Cuban issue, 43, 62, 69, 77, 81,

105, 151, 231; and Treaty, 43; and
Manila, 44, 46–47, 48, 50, 119, 128,
128 n., 131, 139, 173, 200; as limit
on negotiations, 51, 66, 75, 76, 84,
85, 98, 105, 108, 111, 118 n., 118–
119, 122, 138, 142, 151, 178, 179;
French text of, 51, 128; on Spanish
sovereignty, 76; debate on 4th article
of, 77; on Guam, 81; Montero Ríos
and, 93; U.S. to support cost of, 108;
on Puerto Rico, 110; and Philippine
issue, 128 n., 129, 130 n., 151, 154,
200; yellow book on, 132, 137;
Münster on, 142; transactions preceding, 155, 156; on German rights
in Carolines, 164; terms of, listed,
231–232; mentioned, 172
protocols, daily: SEE minutes of joint
sessions
public opinion: Montero Ríos on, 83;
and Cuban debt, 87; and Fashoda
crisis, 127; and Spanish Philippine
proposal, 154; and U.S. acquisition
of Philippines, 191; and final treaty,
221 n.; McKinley on, 133 n., 140 n.
—, European: on Spanish-American
War, 37 n., 177 n.; and threat of
rupture, 80; and Cuban bonds, 97;
on Spain, 133 n.; Germany and,
177 n.
—, French: and Dreyfus Affair, 92
—, U.S.: and Philippine issue, 25 and
n., 48–49, 82 n., 102 and n., 117,
119, 151, 154; Frye on, 27; Reid on,
29–30; and Luzon, 42; on tariff, 66
and n.; on Cuban issue, 78, 96–97,
98–99, 114, 117; and threat of rupture, 80; and expansionism, 89 n.;
Day and, 102; McKinley and,
102 n.; and exchange of concessions,
115; and Spanish American War,
115–116, 177 n.; and *Maine,* 116 n.;
and Treaty, 140 n.; and duty of
American Commission, 147; on Mindanao, 166; on Germany, 177 n.;
among Catholic sympathizers, 192;
on Veragua pension, 206; and rejection of U.S. articles, 207
public works: in Cuba, 118, 121,
132 n., 133 n.; in Philippines, 132 n.–
133 n., 151, 158 n., 235; U.S. concessions on, 118 n.
Puerto Rico: Day on retention of, 27;
Reid on, 40; and orders of discussion,